THE
WAR
THAT
NEVER
ENDED

ROBERT CRUDEN

Lewis and Clark College

PRENTICE-HALL, INC.

Englewood Cliffs, New Jersey

THE WAR THAT NEVER ENDED

The American Civil War

Library of Congress Cataloging in Publication Data

Cruden, Robert.
  The war that never ended.

  Bibliography: p.
  1. United States—History—Civil War—Influence.
  I. Title.
E468.9.C93 1973   973.7   72–5672
ISBN 0–13–944363–0
ISBN 0–13–944355–X (pbk.)

THE WAR THAT NEVER ENDED: THE AMERICAN CIVIL WAR

Robert Cruden

© 1973 by Prentice-Hall, Inc.
Englewood Cliffs, New Jersey

Printed in the United States of America

10 9 8 7 6 5 4 3 2 1

PRENTICE-HALL INTERNATIONAL, INC., *London*
PRENTICE-HALL OF AUSTRALIA, PTY. LTD., *Sydney*
PRENTICE-HALL OF CANADA, LTD., *Toronto*
PRENTICE-HALL OF INDIA PRIVATE LIMITED, *New Delhi*
PRENTICE-HALL OF JAPAN, INC., *Tokyo*

In Grateful Memory

CARL F. WITTKE
HARVEY WISH
Scholars, Teachers, Friends

CONTENTS

PREFACE

To many Americans the story of their Civil War is such an oft-told tale that they are frankly bored with it. This is a pity, especially because the war tells us much about ourselves, much that is relevant to our own day. I have attempted to probe some of these meanings by centering attention on people rather than on political and military abstractions, by looking at how fallible human beings, North and South, thought and behaved during the nation's first total war. The conflict involved nearly everyone in the country: men, women, children; whites, blacks, Indians; workers, planters, farmers, professional people, businessmen as well as soldiers and politicians. For reasons of space I have confined my discussion to blacks, soldiers, workers, businessmen, planters and farmers, and, necessarily, to the roles of rival governments. It is needless to say that the treatment in a short work like this falls short of being exhaustive.

To make these wartime people understandable it was necessary to review the developments of preceding decades which helped make them what they were. Here I have enjoyed the benefits of recent scholarship, which has demonstrated that at the heart of the mounting sectional tensions which eventually snapped in war were the issues of race and slavery. Related to them were moral and ideological considerations which played no small part in bringing on the conflict. Race and slavery may not have been the sole causes of the war, but the war cannot be explained adequately without them.

Finally, I have tried to appraise some long-range consequences of the war which still confront us with major problems, for indeed the Civil War was a war that has never ended.

This book was prompted by requests from students over many years for a short history of the Civil War which would concentrate on its human aspects without ignoring other vital features of the conflict. To those students, my thanks.

It is also a pleasure to acknowledge the support and understanding of President John R. Howard of Lewis and Clark College, and of my colleagues: Nosratollah Rassekh, Anthony Ostroff, and John Brown. My special gratitude to James M. McPherson of Princeton University who read the manuscript for the publisher: he saved me from many errors and made suggestions which make the book more coherent and more readable. To James Pirie, librarian, Lewis and Clark College, and Clyde Haselden, librarian, Lafayette College, my thanks for helping solve problems of illustration. I also owe thanks to my typist, Virginia Diegel. Above all, my appreciation to my wife, Janet, whose aid and encouragement were invaluable.

ROBERT CRUDEN

Portland, Oregon

THE

WAR

THAT

NEVER

ENDED

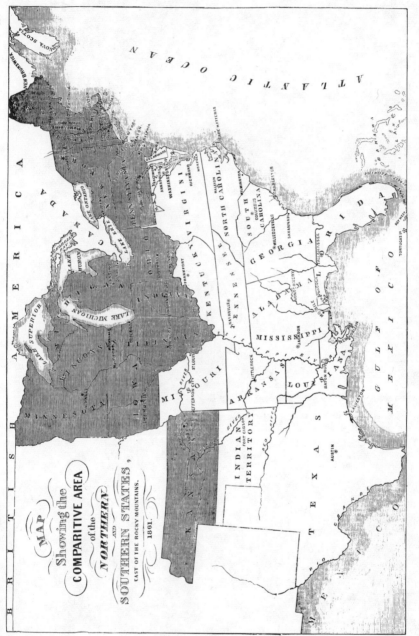

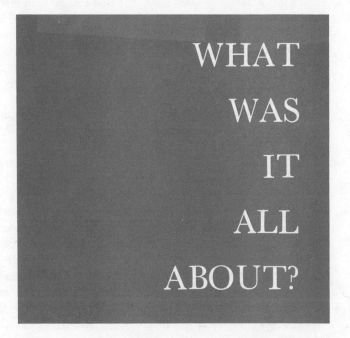

WHAT WAS IT ALL ABOUT?

Today it is a commonplace that the Civil War was probably the single most significant turning point in the domestic life of the American nation. It settled once and for all the nature of the Union on the basis of national supremacy. Historians continue to debate the issue of whether it hindered or hastened industrialization, but it is clear that the war ushered in the dominance of business values in economics, politics, social life and thought which has since characterized American society. The war ended slavery and brought the United States face to face with a new problem: the role of free black people in a presumably democratic society.

In disrupting traditional Southern society, the war aided the emergence of a new breed of Southern leaders, concerned, like Yankees, with railroads, banks, mining, and manufacturing. By opening the way for the first transcontinental railroad and for adoption of a "free land" public policy (the

Homestead Act) it expedited settlement of the West. The war also witnessed the first major federal aid program for higher education: the Morrill Land Grant Act.

It was a war of masses—it is estimated that more than three million men eventually served in the contending armies—operating over vast territories from Pennsylvania to Texas. For the first time in history the strategic use of railroads was demonstrated, while widespread use of the telegraph made possible the coordination of far-flung armies and brought the fighting and home fronts closely together. In the words of Thomas A. Palmer, the Civil War was "the first occasion when the achievements of the Industrial and Scientific Revolutions were put to large scale military use." [1] The war also saw application of the doctrine of total war, in which all the resources of the nation—political, economic, social, cultural, diplomatic and military —were concentrated on breaking the enemy's will to resist, including carrying war to the enemy's civilian population.

The American conflict had international repercussions. Helmuth von Moltke, the Prussian military theorist, drew on the American experience to confirm his own ideas on the strategic value of railroads and telegraphs— ideas he put into effect in the Prussian wars against Austria (1866) and France (1870). British military thought was perhaps even more strongly influenced. If military men made use of the war in one way, European liberals and socialists made use of it in another: the outcome of the war buoyed their hopes for a new day in Europe. The International Workingmen's Association, in which Karl Marx was the dominant figure, proclaimed that "the workingmen of Europe felt instinctively that the star-spangled banner carried the destiny of their class." Citizens of Brussels, after extolling the merits of American democracy, declared, "These teachings which Young America gives us will not be lost on Old Europe." Similar sentiments were expressed by organizations of democratic Poles, Italians and Spaniards. In the world of international diplomacy, the United States attained new stature. Henceforth it was treated, if not as a world power, certainly as a great power.

For such sweeping changes there was a price: more dead in service— 622,000—than in all other American wars until Vietnam, and a nation bitterly divided racially and sectionally, whatever the unity of its political institutions.

How did a war of such magnitude develop?

[1] Thomas A. Palmer, "Military Technology," in *Technology in Western Civilization* (Vol. I), eds. Melvin Kranzberg and Carroll W. Pursell, Jr. (New York: Oxford University Press, 1967), 497.

No one really *knows*. Men of that day differed on the war's basic causes, and historians since have come no closer to consensus.

According to the viewpoints of writers from that time to our own, the war grew out of a moral conflict so basic that it could be resolved only through violence: slavery versus freedom, oligarchy versus democracy, property rights versus human rights. Or, out of a constitutional crisis equally fundamental: national authority versus states' rights, nationalism versus particularism. Or, out of the resolve of a new nation to assert its independence from an oppressive mother country, as in 1776.

To others, the conflict was the outcome of economic and political issues: Northern and Southern rivalry for control of Western public lands, deemed essential for the expansion of both sections; or from Northern determination to make the South subject to Northern economic interest; or from Southern resolution to transform the Union into a vast slave state.

Still others held that the war was "needless," the product of fanatics and agitators in each section who made compromise impossible. Or that it resulted from failure of leadership in both sections. Or that it came from the South's resolve to keep the South "a white man's country." Or that it was the inevitable consequence of the existence within one country of two antagonistic social systems, each of which was willing to go to war rather than yield up its own way of life.[2]

We need not appraise the validity of these views in this discussion. Suffice it to say that each has varying measures of truth in it, and that no one in itself is sufficient to explain the coming of the war. Rather, it appears that the war came about from the convergence of many conflicting forces of such magnitude and intensity that they could not be contained peacefully within the existing structures of American society. With that in mind, let us briefly examine *how* these forces functioned. In so doing we have at hand an effective conceptual tool—sectionalism—which is at once broad enough to comprehend a wide variety of factors and narrow enough to provide an edge for analysis.

By sectionalism we mean that, within the nation, different economic, social, and ideological systems became located in specific geographical areas. This stimulated in each case the emergence of a sectional consciousness, just as the confinement of workers to proletarian ghettoes in Britain and Europe aided the rise of a socialist class consciousness. The sectional consciousness gave rise to specific responses to successive national issues in line with the interests and needs of the dominant groups in each section. Each section attempted to identify its interests with the national interest, and each section sought to shape national policy toward its own ends. To make

---

[2] For a comprehensive summary of many interpretations, see Thomas J. Pressly, *Americans Interpret Their Civil War* (New York: The Free Press, 1965).

a complex situation more complicated, there were three, not two, sectionalisms: Eastern, Southern, and Western. We cannot really speak of a "Northern" sectionalism until the 1850s, when for reasons discussed later, East and West drew together vis-à-vis the South. Such a development underlines the fact that in the struggle for control of national policy the role of the rapidly filling West was crucial: in attempting to control national policy the older sections increasingly had to woo Western support.

To understand this situation we must sketch the major aspects of each section, bearing in mind that we are dealing with three *dynamic* sections, each in process of change, each inherently expansionist, economically or territorially or both. Of necessity, our discussion will require over-simplification, for within each section there were several smaller "sectionalisms." Nevertheless, there were some common characteristics present within each section and it is with these that we are concerned.

THE EAST

The East, embracing the states along the Atlantic seaboard from the Canadian border to the Mason-Dixon line, was, in 1800, a relatively stable society of about 2,635,000 people. It was dominated by seaboard merchants, bankers, and wealthy landowners who contrived to keep the farmers, artisans, and laborers "in their place" socially through the sanctions of a class society and politically through property and taxpaying qualifications for voting and holding public office. Two interrelated major forces changed all that: the Industrial Revolution and the upsurge of what one editor called "the Subterranean Democracy." The editor referred to the successful thrust of the poorer farmers and urban workers to get voting and office-holding rights. As he conceded, the change meant little for the masses "but a change of masters," but the change was nonetheless significant: in place of the old Masters of the Mart were the new Lords of the Mill and Mine, driven by the dynamics of their own system to seek expansion and to mold the national policy to serve their own (and as they believed, the nation's) interests.

The Industrial Revolution began in the East, and as it developed, industry swept trade aside as the most dynamic element in the economy. From small beginnings at the turn of the century, manufacturing by 1860 was employing 940,000 men, women, and children in 74,000 establishments with a capital investment of $693,000,000. The value of the products was said by the census to be nearly $1,270,000,000. The coal and iron necessary for manufacturing expansion were readily available. Existing mines were enlarged and new ones opened so rapidly that in 1860 Pennsylvania alone produced nearly 11,000,000 tons of anthracite; another 9,000,000 tons of bituminous coal were also produced, much of it from the same state. National production of iron ore reached nearly 3,000,000 tons by 1860.

How were the raw materials to get to the factories? How were the products of the factories to reach their markets? The transportation problem was met first through large-scale canal building and then through the rapid development of a railroad network: mileage of the latter increased from 2100 miles in 1840 to more than 10,000 in 1860.

The massive economic growth was made easier by new legal devices. State legislatures adopted the principle of limited liability in chartering corporations and passed laws which made such chartering a matter of routine rather than of granting specific authority in each case. Thus, corporations mushroomed, attracting to themselves the investments of thousands of ordinary people now assured that in case of failure the investors' liabilities would be strictly limited.

For a time the course of expansion was limited by an inadequate labor supply, but with crop failures in Europe in the 1830s and 1840s, especially the Irish famine of 1845, and consequent mass immigration to the United States, the labor shortage disappeared. Thanks in large part to such immigration, the East's population in 1860 was 10,594,000—four times as many as in 1800, despite a massive migration of native born Yankees to the West in the intervening years.

Such population growth bred its own tensions, but such tensions were accentuated by the concomitant growth of industrialism, which bred conflicts of its own.

For example, a new dimension of social cleavage was introduced into American society in the form of two new classes: industrial capitalists and propertyless proletarians. The former was of no mean proportion, if we include in it not only those who controlled the new sources of wealth but also the thousands of stockholders, managers, engineers, foremen, lawyers, and others who shared industry's growing prosperity and so identified their interests with those of the captains of the new order.

The proletarians were something new in two ways. There had always been a group of propertyless laborers, of course, such as longshoremen and farm laborers, but they were relatively few and usually of native stock. Even black laborers shared a common American background. Then came the mass migration of the 1840s; soon the urban centers of the East were filled with poverty-stricken foreigners, speaking strange tongues, professing an alien and dreaded religion, willing to work at any wage—a circumstance of which industrialists took full advantage. It took no Karl Marx to perceive here a flaw in Eastern society: Southern spokesmen such as John C. Calhoun and George Fitzhugh noted the exploitive relationship and used it to hammer home their defense of slavery—planters enslaved only blacks, they noted, while Yankees enslaved white people!

Factory owners might rejoice at the plentiful supply of cheap labor, but other Americans saw in the immigrants a menace to their country, to the Protestant religion, to morality, and law and order. Soon there were anti-Catholic secret societies, anti-Catholic riots, and the organization of an anti-Catholic, anti-foreign political party, the "American" Party, which for a time controlled governors and legislatures in several Eastern states. The Irish, principal victims of the xenophobia, responded by clinging closely to the Democratic Party, the only native organization which welcomed them, deepening their identity with their Church, and attacking black Americans. Often the reason for the attacks was competition for jobs, especially on the docks, but perhaps equally important was the fact that Negro-baiting helped the Irish identify with their persecutors: long before the advent of the Irish, native Americans rioted against blacks in Eastern cities. To be anti-black, in many Irish eyes, was to be American!

If some Americans blamed their troubles on immigrants, others felt themselves threatened by industrialism itself. Those who clung to the old order for sentimental reasons or for reasons of social and political power doggedly, if unsuccessfully, fought the new way of life which they feared and despised. Skilled artisans, fearful of the new technology which undermined their skills, pay, and social status organized unions and went on strike, as did many of the less skilled textile mill workers.

Still others resented industrialism because of the ill omens it augured for their country: pollution of rivers and air, the scarring of the countryside by mines and quarries, the teeming slums spreading like cancer in factory towns, the new breed of businessmen who seemed devoid of scruples. The alienated believers in the old order found spokesmen in intellectuals outraged by the new order's degradation of humane values. Heeding his own "different drummer" Thoreau hied himself to Walden Pond, observing that the great end of industry was not to meet human needs "but that corporations may be enriched." Emerson violently attacked "Trade, with its Money, its Credit, its Steam, its Railroad," which threatened to impose on man "a new universal Monarchy more tyrannical than Babylon or Rome." More activist folk, swept up in a great revival of evangelical Protestantism, worked in a host of reform movements to make society more Christian, to mitigate the abuses of industrialism, and to refashion society closer to their hearts' desire: temperance, sexual "purity," women's rights, protection of children, care for the mentally ill, Utopian socialism, and of prime importance, abolition, of which we shall say more later.

While the Industrial Revolution was transforming economic and social life, it helped accent an equally basic force that was changing political life: the pressure of the disenfranchised for a voice in government. In the first thirty years of the century, state after Eastern state (with the exception of

Rhode Island) dropped property qualifications for voting and officeholding. Thus was created a new political constituency of urban workers and poorer farmers which looked to political action to remedy its grievances. As the new elements asserted themselves, the grand coalition of the National Republican party, embracing within itself the Federalist tradition of government by "the rich, the well-born and the educated" and the tradition of Jeffersonian democracy, came apart. The bitter internal feuds that racked the administrations of Andrew Jackson brought the process to a head. Two major parties emerged: Democrats and Whigs.

The Democrats made their appeal to urban workers, especially immigrants, poorer farmers and small businessmen; the Whigs to industrialists, the great merchants, the well-to-do farmers and the burgeoning middle class. Thus, the Democrats generally stood for locally controlled banking to aid farmers and small businessmen; a low tariff, to keep living costs low; and laws to protect the worker and immigrant. The Whigs wanted a national bank to regulate the flow of credit and provide a stable national currency; a protective tariff to aid industry and indirectly provide a domestic market for farmers; and federally subsidized public works programs to develop a national market.

Whigs generally enjoyed the support of black voters in those states in which blacks could vote: many Whig leaders were abolitionists and Democrats were openly hostile to blacks. Democrats countered by disfranchising blacks in New York and Rhode Island, although in the latter case the action was rescinded when Whigs recaptured control of the state. Ironically, in view of the Democratic claim to represent the "common man," few social reformers were attracted to the party; most, including the abolitionists, when they were interested in politics at all, tended to be Whigs.

Both parties accommodated themselves to industrialism; they differed on means, not ends. Neither questioned the basic values of the new order. Whigs were outspokenly in favor of it, and in practice Democrats showed themselves no less eager than Whigs to grant charters and ease the process of incorporation. This aspect of the Democratic Party disillusioned many spokesmen for labor; some turned to independent political action, while others, clinging to the party, turned to the national party's most trenchant critic of Northern capitalism, John C. Calhoun, spokesman for the Southern slaveholders. Here was the man to save white labor from capitalist oppression! This identification of the cause of white labor with that of the slaveholders was to last long beyond the election of 1844, when it was so openly expressed.

But the issue of slavery, or rather, expansion of slavery into the territories, however much it confused workingmen trying to cope with the problems of industrialism, came to transcend all other issues, no matter how desperately politicians sought to cool it. By the 1850s "Free Soilers" had bolted the Democratic Party; Whigs were torn between "Conscience" and "Cotton" Whigs; and even the "American" Party foundered on the issue. The period of political disintegration came to an end with the organization of the Republican Party in 1854 and its remarkable showing in the presidential election two years later. Now the dissident Democrats, Whigs, and Know-Nothings bent on curbing expansion of slavery and on ending Southern domination of the national government were gathered under one banner. On the other hand, the Democrats continued to attract workers and immigrants, pitched their appeal on grounds of class and race and worked more closely with their Southern counterparts. The division between the parties deepened, for the issue of slavery added a moral dimension to political issues which made compromise increasingly difficult. Indeed, the moral issue had proved so intractable that the major Protestant denominations—Presbyterian, Methodist, and Baptist—had already split irrevocably on it.

The East, then, was a section in stress, marked by a ferment of opinion, dissension, disorder. Some Southerners, typified by George Fitzhugh, interpreted this as weakness and decay, preliminary to social collapse. Yankees, and some British travelers, such as Alexander Mackay, saw in it the strength and vitality of a young people destined to make its mark in the world. As Mackay noted, "When they look to the future, they have no reason to doubt the prominency of the position, social, political and economical, which they will assume. But they are in haste to be all of that they are yet destined to be." And what they were destined to be, thought Yankees, were harbingers of freedom and democracy to the world.

Here, perhaps, is the sentiment which bound the conflicting elements of the East together: pride in their country and in its mission, and in the primacy of freedom both at home and abroad. The fact that this devotion to freedom had its roots in the aims of diverse and often conflicting interests made it all the more viable. Businessmen seeking greater profit, workers demanding better wages, farmers wanting easier credit, social reformers trying to improve society, women battling for equal rights, and abolitionists working to end slavery—all needed freedom and all used freedom to attain their ends. In the course of such struggle each was compelled to identify himself or herself with freedom as an abstract good. To be sure, there were frequent mob outbreaks against spokesmen for unpopular views, but in the East there was none of that organized suppression of opinion which came to characterize the South. And the Southern view that the uses made of freedom were signs of degeneration turned out to be a fatal misjudgment.

So far we have been discussing a particular kind of East—the white East. There was also a black East—small, numbering in 1860 only 156,000 in a population of nearly 10,600,000, but nonetheless significant. Its elite of business and professional men included Dr. James McCune Smith, a graduate of the University of Glasgow, who challenged the racist theories of John C. Calhoun; Henry Highland Garnet, abolitionist pastor of a white Presbyterian church in Troy, New York; Dr. Martin R. Delany, whom Theodore Draper calls "the founding father of American black nationalism;" James Forten of Philadelphia, whose ownership of a thriving sailmaking establishment did not deter him from militant promotion of black interests; and Frederick Douglass, the internationally famous abolitionist who went on to become, in the words of August Meier, "the most distinguished Negro in 19th century America." [3] Most blacks, like most whites, attained no historical distinction. A considerable number of them were skilled craftsmen, or engaged in the lucrative callings of barbers, waiters and hotelkeepers, but most were poorly paid laborers and domestics.

Small though it was, the black presence was resented. White craftsmen generally excluded blacks from their unions, and effectively barred them from better-paying jobs by refusing to work with them. If public education were provided for blacks at all, it was on a segregated basis. Private black schools were driven out of existence in Connecticut and New Hampshire by legislation and mob action. Racism in the churches led to organization of separate black churches among Methodists and Baptists. The fact that blacks could vote irked so many whites that by the 1840s five states had either wholly or partially disfranchised them. Residential segregation was general, with the mass of poor blacks restricted to slums. Anti-Negro riots flared sporadically in Northern cities. As early as 1813 James Forten complained about police persecution of blacks. In short, Northern whites, while conceding black freedom, were not prepared to accord black equality. Indeed, no less than Southern whites, they believed that blacks were inherently inferior to whites. And, like Southern whites, they dreaded the prospect of racial "amalgamation"—a fear which anti-abolitionists did not hesitate to exploit.

Like the white East, the black East was in process of change—symbolized by the publication in 1829 of David Walker's famous *Appeal . . . to the Colored Citizens of the World*. Walker, a Southern-born free black who made his living as a used clothes dealer in Boston, upbraided many of his fellows for their apathy and even hostility to abolition. More significantly, he struck a new strong note of militancy. Whites, he said, could bring about abolition and grant equality to blacks—or blacks would do it themselves through violent revolt. The new black mood thus represented coincided with the rise of activist abolitionism among whites (typified by William Lloyd Garrison) and each reinforced the other.

Indeed, as Benjamin Quarles has noted, the black role in abolition was

[3] Theodore Draper, "The Father of American Black Nationalism," *New York Review of Books*, March 12, 1970, p. 33; August Meier, "Blueprint for Black People," in *Frederick Douglass*, ed. Benjamin Quarles (Englewood Cliffs, N.J.: Prentice-Hall, Inc., 1968), p. 143.

crucial in many respects.[4] Black subscriptions helped keep Garrison's *Liberator* alive in its early critical years. Blacks manned many of the stations on the Underground Railroad, and its black agents, such as Harriet Tubman and Sojourner Truth, penetrated the South more effectively than did whites. Vigilance committees in the major cities sheltered fugitives and helped establish them in relatively safe communities. Lecturers like Frederick Douglass and William Wells Brown won wide audiences for the abolitionist message, and dramatized the issue of slavery such as no white could have done. Blacks played such a prominent role in rescuing captured fugitives, according to Quarles, that up until 1850 "it had been a business conducted almost exclusively by Negroes."

Black abolitionists, like white, were divided on issues of policy. Some followed Garrison in his emphasis on the moral issue, his distrust of politics and politicians, and in his advocacy of "No Union with Slaveholders." Others, no less concerned with moral issues, were bent on using political action to mobilize public sentiment and thus eventually bring about emancipation. A few, typified by Henry Highland Garnet, advocated armed action to overthrow slavery. Garnet's call drew only limited favorable response, and gradually many blacks, most notably Frederick Douglass, long an admirer of Garrison, drew away from the Garrisonian position. They perceived that underneath its seeming militancy the slogan of disunion meant the perpetuation of slavery. The slogan grew out of the troubled consciences of whites; their sense of guilt would be assuaged when they no longer lived in a common country with slaveholders. But a separate South would be a slave South, and blacks, having no sin of slavery to atone for, could see clearly both that slavery must go, and that the fate of the free black was inextricably interwoven with the fate of the slave.

This struggle for black rights and for emancipation found expression in many ways, outside of interracial abolitionist groups. Local and state organizations of blacks were founded, and national conventions, beginning in 1830, gave voice to black protests not only against slavery but also against anti-Negro violence, prejudice, and discrimination in East and West. Several black newspapers appeared, notably *Freedom's Journal*, which made its appearance in 1827, *The Colored American*, and later, Frederick Douglass' *North Star*, to express black viewpoints on current issues. Petition movements were organized to present black complaints to state legislatures and the national Congress. Societies were organized for various ends: to set up schools and libraries for blacks; to promote temperance; and encourage self-help by providing mutual aid for members in time of need. In short, excluded from active participation in white society, blacks developed their

[4] Benjamin Quarles, *Black Abolitionists* (New York: Oxford University Press, 1969), *passim*.

own forms of organization and expression: they no longer passively accepted the white definition of their "proper place" in American society.

THE SOUTH

The South, no less than the East, was transformed in the 60 years prior to the war, although in different ways. In 1800 it extended from the Mason-Dixon line south to the limits of Georgia and westward through the relatively new states of Kentucky and Tennessee; in 1860 it embraced that area plus Florida and the territory from Georgia to the western frontier of Texas. Its white population increased more than four times—from 1,700,000 in 1800 to more than 7,000,000 in 1860. This population was almost entirely native-born and of Anglo-Saxon descent: the census of 1860 listed only 391,000 foreign-born in the South, compared with 2,000,000 in the East. The black population expanded no less, from 918,000 in 1800 to 4,000,000 in 1860. The Indian population, including the highly advanced Cherokees, had all but disappeared, stripped of their lands through fraudulent "treaties" and persuaded or compelled to leave their ancestral homes for the Indian territory beyond the Mississippi.

In 1800, the South was predominantly rural, engaged in the production of foodstuffs and staples such as cotton, rice, and tobacco, dependent on black slaves as its labor supply, dominated by a planting aristocracy which not only maintained political control but also set the tone for society as a whole. It was an aristocracy imbued with the spirit of the Enlightenment: skeptical, tolerant, patriarchal in relations with its slaves, and hopeful that ways could be found to end slavery without disrupting society.

By 1860 the South, while still agrarian, was integrated into the industrial economies of both Old and New England and subject to the caprices of a world market over which the South had little control. In the interim the political hegemony of the planters had been challenged by the democratic power of farmers and mechanics. And slavery itself, at the very time it was becoming most profitable and essential—or so it seemed to the planters, was challenged by the rise of abolition in the West and East and a mounting tide of hostile criticism in Britain—a criticism to which the planters were extremely sensitive. The planters, and Southerners generally, responded after the 1830s by abandoning the principles of the Enlightenment, uniting in defense of slavery as a positive good, the suppression of anti-slavery sentiment in the South and attempting to silence critics elsewhere in the United States.

How this came about may be traced to several major developments which joined and reinforced each other to change the South.

First, the "invention" of the cotton gin in 1793 made possible the profitable cultivation of short-staple cotton, the kind best suited for the vast upland areas of the seaboard states and to the great "black belt" of the interior states. This was so because it increased fantastically the productivity of slave labor in the time-consuming process of separating seed from fibre. Hand labor produced at best two pounds of fibre a day. The new machine increased this to 10 pounds; when water power was used, instead of human or animal power, the gin turned out 1,000 pounds; and later improvements doubled that output. This low-cost cotton met so admirably the needs of Britain's booming cotton textile industry, as well as those of the developing textile industry of New England, that in a short time cotton was not only the mainstay of the Southern economy but also the largest single item in the nation's exports.

The increase in production was phenomenal: from 73,000 bales in 1800 to 3,841,000 in 1860. In the latter year total exports of United States merchandise were valued at $334,000,000; cotton alone accounted for $192,000,000. (By comparison, wheat exports were valued at only $4,000,000.) There was ample ground for Southerners to proclaim, as they did increasingly, that "cotton is king." The corollary was that cotton was king so long as labor was enslaved, for the boom in cotton made slavery profitable. Planters, such as Jefferson Davis, came to believe that Southern prosperity was firmly rooted in slavery.

Cotton may have been king, but it was a limited monarchy. Cotton's very success bound it to a free world market over which Southern planters had little control. They prided themselves on being a people superior to the money-grubbing Yankee capitalists; the reality was that, like the Yankees, they were part of a capitalistic world. But while the Yankees were building an industrial society, the South was essentially colonial, providing the raw materials for industry, both at home and abroad. When the Liverpool cotton market sneezed, the South caught cold; and when Liverpool got a cold, the South was prostrated, as in the "hungry forties," when cotton at wholesale went to 5.6 cents a pound (in 1845) compared to 16.5 cents in 1836.

This cycle caught the planter in a vise. Unlike the Yankee mill owner, who laid off his workers in depression times, leaving them to be supported by private or public charity, the planter had to maintain his labor force, or sell it off at falling prices. This led planters to use that labor to produce more cotton, even when the market was glutted. This, of course, helped to drive down prices still further, until the swing of the business cycle ushered in a new period of prosperity.

Such conditions made the plight of the small planter increasingly difficult. Only those with adequate credit or capital could weather crises which came periodically, and there were other reasons why the big plantation overcame the small. The wealthy knew of and could afford application of modern techniques; only they had the means to maintain the levees along the river bottoms, which in effect gave them a monopoly on the best land; they could, and did, organize labor more efficiently than could small planters, and bring some measure of management expertise to bear on the problems of cotton production. Thus, they were best able to take advantage of improved conditions, often by taking over the land and slaves of less fortunate neighbors. Indeed, concentration of wealth had proceeded so far by 1850 that, according to William E. Dodd, the noted Southern historian, the one thousand richest planter families "received over $50,000,000 a year while all the remaining 660,000 families received only about $60,000,000." [5] Contributing to this was the rise in the prices of both cotton and slaves after 1845, which added substantially to the wealth and power of those able to survive the Panic of 1837.

For a time there was opportunity for the small planter. The opening of the fertile lands of the southwest for settlement after expulsion of the Indian peoples made it possible for men of slender means to acquire plantations and for those of moderate circumstances, such as Joseph E. Davis, the brother of Jefferson Davis, to amass fortunes. Such "new men," together with older planters who had migrated West, and Yankees who came south to share in the "flush times," had little in common with the tradition of the seaboard aristocracy. Despite their affection for some of those traditions, they were as hard-headed and as hard-fisted as the Yankee mill owners. They knew that their position rested on cotton and slavery, and they were about as ready to give up one as the other. They gave substance to the new slavery ideologies which were developed by intellectuals in Virginia and South Carolina.

It should be noted that even in the Southwest, the process of concentration asserted itself, as the great landowners steadily encroached on the lands of the less wealthy. The small planters, desperately trying to edge their way up the social ladder, sought relief in demanding reopening of the African slave trade, the opening of the territories of the United States to slavery, and the suppression of anti-slavery sentiment everywhere. Since their own situation was desperate, they were willing to press their point to crisis, to secession. The great planters, sensitive to the dangers involved, were much more cautious.

With the development of the Southwest, another change appeared in the South: a division of function between the Upper South of Virginia, Maryland, and North Carolina on the one hand, and the Deep South on the other. For various reasons the need for slaves in the Upper South declined in the early decades of the century while their numbers increased. The consequent surplus put a strain on planters, but the opening of the new lands provided a lucrative market. Every year, thousands of unhappy

---

[5] William E. Dodd, *The Cotton Kingdom* (New Haven: Yale University Press, 1919), p. 24.

blacks were "sold down the river" to the Black Belt. In 1831, Thomas R. Dew, professor of political science at William and Mary College, explained to the Virginia legislature that it could not afford to give up slavery—as had been proposed—because the state profited almost as much from the sale of slaves as from its entire tobacco crop. In short, the growing domestic slave trade helped to bind together the genteel, patriarchal Old South and the tough, aggressive New South of the West.

The development of the cotton culture and its expansion into the Southwest help explain changes in the South. A psychological element, so deep and pervasive as to become an historical force in itself, also played a role. It had long been an article of planter faith that the civilizing influence of slavery had transformed savages into happy beings who, under white supervision, fulfilled the role to which God in his infinite wisdom had assigned them. Virginians, in particular, pictured themselves as kindly, indulgent masters who, in tempering the cruelties of slavery, had won the affection and loyalty of the slaves—a belief shared by many planters elsewhere.

This euphoria received its first jolt in the 1790s, when blacks in Santo Domingo bloodily and successfully destroyed slavery and eventually established themselves as the independent republic of Haiti—which, incidentally, was not recognized by the United States until after the Civil War had begun. The slave rebellion in itself was sufficient to alarm mainland whites but the tales told by planter refugees set off a panic which resulted in some states banning the entry of any West Indian blacks, including slaves held by refugees. Then in Virginia, in 1800, came Gabriel's aborted insurrection, for which he and 35 others paid with their lives, followed by other outbreaks climaxed with the famous rebellion in 1831 of Nat Turner—again in Virginia. If such things could happen in Virginia, who was safe?

The results were fear, hysteria, tension, prolonged over such a time as to take on aspects of collective paranoia. Slave "plots" were "discovered" with alarming frequency, the accused duly punished and informers suitably rewarded with freedom and cash. It is difficult to say how many such plots were authentic. In any case, the white South reacted on the basis of its fears. Slave codes were made more rigorous. Restrictions on free blacks were intensified. The teaching of blacks to read and write was made illegal. No black meeting could be lawfully held without a white person in attendance. Curfews were established for blacks. The black church was driven underground, to become the "invisible institution" of slavery. And, of course, any public criticism of the "peculiar institution" was outlawed.

Naturally, planters were hardly to be expected to believe that slavery itself was at the root of rebellion. It was psychologically necessary for them to believe that slaves were indeed content and happy. It followed, then, that some alien, malign force was at work subverting the slaves. That force was not far to seek: an abolitionist conspiracy to sow disaffection and sedition in the South. Proof? The sending into the South copies of David Walker's *Appeal* of 1829 and William Lloyd Garrison's *Liberator*, which began publication in 1831, just eight months before Nat Turner's uprising. It was a simple case of cause and effect: propaganda in Massachusetts brought bloodshed in the South. As abolitionism grew the Southern mind saw its society as undermined by subversion, threatened with black insurrection, and beleaguered from without by growing hostility. That no major uprising took place after Nat Turner's and that abolitionists for many years were a small, unpopular minority in the West and East, were of little significance. White Southerners *thought* they were endangered, and what they thought made the historic difference.

And all white Southerners felt threatened—not simply planters: black insurrection menaced all whites. Thus an issue was presented which transcended all others, an issue which bound all whites together, regardless of class. The deep cleavages of Southern society were thus glossed over, the promising democratic revolution aborted (as we shall see), and leadership preserved in the hands of the great planters.

Immediate white response took two major forms: outright repression of anti-slavery criticism, even if not abolitionist oriented; and the elaboration of a social philosophy which held that black slavery was the best foundation for white civilization.

Suppression of dissent in the South was relatively easy. Mob violence, legislation, actions of boards of trustees and other agencies of authority, together with a hostile press and public opinion, silenced or drove out of the South those editors, preachers, teachers, and others who did not publicly conform to official orthodoxy. This treatment was not confined to the issue of slavery itself. Gradually there emerged an orthodox line in religion, history, economics and political theory, for all these were drafted in the cause of demonstrating the goodness of slavery. Some latitude was permitted "scientists" like Josiah Nott and George R. Gliddon, who challenged the traditional Christian view of a single creation of man. Their view that there were several "types" of mankind was discussable because they "proved" that of all the types the black was the most inferior. "Dangerous" books, such as Hinton R. Helper's trenchant criticism of slavery as dangerous to the Southern people, *The Impending Crisis of the South*, were publicly burned. In some states possession of such a work was made a felony. In Georgia the circulation of material intended to cause revolt among slaves was punishable by death! Campaigns were carried on to discourage students from attending colleges outside the South, and in Southern schools to use only textbooks reflecting the official Southern outlook.

Such measures, effective though they were, did not get at what Southerners felt to be the source of contagion: abolitionism elsewhere. Appeals to authorities in the East to suppress the agitation were fruitless, although during the Jackson Administration the postmaster in New York withheld the dispatch of "incendiary" publications. More successfully, Southerners used their power in the federal government. For eight years the House of Representatives refused to consider anti-slavery petitions, despite the constitutional proviso to the contrary. For more than 25 years there was, in the words of Clement Eaton, a "virtual censorship of the mails crossing the Mason-Dixon line" which rested upon "the acquiescence of the federal government." [6] Amos Kendall, the slaveholding postmaster-general in Jackson's cabinet, explained that while "we owe an obligation to the laws, . . . we owe a higher one to the communities in which we live." Many years later, in 1857, the attorney-general of the United States held that no postmaster was required to deliver mail which might cause unrest among slaves.

A consequence of this repression was that the Southern mind was increasingly insulated from the currents of thought and opinion flowing in the nineteenth-century world, and was thus more and more out of touch with the realities of that world—as the Confederacy was to discover to its disadvantage during the war. However, for a generation prior to the war the white South had its own version of reality, generated by such leading intellectuals as John C. Calhoun, perhaps the most ingenious political theorist in American history; Thomas R. Dew, professor and later president of William and Mary College; J. D. B. DeBow, at one time a professor at the University of Louisiana and editor of the powerful *DeBow's Review*; and George Fitzhugh, the Virginia lawyer who buttressed his defense of slavery with a sharp indictment of the inhumanity of free, capitalist society. Their gospel was faithfully expounded by a host of preachers, teachers, editors, and politicians and became the orthodoxy accepted by the mass of Southern whites.

The new philosophy was a deliberate rejection of the values of the Enlightenment set forth in the Declaration of Independence, such as the natural rights of man, so dear to an earlier generation of Southerners. The idea that "all men are born free and equal" was "unfounded and false" argued Calhoun. Rather, men were born into a social order which protected them; they in turn were subject to its laws and institutions. Such rights as men might possess were not "natural rights" but those granted by society in varying degrees according to the contributions made by individuals. Liberty was such a right, but when liberty came into conflict with society's responsibility to protect its members then "liberty must, and ever ought to, yield to protection."

As for equality, it was obvious that men were unequal in character, talents and condition; such inequality must be recognized by society since

[6] Clement Eaton, *The Freedom-of-Thought Struggle in the Old South* (New York: Harper & Row, Publishers, 1964), p. 197.

it was "indispensable to progress." Inequality provided the spur for individuals to improve themselves and thus indirectly improve society. It followed then that power rightfully belonged to those who contributed most to society: in terms of character and talents they had proved themselves fit to rule by succeeding in what Herbert Spencer later called "the survival of the fittest." This, of course, provided a rationale for planter rule in white society; its assumptions likewise provided moral and other sanctions for slavery.

The connection was put bluntly by Dew: "The exclusive owners of property ever have been, ever will and perhaps ever ought to be, the virtual rulers of mankind. . . . It is the order of nature and of God that the being of superior faculties and knowledge, and therefore of superior power, should control and dispose of those who are inferior. It is as much in the order of nature that men should enslave each other as that other animals should prey upon each other." [7]

Advocates of the enslavement of blacks found other justifications. Clerics cited appropriate Biblical passages to show that slavery had divine sanction. "Scientists" proved the inherent inferiority of blacks. Blacks were incapable of intellectual achievement: their mental growth stopped at puberty; thereafter they were creatures of passion. Proof? Although blacks had lived for thousands of years in Africa they had never developed a civilization. Slavery, however, had taken these savages, provided them with the kind of work suited to their character, given them guidance by civilized whites, and so brought them to a high point "never before attained by the black race in any age or country." Thus, Calhoun argued, it was a "positive good" for both races, benefiting both and providing "the most safe and stable basis for free institutions in the world." James Henry Hammond of South Carolina carried the argument a step further. Slaves, he said, were "happy, content, unaspiring," the mudsills of society who made possible the class of whites "which leads progress, civilization and refinement."

Another body of argument held that without slavery the South was doomed. Dew and Jefferson Davis expounded the notion that only through slave labor could the South develop economically. Calhoun asserted that slavery was the only basis on which whites and blacks could coexist peacefully; abolition would lead to race war, in which the South would be subject to "slaughter, carnage and desolation." The result would be a reversal of proper race relations: the blacks "and their Northern allies would be the masters, and we the slaves."

DeBow, while subscribing to such beliefs, touched upon an aspect rarely discussed by pro-slavery spokesmen: the benefits of slavery to poorer whites. Wages and living conditions in the South were better than in the

---

[7] Quoted in William E. Dodd, *The Cotton Kingdom* (New Haven, Conn.: Yale University Press, 1919), p. 53.

North, he said, while workers were saved from the blighting effects of factory work. Poor men in the South, freed from competition with foreign, pauper labor, could accumulate wealth and become slaveowners. And most important, in the South, the poor man "preserves the status of a white man, . . . The poor white laborer at the North is at the bottom of the social ladder, whilst his brother here has ascended several steps and can look down upon those who are beneath him, at an infinite remove." [8]

These defensive arguments were supplemented by aggressive criticism of free society, best exemplified in the work of Fitzhugh. Drawing on a wide range of sources, Fitzhugh charged that free society, as represented in the industrial states of Western Europe and the United States, had proved a failure. The masters of capital had only one god—profit—and in its pursuit they made both themselves and the workers less than human. The mass of workers were no better than slaves, for they were utterly dependent on employers; and in many respects they were worse off than black slaves. Black slaves were sure of their livelihood, in good times and bad, in sickness and old age, for it was in the interest of their owners to take care of them. "Free" white workers were turned out to fend for themselves when their labor was no longer profitable. Labor resented this exploitation, and out of this resentment would come revolution, social collapse, and eventual re-integration. "Slavery will everywhere be abolished, or everywhere reinstituted."

Fitzhugh had little doubt as to the outcome, for "Slavery is the natural and normal condition of the laboring man, whether white or black." The South had no need for white slaves, for "we have black ones." Elsewhere the form of slavery for whites would be more benign than for blacks, for white laborers needed slavery for protection, while blacks required slavery for their governance. Nevertheless, black slavery showed the way to other societies. The interests of labor and capital were united, both worked in harmony for common ends, and the result was "the oldest, the best and most common form of Socialism," a form that combined the best features of both socialism and free competition. Thus, in contrast to the dissension-plagued North, in the South "all is peace, quiet, plenty and contentment." [9]

Not quite. The white South had its own share of dissension. Three-fourths of the whites owned no slaves, and many of them bitterly, if im-

[8] For an excellent collection of pro-slavery arguments, see ed. Eric L. McKitrick, *Slavery Defended: The Views of the Old South* (Englewood Cliffs, N.J.: Prentice-Hall, Inc., 1963).

[9] For a recent edition of Fitzhugh's major works, see ed. Harvey Wish, *Ante-Bellum: Writings of George Fitzhugh . . . on Slavery* (New York: Capricorn Books, 1960).

potently, hated the plantation system. It not only nurtured the growth of a black population in a white man's country; it also, by encompassing the better lands, forced yeoman farmers to less hospitable soil. Artisans and mechanics may have envied the aristocratic way of life, but they resented the aristocratic contempt for labor and they fought, with some measure of success, the slaveowners' practice of hiring out slave craftsmen to employers. Strikes were not as frequent as in New England, but strikes there were, often broken by the use of slaves—as at the Tredegar Iron Works in Richmond, Virginia, which used a strike to replace its white working force with black slaves.

A steadily mounting grievance of poorer whites was lack of an adequate public school system, which doomed many of their children to illiteracy while the sons of planters enjoyed the services of tutors and the benefits of college education usually in the North or in Britain. Mountaineers loathed the lords of the plantations—a fact which was to cause no little difficulties for the Confederacy later on. Urban businessmen were restive under taxation systems which favored landowners and banking laws which made business difficult and precarious. And many farmers and mechanics, adhering to the strict morality of their Baptist and Methodist churches, looked askance at the presence in their midst of more than 400,000 slaves of mixed descent, mute testimony to that which they most abhorred—interracial sex.

Such feelings surfaced during the democratic upsurge which disrupted traditional patterns in the South as much as in the Northeast. The disfranchised masses of small farmers and mechanics won their struggle for political rights over bitter opposition; by the 1840s every Southern state, except Virginia and South Carolina, was in some measure politically democratic. As in the Northeast, a new type of politics emerged, and a new type of politician, who voiced the demands of their constituency for public schools, equitable taxation, and acceptance of social responsibility for the criminal, the mentally ill, and the aged poor. While the new voters generally flocked into the Democratic Party, the wealthier planters and urban middle class voted for the conservative Whigs. For a brief time the South experienced vital two-party politics, but the rending issue of slavery doomed Southern Whigs as it did Northern. Planters and other conservatives, if they were to preserve their influence, had no alternative save to join the Democrats.

This they did with misgiving, for they feared and despised the raw appeals to class prejudice made by many Democrats. They soon found their misgivings groundless: Democrats, like Whigs, had no intention of upsetting the social order, however radical their rhetoric. Radicals as well as conservatives voted for legislation to tighten up slave codes and to restrict the freedom of free blacks. No legislature, whatever its composition, sought to change constitutional prohibitions against free black voting. In the three states where such voting had been permitted—Tennessee, Maryland, and North Carolina—it was prohibited by 1835.

Why the lack of basic change? Many answers are possible. The winning of political reforms and the growing prosperity after 1845 blunted the drive for social reform. The new voters and their leaders were often poor with scanty education, lacking any save a vague sense of democratic ideology for changing things; ill at ease and inexpert in the ways of exerting power, and thus easily influenced by expert politicians who served the planters. Further, the basic source of power remained with the planters: a power that was growing with the cotton economy and with the concentration of wealth in the hands of the greater planters. These knew well how to use that power to manipulate popular leaders, in ways reminiscent of those used by the Roman patricians to manipulate the leaders of the plebs: flattery, social acceptance, financial aid, even marriage into the aristocracy. The careers of Albert Gallatin Brown in Mississippi and Joseph E. Brown in Georgia provide forceful illustrations of how men of the people could be transformed into spokesmen for the planters.

Such transformation was made easier because the planters proved flexible on reform. Like the English aristocrats of 1832 they were willing to make concessions as long as their power was left untouched. Thus, some public school systems were established and measures adopted for humanitarian reform. But the schools were inadequately financed and the other measures minimal, sufficient to quiet popular unrest but far short of meeting Southern society's needs.

Another, and perhaps more basic force was at work. The radical Democrats perceived, however dimly, that execution of a program to benefit the mass of Southern whites was impossible without dislodging the planting aristocracy, and that called for destroying the basis of its power: slavery. Hinton R. Helper, no supporter of black rights but an eloquent spokesman for poorer whites, put the issue clearly in 1857. If the non-slaveholding people of the South were to gain their ends, he said in *The Impending Crisis of the South,* their first step must be to "devise ways and means for the complete annihilation of slavery."

This was revolution, and few whites were ready for that. Even less were they ready for a revolution that would free black people. It was an article of faith with them that blacks could live with whites only in subjection, and however much one might dislike it, slavery provided the means. Poor mechanics as well as wealthy planters were agreed that the South must remain "a white man's country."

So much has been written about the planters' life style—their lavish hospitality, their sense of *noblesse oblige* in public service, their sensitivity to personal honor and quick resort to violence in its vindication, their dalliance with slave women and dehumanization of white women into symbols of racial purity—that it seems needless to discuss it further. Yet some comments are in order. It was, essentially, an attempt to emulate the society of British landed gentry and that of the Old South's plantation aristocracy of the eighteenth century, in which great land ownership, and in the South, ownership of many slaves, bestowed the cachet of prestige. Such an outlook was basically inconsistent with the nineteenth-century planter's role as a vital part of world wide capitalism, and this he rarely perceived. So, in an era which demanded bankers, engineers, scientists, and technicians, the planter's white sons, in good traditional fashion, were educated for law, politics, the church, the army, and the plantation. There was symbolism in the devising of the cotton gin, not by a planter, but by the visiting Yankee, Eli Whitney.

The same aristocratic bias—as well as a desire for quick profit—led planters to invest their capital in land and slaves, although the development of the South called for industrialization and the diversification of its economy. The need to develop technologically was pointed out in 1845 by William Gregg of South Carolina, a successful cotton textile manufacturer, and it was repeated time and again by conventions of Southern businessmen. Some progress was made, but even in 1860 there were fewer cotton spindles in the entire South than in the center of the New England textile industry, Lowell, Massachusetts. Likewise, the vast coal and iron deposits of Alabama and Tennessee were largely undeveloped. Merchants, rather than planters, provided the stimulus for the building of 9,000 miles of railroad, with the aid of state and federal subsidies.

Southern businessmen, then, were beginning to see that Southern interests might not be necessarily identical with planters' interests, but their power was much less than that of their Yankee counterparts, and they were caught in the web of slavery. Many industrial and mining enterprises used slave labor, and businessmen, no less than other whites, looked on slavery as the only viable system of race relationships. Thus they too were infected by the feelings of race pride, race fear, and persecution by a hostile world which contributed to the rise of a Southern nationalism in the 1850s.

Increasingly Southerners thought of themselves as a people apart from and even oppressed by other Americans. They occupied a distinct territory and gloried in a common Anglo-Saxon blood; they spoke the same tongue and shared a common orthodox view of Protestantism; they had their own traditions, their own lifestyle, their own institutions—especially the "peculiar institution"—which distinguished them from the rest of the country. In short, they had the strongest of sectional identities. Even the vaunted doctrine of state's rights became, as U. B. Phillips, perhaps the most famous Southern historian, pointed out, not an end in itself but a means through which to promote Southern rights, to develop a consciousness of Southern nationality.[10] Henry Timrod, the Southern poet, in proclaiming in 1861 that "At last we are a nation among nations" sounded the note of Southern nationalism, that the war was one of national liberation.

Within that "nation," but not of it, were 4,097,000 blacks, more than a third of the entire Southern population. Of these, 3,838,000 were slaves, and of these 411,000 were of mixed descent—some so white, in fact, that they were sometimes mistaken for white family members, as William Wells Brown, the fugitive slave who became a leading abolitionist, attested from his own experience.

The blacks were the progeny of the only large body of unwilling immigrants in our history, brought here against their will from the aptly named Slave Coast of West Africa. They were not savages. On the contrary, they were the products of a long history of civilization, living in highly developed agricultural and commercial societies, with complex social structures, well-organized governments and fairly sophisticated religious beliefs. They were familiar not only with the oral traditions of their peoples but, in some cases, also with written, for with the Moslem invasions of West Africa had come schools, universities, and the widespread use of Arabic as a written and spoken tongue. Among those kidnapped for American slavery were experienced farmers, skilled artisans and artists, even princes and priests who had fallen victim to rivals or been captured as prisoners of war. On this side of the water they were stripped of their names—their personal identities—and widely dispersed over farms and plantations. They were also stripped of their history—their collective identity—and reduced to chattels, to be bought, sold, bred, and disciplined like so many cattle.

Slavery, like the South generally, was changing. Its center shifted from the Atlantic seaboard to the Black Belt of the Southwest. At first distributed among countless farms and small plantations, increasing numbers of slaves tended to be held on larger units as the plantation system spread. According to the 1860 census, a fourth of the slaves lived on plantations with more than 50 slaves, while less than half lived on those with fewer than 20 slaves. Even this picture does not accurately portray the concentration of ownership, for census returns were based on counties, so that planters with holdings in more than one county—and there were many such—were listed as separate slaveholders. In short, as the units' of production grew, slavery developed the same type of impersonal relationship between master and slave that characterized the relationship between Yankee industrialist and worker.

This impersonality was accentuated by the growth of the domestic

[10] U. B. Phillips, *The Course of the South to Secession* (Washington, D.C.: American Historical Association, 1939), pp. 156–57.

slave trade which accompanied the spread of the cotton kingdom to the Southwest. A whole class of traders, brokers, and commission agents emerged to handle the buying of slaves in the Upper South and their sale in the Deep South. It was formerly thought that the slave traders generally were of a class and character that caused planters to despise them, but Kenneth Stampp has shown that the trade was engaged in by men from every stratum of Southern society, and that many of them were socially acceptable to the aristocracy.[11] The trade did offer an opportunity for poorer whites to make their way into the planter class, and despite the speculative and often unscrupulous character of the trade, some were eminently successful. Nathan B. Forrest, later a Confederate general and still later the national leader of the Ku Klux Klan, and Isaac Franklin, who profited sufficiently to buy plantations in Louisiana and Tennessee, are cases in point. For the blacks "sold down the river," uprooted from familiar scenes and separated from families and friends, inspected, handled, and put through their paces for prospective purchasers, it was a fearful revelation of how inhuman slavery could be. It also impressed on them how little they counted as human beings.

The same lesson was impressed on them, in different ways on the plantations, of course, although it took on a special character with the concentration of ownership and the growth of large plantations. Owners could not manage all their holdings, and some were not interested, so that actual management often fell into the hands of experienced men, the overseers. Just as the prestige and income of Yankee factory managers rested on records of output, so did those of the Southern overseer. This meant that the long-range interest of the master in treating slaves humanely, even if only from economic considerations, conflicted with the short-range interest of the overseer in producing record bales of cotton, regardless of effects on the slaves. Usually the overseer won, for with the planter as with the Yankee mill owner, the immediate profit was the determining factor. Thus, economic factors, as well as the growing rigor of the slave codes, tended to make slavery harsher than before—at the very moment when opinion in Europe and in the North was becoming more critical of the institution.

At the same time, however, slavery as purely a plantation system of labor gave way to differentiation. Since blacks proved they could be trained, they were used in increasing numbers in a variety of occupations. The coal, iron, and lead mines of Virginia and Kentucky; textile mills of the Deep South; iron works, foundries and tobacco factories of the Upper South; railroad and other heavy construction—even the cattle ranches of Texas—all used slave labor. In the cities and towns slaves were to be found in

[11] Kenneth M. Stampp, *The Peculiar Institution* (New York: Vintage Books, 1956), pp. 267–71.

many occupations: domestics, longshoremen, draymen, carpenters, shoe-makers, tailors—even typesetters. While many such blacks were owned by their employers, a considerable number were hired out by their masters (at fees which effectively undermined white wage standards), and some were even permitted to hire their own time. That is, they made their own job arrangements, paid their masters a fixed amount of money, and kept the remainder, if any. In this way some slaves were able to buy their own freedom. More significantly, the practice subtly subverted the institution of slavery—a fact lamented time and again by public officials and editors. A realization of this danger, combined with the hostility of white workers whose jobs were threatened, resulted in legislation curbing the number of occupations in which slaves (and even free blacks) could work, but the practice continued.

If some aspects of slavery were less galling than others, it was still slavery. The industrious artisan striving to buy his freedom could be swindled with impunity by an unscrupulous master. The young mason enjoying the relative freedom of town life could be sold off as a plantation hand when prices were right. And in the towns, where the hold of the master was weak, public authority took its place. A thousand and one regulations covered the slave's behavior, violation of which usually resulted in floggings or other exemplary punishment. In the towns, as on plantations, slaves had to be kept in fear.

Nevertheless, slaveowners persuaded themselves and others—and not only in their own time—that the slaves were happy. Time and again they described their slaves, with every appearance of truthfulness, as warm, affectionate, happy-go-lucky, eternally grinning and chuckling, without a care in the world. But, as Stanley M. Elkins has pointed out, this "Sambo" stereotype was a white creation—a black adaptation to the rigidities of the slave system.[12] To survive, black slaves had to play the role expected of them by their masters, and so well did they play it that whites accepted it as genuine. Certainly, with some blacks the role-playing became so realistic as to become reality itself. With others, it was only a role, discarded once they led real lives with their fellows in the towns and on larger plantations, where they were less under the immediate surveillance of master or overseer. In such circumstances they developed their own cultures, with their own values, standards and social expectations, and communicated through a slave patois with manifold nuances of meaning which escaped those whites who complacently assumed they understood the black mind.

The outward slave response to slavery took many forms. Some adapted well, became in fact the "Sambo" of the stereotype. Some sought escape through sex, alcohol, and pietistic religion. Others resisted. Some slave

---

[12] Stanley M. Elkins, *Slavery: A Problem in American Institutional and Intellectual Life* (Chicago: University of Chicago Press, 1959), pp. 131–32.

rebellions did occur, and others were planned but exposed before they could be carried out. Thousands of slaves fled, especially after intrepid black abolitionists penetrated the South to organize escapes. Those discontented but unable or unwilling to risk escape, with its drastic punishments if one were captured, struck back in their own ways. They dawdled on the job; they damaged tools and implements; they maimed livestock—all with a show of stupid docility which infuriated and confused masters and overseers. In extreme circumstances, slaves resorted to murder and arson. Perhaps the best testimony to the slaves' response was produced by the war: as soon as Union armies neared, slaves streamed off the plantations!

In addition to black slaves, there were nearly 260,000 free blacks (many of them of mixed descent) in the South. Some were wretchedly poor, eking out a precarious existence in marginal jobs; others were relatively well off as skilled artisans, farmers, or planters; and a few, like William Johnson, the fabled barber of Natchez, Mississippi, amassed modest fortunes. In Charleston and New Orleans there were black communities of distinction, the members of which were often linked through illicit family ties to the white aristocracy, and who thought and behaved like their white counterparts. At the other end of the scale were the blacks who were permanent public charges, including not only the normal number of unemployables but also sick or worn-out slaves, belatedly freed and dumped in the cities by their masters.

Whatever exceptions might be made in individual cases, white Southerners looked askance at the free black presence. As a group they were regarded as vicious, immoral, criminal, and next to abolitionists, the most dangerous threat to slavery. Whites believed that free blacks helped instigate slave plots, a belief strengthened by the Denmark Vesey "plot" of 1822, for Vesey was a free artisan.[13] White attitudes were soon reflected in laws. Freedom of movement of free blacks was drastically restricted. They were forbidden to carry firearms. They could not legally entertain slaves. School sessions and church services were prohibited unless responsible white persons were present. The better paying jobs were gradually closed to them by law or by violence. By the late 1850s at least five states provided for easy re-enslavement of free blacks. In fact, re-enslavement had always been a threat. Towns and cities used it as punishment for legal offenses. White kidnappers carried on a profitable trade in free black flesh with virtual immunity: they claimed their victims were fugitive slaves, and of course, no black could testify against white men!

13 Richard C. Wade, *Slavery in the Cities: The South, 1820–1860* (New York: Oxford University Press, 1964), pp. 225, 250–51. For Thomas R. Dew's view that free blacks were "worthless and indolent" while "admirably calculated to excite plots, murders and insurrections," see Eric L. McKitrick, *Slavery Defended*, pp. 30–31.

THE WEST

The West, by which we mean the Old Northwest, was an area of nearly 250,000 square miles lying north and west of the Ohio river, which eventually made up the states of Ohio, Indiana, Illinois, Michigan, and Wisconsin. Long before settlement became important the significance of the section was indicated by the Continental Congress when it adopted the famous Land Ordinance of 1785, setting forth public land policy, and the Northwest Ordinance of 1787, providing the basic conditions under which territories of the United States were to be organized and later admitted to the Union as states. In addition, the ordinance prohibited slavery in the territory, setting the precedent that the national Congress had authority to regulate slavery in the territories.

When these ordinances were adopted, there was only a sprinkling of settlers to contend with the Indian peoples for dominion over the vast expanse of forest, swamp, and prairie. Successive waves of settlement, backed by the usual force and fraud from Washington, drove the Indians beyond the Mississippi to lands as yet uncoveted by whites. By 1850 few red men remained; their hunting, fishing, and planting grounds were now occupied by 4,500,000 whites—a rate of population growth far beyond those of the East and the South. It was a diverse population. In addition to those born in the section, there were 472,000 who had come from the South; 718,000 from the Middle States; and 172,000 from New England. Some 527,000 came from Europe, mainly Ireland, Germany and Scandinavia.

This made for other diversities, for each group brought with it an attachment to its own way of life. Nevertheless, there were elements which bound Westerners together and gave them a special character that was neither Southern, nor Yankee, nor foreign. They were migrants who, frustrated by developments in their homelands, had moved west in the hope that cheap land and hard work would bring success. They were not rich, but neither were they poor. It required ready capital to move family, household goods, tools, and equipment to the new land. And, after 1820, when Congress abolished credit in public land sales, cash was needed to buy land.

Far removed from the centers of wealth and culture, involved every day of the week in work which left them little leisure, Westerners were practical minded, scornful of too much "book learning," and fiercely egalitarian. No man was better than any other, they held, and they were determined to permit no relapse on their soil into the class systems of South and East with which they were all too familiar. They may have patterned their state constitutions after those of the older states, but they kept power in the hands of the common people, with the exclusion, of course, of blacks and women. All white males could vote and hold office.

Legislatures were given wide powers while authority of governors was limited. Wisconsin even provided for popular election of the judiciary!

The Western insistence on political democracy was a manifestation of an even deeper commitment to economic democracy. Land was wealth, and Westerners wanted that wealth easy to come by, especially since it was being threatened by Eastern land speculators. Most of the land was in the hands of the government, and Westerners were convinced that it belonged to them and their children—were they not the people who could make best use of it? Were they not entitled to it through settlement? Given the situation, the only way in which the land could be transferred into the hands of the people was through political action. Divided, like other Americans, on such issues as tariff, and banking and currency, Westerners were united on a free land policy. As their political power grew in Congress—the West had one spokesman in the House in 1800; 56 in 1860—its role in intersectional politics became pivotal. Wooed first by the South, then by the East, Western politicians were willing to trade votes in return for steady liberalization of the terms on which public land could be obtained.

We should note that the attitude of the Westerners toward land was not that of a mystic peasant attachment to it. Rather, they looked upon land as businessmen: it was a resource to be exploited for profit and sold whenever high prices offered. Thus a constant internal migration as the region began to fill up: already established settlers sold out to newcomers willing to pay the price and moved farther west to take advantage of cheap government land. Or, in the case of crop failures, depressions, or mined-out soil, the presence of cheap land offered an opportunity to recoup one's fortunes. And, of course, it provided the assurance that one's children had at least the means of a livelihood. Free land, then, was as vital to the West as slavery to the South and industrial enterprise to the East.

A major element in the growing estrangement between South and West in the 1850s was Southern pressure to extend slavery into all the territories. Slavery, as such, presented little problem to Westerners. Indeed, a disguised form of slavery existed in Illinois and Indiana for many years, despite the Northwest Ordinance. The whites generally had little love for blacks: legislation and custom bore harshly on "free men of color." The West turned against slavery only when its threatened extension into western public lands presented a menace to the Western way of life, based as it was on free land and free farmers.

Western insistence on free land grew, in part, out of changes in the West itself. These transformed the region from an isolated area of subsistence farming to a booming territory of market farming which was as much involved in the capitalist world as industry in the East and cotton planting in the South. Once the pioneers had drained the swamps, cleared the forests, and broken the unyielding prairie sod, their successors produced a surplus of wheat, corn, hogs, and whiskey. The market was the industrializing East, but the Alleghenies blocked easy access. Westerners, of necessity, had to ship their products down the Mississippi to New Orleans, there to be transported to the east coast. This route, which also opened to Westerners, Southern, Latin American, and European markets, became all the more important after the advent of the steamboat on the Mississippi in 1817, which drastically cut costs of transportation, with consequent benefits to the Western farmer both as producer and as consumer. This strengthened a community of economic interest between South and West which was to last until the 1850s.

The relationship began to erode with the opening of the Erie Canal in 1825 and the subsequent spread of canal systems in the western states, linking the farming hinterland of the Great Lakes with the Atlantic seaboard. Slowly at first, but with increasing momentum, commodities from the West began flowing eastward instead of southward. Then in the 1840s came three developments which hastened the process. The collapse of the economy in 1837 and the prolonged depression which ensued meant disaster for Western farmers. With the domestic market limited, their attention turned to foreign outlets, and particularly to Great Britain. In Britain the need for cheap food was apparent and the Anti-Corn Law League was conducting massive agitation to repeal the laws restricting import of foreign wheat. On this continent abolitionists told the farmers their plight was due to domination of the federal government by Southerners, who saw to it that world markets for cotton were cultivated while markets for western wheat were neglected.

The Southern-oriented Polk Administration, elected in 1844 just as the depression was lifting, was preoccupied with its plans for expansion into Mexico and in its dispute with Britain over the Oregon country. It felt the necessity for cementing a South-West political alliance while at the same time heeding demands of the planters for lower tariffs. The outcome was the Walker Tariff of 1846, sharply reducing import taxes, and in effect widely expanding the American market for British manufactures. That same year, for domestic reasons as well as in consideration of the American action, Britain repealed the Corn Laws, giving Western farmers access to Europe's single biggest market. In 1844 the United States exported 1,000,000 bushels of wheat; in 1847, 4,000,000; and, with fluctuations from time to time, reached a record high of 15,000,000 bushels in 1857. Farmers profited even more than these figures indicate because of crop failures in Europe in the late 1840s, which sent wheat prices soaring. Such golden opportunities called for land, and more land—and to the Westerners this meant free land.

These developments might have tightened the economic ties between West and South but for another development: expansion of the Eastern railroad network into the West while Southern railroad builders provided little competition. In 1847 there were only a few hundred miles of railroad in the West, but a heavy infusion of Eastern capital brought about so much building that by 1860 there were 9600 miles of track, tying East and West in a thriving relationship. Some Westerners and Southerners tried to modify the situation through the Illinois Central, linking Chicago with New Orleans, but their move came too late to count, and in any case the advantage lay with the East-West routes. These provided more direct connection with Europe and thus transportation costs were lower than those of the circuitous route through New Orleans. Wheat and flour spoiled less in New York and Boston than in the humid warehouses of the South. Credit was cheaper and easier to get in the East than in New Orleans.

Thus, a new community of economic interest, binding East and West together, supplanted the older South-West community. A larger consequence was foreseen as early as 1847 by an Easterner, who told Alexander Mackay, the British traveler: "This is what we have effected by tapping the West. We have united it to us by bonds of iron, which it cannot, and which, if it could, it would not break. By binding it to the older states by the strong tie of material interests, we have identified its political sentiment with our own." [14]

There were still other elements of change in the West. While the bulk of the population remained rural, an increasing proportion lived in fast-growing towns and cities. After the opening of the Erie Canal such settlements as Detroit, Cleveland, Milwaukee and Chicago boomed as ports through which passed ever-increasing numbers of immigrants—both foreign and native—and a steadily mounting flow of farm commodities and manufactured goods. Industry, taking root to meet regional needs and exploit the West's resources, spurred still further urban growth. Cincinnati became the nation's leading meat-packing center; farm equipment was produced in Canton, Ohio, Moline, Illinois, and Chicago. By 1860 the West had nearly 37,000 manufacturing establishments employing 210,000 workers producing goods valued at $384,000,000. Galena, Illinois, prospered as the center of a lead mining area, while numerous other mining towns sprang up throughout the West atop deposits of coal, iron, and copper. In short, the Industrial Revolution had come West.

Western industrialists and middle class people largely shared the social philosophy of their Eastern counterparts—indeed in many instances they were transplanted Easterners. Disciples of Adam Smith, they believed as religiously in free enterprise, free labor, and free land as they did in government aid for road, canal, and railroad building, for dredging rivers and deepening harbors, and when it suited their interests, for federal aid to private business through protective tariffs. Their prosperity depended upon an expanding national market based on free consumers able to

---

[14] Alexander Mackay, *The Western World, or Travels in the United States in 1846–1847* (London: R. Bentley, 1850), Vol. I, 240.

absorb the products of mine and factory. Willing to allow slavery to continue where it existed, they opposed its extension, for that signified a minimum rather than maximum market.

There was another dimension to their attitudes. Their commitment to free enterprise was based on the assumption that it was an integral part of the larger concept of a free society, the highest form of civilization. The purest expression of this ideal was the United States—except for slavery. This made a mockery of their belief that the principles of the Declaration were not fallacies, but vital principles to be followed by all mankind. The unease this conflict produced was accentuated by the moral issue of slavery. Could a Christian nation sanction the enslavement of human beings? This question, raised by abolitionists, brought about the splits between North and South in the major Protestant churches during the 1840s. Here was a demon which would not down. Westerners took their religion very seriously indeed, especially after the revivals which swept the section in the 1820s. Abolitionists, with their strong emphasis on personal piety, made the most of it.

There was also a black West. By 1850 there were nearly 46,000 blacks in the region, centered largely in such cities as Cincinnati, Detroit, Cleveland and Chicago, and their number was growing: despite the flight of thousands to Canada after passage of the Fugitive Slave Law of 1850, the census counted nearly 65,000 in 1860. As in the East, most earned their livelihoods at a variety of skilled and unskilled occupations, and a small elite articulated the aspirations of the black community. Among these spokesmen were John Mercer Langston, a member of the Ohio bar; John Jones, a prosperous tailor of Chicago; George DeBaptiste, an active agent of the Underground Railroad in Indiana and Detroit; and H. Ford Douglass of Illinois, who later became one of the few black commissioned officers in the Union army.

Most Western blacks were free, but slavery did exist for a time in the area, despite the Northwest Ordinance. A pioneer mining promoter moved into the Galena lead mining region of Illinois in 1822 with 150 slaves as well as other personnel, and as late as 1840 the Census reported more than 300 black slaves in the state. More commonly, in both Illinois and Indiana, blacks were held to long-term labor contracts which in effect made them slaves although technically they were free. Richard C. Wade has noted the complaint of the governor of Illinois in 1828 that "our negroes" were fleeing to St. Louis to escape such bondage—despite the fact that Missouri was a slave state—and his request that the mayor of the city help in their "capture and return." [15]

[15] Richard C. Wade, *Slavery in the Cities*, p. 220.

Western white attitudes toward blacks may be summed up in the observation that while Westerners wanted no slavery, neither did they want free blacks. Illinois and Indiana eventually banned their legal entry. Other states, Ohio for example, required newcomers to post prohibitively high bond—supposedly to make sure they kept the peace and did not become public charges. That such laws were infrequently enforced does not disguise the animus behind them. There were still other legal discriminations. Only Indiana permitted free blacks to vote, and that right was rescinded in 1851. Blacks could not serve as jurors, and in some states could not testify against whites in court—which made black men easy pickings for unscrupulous whites. Public schools were closed to black children, although their parents paid school taxes. Segregation in housing became as much a feature of Western towns as it was of Eastern and Southern cities. Mob violence, while not as pronounced as in the East, was still to be feared in towns on the Ohio River. Blacks were driven out of Portsmouth, Ohio, in 1830; Cincinnati blacks were victims of major white riots in 1829, 1836, and 1841. Private black schools were forcibly closed in some places. In short, Western democracy was not for blacks.

Blacks thought otherwise. They, too, had staked out a claim to American democracy; blacks had fought in the Revolutionary War and the War of 1812; their labor had helped develop the nation, and their taxes went to support government. At first they had few alternatives save to accept subordination, but as their numbers grew and an educated leadership emerged, they became more militant. Local and state societies of blacks were organized, devoted to promotion of black rights. Members demanded suffrage for blacks, on the hallowed ground of "No taxation without representation," the opening of public schools to black youngsters, and the ending of discrimination in the courts. In the meantime, blacks organized and financed their own schools in many communities and formed mutual benefit associations to aid members in distress. They failed to gain the suffrage, but they finally won concessions on schools in Ohio, Michigan, and Wisconsin—although the funds allocated were inadequate and segregation was the rule. Another success was scored in Ohio in 1849 when the state's oppressive Black Laws were repealed: free black immigration was permitted, and blacks were allowed to testify in court against whites. Western blacks, like Eastern, were developing their own sense of community, producing their own leaders, and through struggle creating a sense of their own worth and dignity.

Nowhere was this more evident than in black abolitionism. Blacks were active in existing interracial abolition societies but when necessary they set up their own organization. Underground Railroad operations, shuttling fleeing slaves from the Ohio River to the lake ports of Detroit, Toledo, Sandusky, and Cleveland, were many times engineered by blacks, for fugitives felt more secure among their own people than among whites.

All-black vigilance committees functioned in Detroit, Cleveland, and other towns to protect fugitives from capture and to expedite them on their way to Canada.

Militancy sometimes went even further. In 1849 an Ohio black convention voted to circulate Henry Highland Garnet's call for armed resistance to slavery, in sharp contrast to the repudiation of the speech by the New York state convention to which it was addressed. Nor was militant action lacking. Black informers, whose activities menaced the efforts to help slaves escape, were given community punishment when caught, with tar-and-feathers or flogging the usual result. In 1833 Detroit blacks successfully battled police to free fugitives. Thirteen years later in Chicago, both black and white abolitionists united in wresting two fleeing slaves from the authorities. In 1859, the black Charles Langston, brother of the more famous John Mercer Langston, was one of those convicted for helping in the celebrated Oberlin-Wellington rescue of a black man seized under the federal Fugitive Slave Law. Western blacks, like those in the East, perceived that the struggle for emancipation was inseparable from the struggle for equal rights—a point which many white abolitionists did not appreciate.

Abolition and Anti-Slavery

The abolitionists who emerged in the 1830s were a different breed from those of an earlier generation who had hoped to bring about voluntary liberation of the slaves by touching the hearts of slaveholders. The new men—and women—were in a sense a response to the Southern developments which indicated that such hope for an end to slavery was illusory. They were, also, a product of the growing anti-slavery feeling which surfaced during the bitter controversy over the Missouri Compromise of 1820. More immediately, they were the offspring of the intensely pietistic religious revivals which swept the country in the 1820s and 1830s. Most of the converted were content to lead "redeemed" lives in terms of personal piety, believing that social regeneration must wait upon universal individual redemption.

For the new abolitionists this was not enough. Godliness, they insisted, required not only that individuals forsake sinful ways but also that the nation purge itself of its social sin—slavery. The true Christian, as Charles G. Finney, the master evangelist from Oberlin, reiterated unceasingly, *must* be anti-slavery. This integration of personal and social morality afforded abolitionists a psychological base from which to appeal to thousands of folk in East and West already sensitized to moral issues by the evangelism of the revivals. And abolitionists, confident of the righteousness of their case, were further encouraged by the successful campaign of British abolitionists to end slavery in the British West Indies.

Through pamphlets, newspapers, mass meetings, church services, evangelistic rallies, and private discussions they spread the gospel. They received invaluable assistance from their enemies. Southern editors and politicians helped provide William Lloyd Garrison, epitome of the new militant abolitionism, with an unwarranted national and international reputation as the father of American abolition. The refusal of Congress to consider anti-slavery petitions provided abolitionists with a cause to which they could rally numerous citizens, such as the aged John Quincy Adams, who were less concerned with abolition than with the constitutional rights of American citizens. Censorship of the Southern mails also helped abolitionists to dramatize the slave threat to American liberties, as did the demands of Southern states that anti-slavery propaganda be suppressed in the North. Even more significant in this respect was the federal Fugitive Slave Law of 1850, which aroused even Northern conservatives, such as Richard Henry Dana of Boston, the noted lawyer and author of *Two Years Before the Mast*. In this sense, the abolitionists were the spark-plugs of what came to be a much broader anti-slavery movement, made up of men and women who differed in their interpretations of the movement but were at least united in fighting the extension of slavery.

Abolition, like every major social reform movement, attracted its share of fanatics and crackpots. The fact that the anti-slavery movement for the most part was made up of sober, respectable, successful middle-class citizens is often overlooked. Dwight L. Dumond, who made an exhaustive study of the movement, pointed out, with perhaps some exaggeration, that abolition was "initiated and carried through at great personal sacrifice by men of property and high position in religious and educational institutions, in public life, and in the professions." [16]

Even a partial list of those attracted to abolition shows its middle-class appeal: Lewis and Arthur Tappan, successful New York merchants; Gerrit Smith, one of the greatest landowners in New York; Joshua Giddings and Benjamin Wade, rising young lawyers of Ashtabula County, Ohio; Arnold Buffum, New England hat manufacturer; William Ellery Channing, the distinguished Unitarian leader of Massachusetts, and his radical successor, Theodore Parker; and Theodore D. Weld, son of a Yankee Congregationalist minister, who supplied the practical organizational talent which gave point and strength to scattered anti-slavery sentiment.

These are all Easterners and Westerners. Actually, a surprisingly significant impetus to abolition came from Southern exiles. The roll of such men is too long to call here. Let a few examples suffice:

Levi Coffin of North Carolina went to Indiana in 1826, and there became a notable figure in organizing escapes of fugitive slaves. Edward

---

[16] Dwight L. Dumond, *Anti-Slavery: the Crusade for Freedom in America* (Ann Arbor: University of Michigan Press, 1961), p. 95.

Coles of Virginia in 1819 brought his slaves West, gave them land and freedom, and later as governor of Illinois blocked adoption of a pro-slavery constitution. Thomas Morris of Virginia went to Ohio in 1795, became active in anti-slavery politics, served in the state legislature, became chief justice of the Ohio Supreme Court, and entered the U.S. Senate in 1833 as the first anti-slavery senator.

Southerners continued to make contributions after the rise of militant abolition, among the most notable being the Grimké sisters of South Carolina and James G. Birney of Alabama. Angelina and Sarah Grimké, daughters of an old aristocratic family, were converted to abolition, freed the slaves who were their family portion, attempted unsuccessfully to promote abolition in their home state, then went North to become leading lights in the new crusade. Birney, who had been chief counsel for the Cherokee Nation in its futile struggle to retain its ancestral lands, was a successful lawyer. Converted to abolition by Weld, he sold his slaves, tried to organize anti-slavery societies in the Upper South, retreated to Ohio under threats of violence, and became one of the outstanding leaders of the movement.

The middle-class character of abolition helps explain its eventual success. Apart from the group of New England reformers gathered around Garrison, abolitionists generally were conservative in their outlook. Most of them, with a few exceptions such as Wendell Phillips, the outspoken clergyman of Massachusetts, and Horace Greeley, the influential editor of the New York *Tribune*, were either indifferent or hostile to the infant labor unions. (Union men charged that the hearts which bled over black slavery were flint over white slavery in the mills.) Most abolitionists were strong believers in individualism and free enterprise: indeed in the 1850s one school of thought justified emancipation on grounds of classical economics —free black labor in the South would prove more productive than slave labor, and thus provide cheaper cotton for New England mills while at the same time elevating the condition of the blacks. The crusaders supported the orthodox churches while striving to reform them from within. They revered the Declaration of Independence and honored the Constitution; they believed that their ends could and should be attained through constitutional means, as well as through moral influence.

In short, abolitionists were never so far apart from their neighbors that dialogue became impossible. The dialogue was so important in spreading the gospel that when Garrison and his followers appeared to threaten it, their opponents were willing to split the movement rather than let the radicals seem to speak for all abolitionists.

The dialogue was not all sweetness and light. Abolition meetings were mobbed again and again; newspaper offices were wrecked; in Alton, Illinois, Elijah Lovejoy, preacher and editor, was assassinated. Less dramatic but nonetheless effective sanctions were enforced in both East and West. Lane

Theological Seminary in Cincinnati banned student activism; dissidents went to Oberlin, transforming it into an abolitionist powerhouse. Harvard College refused reappointment to Dr. Karl Follen because of his anti-slavery views. It turned down employment of Richard Hildreth, the historian, for similar reasons. The Tappans had difficulties with New York banks and insurance companies—to say nothing of a boycott organized against them by Charleston, South Carolina, merchants. A botany teacher in Washington, D.C., charged with intending to circulate abolitionist literature, was threatened with the death penalty; the prosecutor was, ironically, Francis Scott Key, author of *The Star Spangled Banner*.[17] The strength of the abolitionists lay in turning the outrages to account, in alerting the public to the danger to American freedom inherent in slavery, for whites as well as blacks. Through the open violence of mobs and the hidden violence of respectable institutions they never ceased talking to their fellow Americans.

It was on this issue that the movement split. Garrison, consistent with his humanistic idealism, moved from orthodox piety to abolition to extreme positions on a variety of issues. He excoriated the churches, political parties, and the Constitution, which he labelled, as early as 1833, "a most bloody and Heaven-daring arrangement." He took a leading role in the struggle for women's rights, a movement even less popular than abolition. He became an uncompromising pacifist and began to advocate disunion.

This was too much for respectable anti-slavery men. They wanted no part of a movement which in the public mind was tainted with religious infidelity, free love, and hostility to the Constitution. Such sentiment found expression in 1840 when its exponents withdrew from the Garrison-oriented American Anti-Slavery Society and founded their own American and Foreign Anti-Slavery Society. Actually, neither national society was as important as the local and regional societies—and in them there was a mounting demand for political action to give point to moral suasion.

This desire bore fruit in independent political action, such as the Liberty Party, organized in 1839. The party never attracted many voters, but in 1844 it provided just enough popular votes to give the New York electoral vote to James K. Polk, Democrat, and thus send him to the White House. In 1848, as part of a larger Free Soil coalition, it helped make the slave-owning Whig, Zachary Taylor, president. Abolitionists proved that, while they had little mass support, they had sufficient votes to be spoilers. Here was a force that practical politicians had to reckon with.

Perhaps more important in the long run was the growth of anti-slavery sentiment within the established parties—Democrat and Whig. Thomas Morris, transplanted Southerner and Ohio Democrat, the first anti-slavery

[17] Louis Filler, *The Crusade Against Slavery, 1830–1860* (New York: Harper & Row, Publishers, 1963), p. 75.

United States Senator, was elected in 1833. Joshua Giddings, Ohio Whig
and outspoken abolitionist, was sent to the House in 1838. Thaddeus
Stevens, Pennsylvania Whig, made not only abolition, but also equal rights
for blacks, an issue in his state's politics. Charles Sumner and Henry Wilson
(both later United States Senators) successfully pushed anti-slavery policies
in Massachusetts, as did Abraham Lincoln, less successfully, in Illinois.

Democrats were less hospitable than Whigs to the new ideas—early
anti-slavery leaders were read out of the party—but they could not halt the
process of change. In short, within both parties anti-slavery was spreading,
not only because of abolitionist propaganda, but also, and of more importance, because the trend of events (which we shall discuss in the next
chapter) seemed to give point to the abolitionist claim that there was a
"slave power," bent on extending slavery throughout the nation and even
beyond, into Texas, Mexico, and Cuba while it subverted the liberties of
Americans at home. Thus, when the Republican Party was organized in
1854, there was already in existence a considerable group of experienced
anti-slavery politicians, who saw in the new organization not only a means
of realizing personal ambitions but also of attaining their anti-slavery goals.

What were these goals? Here there was considerable confusion among
the general public, for abolitionists themselves were far from being of one
opinion, if we include among abolitionists the diversity of men with anti-
slavery beliefs. Some, like Abraham Lincoln, believed in merely restricting
slavery to the existing slave states, holding that this would eventually lead
the institution to extinction. Still others held out for gradual emancipation,
with or without compensation to slaveowners. The militants called for
"immediate" emancipation, a demand which scared the public and offended
moderate anti-slavery elements. Pro-slavery men made good use of the
demand, conjuring up nightmares of black rebellions, massacres of white
men, raping of white women, racial amalgamation. Explanations by militants as to its meaning were never quite clear. Perhaps the most cogent
was offered by Garrison: "immediate" emancipation was a statement of
moral imperative, not a practical program. Said he: "Urge immediate abolition as we may, it will . . . be gradual abolition in the end. We have
never said that slavery would be overthrown by a single blow: that it ought
to be, we shall always contend."

One reason why so many abolitionists were against immediate emancipation was their belief that freed slaves would not be ready to assume
the responsibilities of free men. Some, sympathetic to the slave though
they might be, shared the prevalent view that blacks were by nature
inferior to whites, and thus advocated the colonization of freed slaves in
Africa or Latin America. Others, conceding the present backwardness of
blacks, attributed it to the degrading influence of slavery. Freedom, they
argued, would bring out the hidden potential of blacks. To this end they

brought to countless platforms such fugitives as Frederick Douglass and William Wells Brown, and sponsored the publication of slave narratives, designed not only to demonstrate the horrors of slavery but also the potential of black people.

The solution to the problem of "immediate" emancipation, first expressed by the seceding students at Lane Seminary, was later generally accepted—it was "gradual emancipation, immediately begun." Private ownership of slaves was to end immediately, slaves were to become free laborers, and "placed under a benevolent and disinterested supervision . . . until ready for intellectual and moral equality with whites." The details of this naive proposal were never spelled out, and few white abolitionists asked blacks what they thought of it. Indeed, white abolitionists generally, including militants, held their black associates at arm's length. Some societies excluded blacks from membership; few white abolitionists met blacks socially; and only reluctantly, under great black pressure, did societies admit blacks, such as Douglass, to policy-making positions. Besides—and this was a sore point with black abolitionists—many white abolitionists were lukewarm or even hostile to the black campaign for equal rights in West and East. Abolitionists could not escape their racist heritage!

There was another aspect of the anti-slavery movement which deserves mention—its contribution to the transformation of Eastern and Western sectionalisms into a Northern sectionalism. If canals, railroads, and the spread of industrialism united East and West in terms of material interest, abolition helped provide a common bond of moral and spiritual goals. Northern sectionalism came to be identified with the moral foundations of the nation as set forth in the Declaration, and thus in Northern minds, was not sectionalism at all, but the very embodiment of the American nation. The North was the inheritor of the Revolution, the representative of freedom, the living example of democracy. Thus, American nationalism, uneasy in the face of rising Southern nationalism, was strengthened by a new infusion of moral idealism. By the same token, the slave South came to be looked upon both as a moral deviant and as an enemy of American principles.

Thus far we have seen three distinct sections—East, West and South —developing and changing rapidly, each according to its own regional dynamics, and then the coalescing of East and West into a distinctive North vis-à-vis a distinctive South, with mounting conflicts of outlook, interest, and policy. How these conflicts reached such magnitude and intensity that they proved insoluble short of war will be discussed in the following chapter.

Good-by to Sumter, February 8, 1861. *Harper's Weekly.* February 23, 1861.

CHAPTER II

FEVER

CHART

OF

A

NATION

Sectional tensions manifested themselves as early as the Constitutional Convention of 1787. From then on their intensity may be measured by the steps taken to resolve them, although, as it turned out, each "resolution" contained within itself the seeds of graver crisis. In this connection it is significant to note that men of such diverse outlooks as Thomas Jefferson, John Quincy Adams, John C. Calhoun, and Abraham Lincoln all agreed that the Union was on shaky ground—and that a basic cause of instability was slavery.

This was so, not because white men were greatly concerned about the fate of black men, but because in nearly every sectional issue which arose the issue of slavery was directly or indirectly involved. Slavery had become such an integral part of the Southern way of life that any sectional controversy was bound to impinge upon it, however remote the actual issue appeared to be from the "peculiar institution." Thus, in 1824, when Congress passed a measure committing the federal government to a road and canal building program, John Randolph of Virginia opposed it on the ground that if such a grant of power to the federal government were lawful then Congress "may emancipate every slave in the United States." Twenty years later Joshua Giddings, the abolitionist Congressman from Ohio, noted the development from a contrary point of view: "Our tariff is as much an anti-slavery measure as the rejection of Texas. So is the subject of internal improvements and the distribution of the proceeds of the public lands. The advocates of perpetual slavery oppose all of them."

In this guise, as the center of a complex of Southern interests, slavery was a major source of dissension in the founding of the nation. At the Constitutional Convention there was no disposition to end slavery, but the Southern demand that slaves be counted as persons for calculating representation in the lower house of Congress aroused the opposition of nonslave states. To grant the demand might well mean Southern domination of the new government, a prospect which neither the Middle States nor New England welcomed. And if Southern property were to be made a basis of representation, why not property elsewhere? Out of this dispute came one of the major compromises which made the Constitution possible: the South, in addition to its white population, could count three-fifths of its slave population for purposes of representation and direct taxation.

In so agreeing the all-white convention conceded the ambiguous position of the black slave in the new republic: he was a man, but only three-fifths of a man. As James Madison of Virginia put it in *The Federalist*, the Constitution regarded "the *slave* as divested of two-fifths of the *man*." In urging adoption of the Constitution with this provision, Madison sounded a note magnified later by planters claiming special protection for slave property—that interference with slavery was an infringement on the rights of property. Madison declared that since the new Constitution provided no branch of government dedicated to protecting the rights of property as such, "some attention ought . . . to be paid to property" in establishing a basis of representation.

In fact, the Constitution afforded slave property protection given no other form of property. A slave was a slave, even if he escaped into a free state. No such state could free him, and he was to be "delivered up on claim" of his owner. The slave was not protected by the extradition provisions, and he had no right to due process. The Constitutional provisions were implemented with a federal fugitive slave law in 1793. The slave South was also placated with a Constitutional requirement putting off abolition of the foreign slave trade for at least twenty years.

In general, the divisions at the convention, so deep that at times it seemed no Constitution would emerge, were not between large and small states, as some school texts still record, but between sections. Madison, who kept faithful notes of the secret meetings, reported that "the real difference of interests lay, not between the large and the small, but between the Northern and Southern states. The institution of slavery, and its consequences, formed the line of discrimination." [1]

The line of discrimination continued and deepened within the new nation. In 1798, on issues unrelated to slavery, two slave states—Virginia and Kentucky—asserted the right of states to judge the legality of acts of Congress, a position later taken up by the slave South to protect slavery. A few years later New England resistance to Jefferson's embargo policy was so violent that Jefferson felt "the foundations of the government shaken . . . by the New England townships." The ensuing War of 1812 occasioned massive resistance in New England, accompanied by threats of secession, justified on the ground that the war, like the embargo, sacrificed New England to Southern slaveholders and Western "wild men."

During these years political leaders in Washington discouraged public discussion of the explosive issue of slavery, but in 1819 their hand was forced when Missouri applied for admission to the Union. Was the state to be free or slave? Dissension was so bitter that Representative James Tallmadge proposed a compromise: protect slavery as it was while providing for gradual emancipation. This occasioned debates so divisive, so shot through with threats of civil war and secession, that the aging Jefferson despaired of the survival of the Union. The outcome was the famous Missouri Compromise of 1820: Missouri came in as a slave state, Maine as a free state, and slavery was banned in the Louisiana Purchase territory north of latitude 36 degrees and 30 minutes—the southern border of Missouri. Thus, the South, the West, and the East were for the moment placated, and white Americans generally took comfort in the thought that the issue of the expansion of slavery had been settled. [2]

But the issue of slavery would not down. In 1828, South Carolina, outraged by the newly enacted "Tariff of Abominations," declared the right of injured states to nullify acts of Congress, and in 1832 implemented the doctrine—actions which had less to do with tariff questions than with staking out constitutional ground for protection of slavery against possible

[1] Max Farrand, ed., *Records of the Federal Convention of 1787* (New Haven, Conn.: Yale University Press, 1911–37), II, 9–10. For a recent discussion see Winthrop D. Jordan, *White Over Black* (Baltimore, Md.: Penguin Books, 1969), pp. 323–25.

[2] For a comprehensive review, see Donald L. Robinson, *Slavery in the Structure of American Politics, 1765–1820* (New York: Harcourt Brace Jovanovich, Inc., 1971).

federal intrusion, as William W. Freehling has pointed out.[3] Also, in the 1830s Texans successfully rebelled against Mexico, established their independence, and sought admission to the Union through treaty as a vast slave territory from which other slave states might be carved. American annexationists, unable to muster a two-thirds vote in the Senate, failed. Then, in 1844, guided by Secretary of State John C. Calhoun, they successfully resorted to a joint Congressional resolution, which required only majority vote. Texas was in, the slave South was generally (but not unanimously) happy, and many people in East and West were outraged at the devious means used to bring into the Union a dangerous addition to the slave power.

Two years later came the Mexican War and the fat was in the fire. With American victory assured, anti-slavery representatives in the House won approval of the Wilmot Proviso, excluding slavery from any territory wrested from Mexico. The Senate, dominated by Southerners and their Northern allies, rejected it. The House again adopted the measure, and again the Senate turned it down. The acrid, violent debates reflected the growing polarization of opinion in the country. Eastern and Western Whigs, supported by anti-slavery Democrats, favored the proviso. Anti-war Southerners, led by Calhoun, pro-war Democrats, and Southern Whigs, who had little faith in President Polk's policies—all now gathered together to defend slavery and the right to extend it. The Virginia legislature resolved "resistance at all hazards and to the last extremity" if the proviso were adopted, and other Southern legislatures followed suit. Talk of civil war and secession ebbed and flowed from Congress to county courthouses, and back again.

As positions hardened, the conflicting outlooks became more clearly defined. The South held that slaves were property, protected by the Constitution not only within slave states but also in the territories, which themselves were the common possession of the states. Slaveholders and slaves could not therefore be lawfully excluded from any territory of the United States. Such exclusion would deprive slaveowners of their property rights and would so alter the balance of the Union against the South that in self-defense it would have to resist. Should such resistance result in civil war, responsibility would rest on those who sought to reduce the South to subordinate status. Further, the Wilmot Proviso masked an abolitionist design to organize on Southern borders a ring of free states to be used in subverting slavery.

Anti-slavery men held just as firmly that slaves were not property in the strict legal sense: they were persons held to service, a distinction im-

---

[3] William W. Freehling, *Prelude to Civil War: The Nullification Crisis in South Carolina, 1816–1836* (New York: Harper & Row, Publishers, 1966), p. 86.

bedded in the Constitution, which nowhere mentions slavery, and recognized by the South when it accepted the three-fifths compromise. As for the right to take such persons into the territories, the precedents were clear that the right was limited. Congress, with Southern support, had barred slavery from the Northwest Territory in 1787. Again with Southern support, Congress had excluded slavery in the territories north of the Missouri Compromise line. Congress had lawful authority to do so, for while territories were possessions of the United States they were not part of it constitutionally, and were thus subject to Congressional regulation until they were accepted as states. Further, the Southern demand represented an attempt to impose slavery in an area where it did not exist. Texas, however deviously admitted to the Union, at least protected slavery in its constitution, but in Mexico slavery had been abolished. By what right could the authority of the United States be used to force slavery on a free people? To which Calhoun answered, the right of the conqueror.

Anti-slavery men were also alarmed by reports that expansionists wanted not only all of Mexico but also Central America and Cuba. Polk, in fact, did propose that Spain be approached with an offer to buy Cuba, which his Secretary of the Treasury, R. J. Walker of Mississippi, thought worth $100 million. Other expansionists, such as Senator Stephen A. Douglas of Illinois, urged Polk to take the island by force, if necessary. There was more to the intrigues however, than Manifest Destiny. The French had just abolished slavery in their West Indian possessions, and it was feared that Spain might follow suit. Neither to Cuban nor Southern slaveholders was this prospect palatable.

No less palatable to Easterners and Westerners was the prospect of a vastly expanded slave empire which would tip the balance of the Union against their interests. What hope would there be then for the yeoman farmer, the industrialist, the free worker? Indeed, what hope could there be for a free way of life? The South, in its defense of slavery, had already demonstrated its willingness to sacrifice the rights of white men. Witness its influence in abrogating the right of petition, and in censoring the United States mail. Witness its campaign to suppress freedom of speech and press not only in the South but also in the other sections.

In such an atmosphere a triumphant nation tried to make up its mind on what to do with the spoils garnered from a feeble and divided Mexico.

It did not have much time. Before the Mexican treaty was signed gold was discovered in California, and the rush was on. California, hardly yet accustomed to being part of the United States, in 1849 was inundated by a hundred thousand fortune seekers—clergymen and thugs, farmers and prostitutes, merchants and bandits—from all over the world. The skeleton frame of government set up by the United States could not cope, and in any case no new legal system reflecting American principles had been established. The consequent anarchy compelled California to seek swift admission to the Union. A constitution was adopted and admission applied for, with the blessing of the new Whig President, General Zachary Taylor, a slaveowning sugar planter from Louisiana, who advised Congress to abstain from "exciting topics of a sectional character."

Southerners, dominated by Calhoun, were in no mood to listen. The vast area of Oregon had just been organized as a free territory. Now California sought admission with a constitution prohibiting slavery forever. To them, this was a defiant bid of the free states to dominate the Union, for California's admission would provide 16 free states as against 15 slave states. Already dominant in the House, the East and West would now control the Senate. "We have borne the insults of the North long enough," said Calhoun, urging other Southerners to resist "until the restoration of all our rights, or disunion, one or the other, is the consequence."

Talk of disunion was not confined to the South—it was so prevalent that Taylor flatly told Congress he would use all the power of his office to maintain the Union should the threats materialize. Southern threats of secession may have been a ploy to force concessions, as anti-slavery men like Joshua Giddings and William H. Seward suggested. Others, aware of the secessionist movements in South Carolina and Mississippi and of the passions stirred by the Mexican War and the Wilmot Proviso, were persuaded, with General Winfield Scott, that the country was on the eve of war.

Apart from the general sentiment of the country, a fear of any possible break-up of the Union, there were powerful forces working for peaceful settlement. The flow of gold from California gave a boost to business, exciting prospects of even greater prosperity to come. To a country which all too well remembered the "Hungry Forties" there was appeal in the plea: Why rock the boat?

Yankee textile barons and Pennsylvania iron masters believed that making concessions to the South would bring in return favorable tariffs. Western and Southern railroad promoters, dependent on federal support for the Illinois Central and Mobile and Ohio projects, strove feverishly for conciliation. Eastern bankers, alarmed by declining British interest in American securities, wanted a settlement to revive British confidence. The great merchants of the Eastern seaboard, worried by Southern threats of a boycott of Yankee goods, advocated compromise. Holders of the bonds and notes of the defunct Republic of Texas, which the financially strapped state could not redeem, wanted a way out which would assure them profit. Finally, the great planters of the South, suspicious of secessionist movements, were ready for a deal which would protect basic Southern interests.

All the pressures of these groups, financial and political, converged on Washington to produce an agreement which would unify the country by taking the explosive issue of slavery out of politics.

This was the Compromise of 1850, a series of individual measures made possible by political log-rolling and much absenteeism, which afforded Congressmen an escape hatch on specific bills on which they did not want to publicly commit themselves. What were its provisions?

1. California was admitted—a concession to the free states.
2. Texas adjusted her boundary claims in favor of the United States, and in return received $10 million from the federal government, a settlement highly satisfactory to Texas bondholders.
3. The new lands gained from Mexico, plus the Texan cession, were organized in the new territories of New Mexico and Utah. They, or any parts of them, could apply for admission to the Union as states with or without slavery, as their white settlers might decide. This was Stephen A. Douglas' doctrine of "popular sovereignty" in practice, designed to take slavery out of national politics. Since slaveowners were not forbidden to migrate to the new territories, it provided Congressional sanction for the extension of slavery and an incentive for planters to occupy them.
4. The organized slave trade, but not slavery, was prohibited in the District of Columbia. Intended to propitiate anti-slavery sentiment, it did little to hinder slave trading. Private sales continued legally, and the organized traders simply moved their business across the Potomac to Virginia.
5. A new fugitive slave law met Southern demands for extension of federal authority to facilitate return of runaways. Alleged fugitives were not permitted to testify, and no proof was required other than a certificate from the claimant or his agent saying that the black was indeed a slave. State courts were forbidden to interfere, and individuals who aided runaways were subject to heavy penalties. The federal commissioners who heard the cases were paid $10 if they found in favor of the claimant, $5 if they decided for the black. If the fugitive escaped while in custody, the commissioner was liable for the value of the runaway.

Black America was appalled at what white America had done. Thousands fled to Canada, and among those who remained there were many, such as Frederick Douglass, who vowed to fight the fugitive slave law to the death. But white America, on the whole, was content: a major threat to the Union had been met successfully. Both parties endorsed the settlement, proponents of the compromise swept the 1852 elections, and secessionist sentiment ebbed in the South. The sectional balance, indeed, now favored the South, for California voters elected pro-Southern Senators and many pro-Southern Representatives. New Mexico and Utah territories both accepted slavery, and the California Supreme Court upheld slavery in that "free state" for several years after 1850.

In the East and West business interests rallied popular opinion behind the compromise. With an eye to Southern votes on tariffs and railroads, they vigorously endorsed the fugitive slave law. The appeal of the independent anti-slavery elements, as represented in the Free Soil Party, dropped sharply, from 291,000 votes in 1848 to 156,000 in 1852. So widespread was white sentiment favorable to the compromise that an opponent, Senator Thomas Hart Benton of Missouri, felt that the "great issues" of the nation had been settled. All that was left, he said, were "puny sectional questions and petty strifes about slavery."

To anti-slavery men these issues were far from petty, and they now had in the Senate two redoubtable spokesmen—Charles Sumner of Massachusetts and Benjamin Wade of Ohio—who had surmounted the wave of pro-compromise sentiment despite, or because of, their outspoken abolitionism. To them the paramount political issue was the fugitive slave law, in which they saw a flagrant Southern attempt to use the authority of the federal government to protect slavery in the free states. They resented not only the use of federal power to return fugitives, but also the law's requirement that free citizens aid slave catchers and the penalties invoked against those who aided runaways. Here again, as in the "gag rule" against anti-slavery petitions and censorship of the mails, was an invasion of the rights of American citizens as well as an affront to their consciences. Many hitherto passive Americans now found themselves agreeing with Ralph Waldo Emerson, himself no activist. The law, he noted, was a "filthy enactment . . . I will not obey it, by God."

The law was barely a year old before such words were translated into action. Abolitionists in Syracuse, New York, rescued an alleged fugitive and spirited him away to Canada. Eighteen rescuers were indicted, and some were tried—and acquitted. Three leaders who were not indicted publicly proclaimed their guilt and demanded trial to test the law. The district attorney declined. The pattern was repeated again and again as resistance spread: capture, rescue, arrests, and refusal of juries to convict.

Thus challenged, the federal government made an issue of law and order, pushing for prosecution and using the armed forces when necessary to return fugitives and thus vindicate the law. This in turn inflamed opinion even more, gaining adherents to the anti-slavery cause and giving strength to the belief that American liberties were endangered by a Southern slavocracy using the national government as its instrument. Legislatures strengthened their personal liberty laws so as to make slave catching a penal offense; Massachusetts went so far as to bar from state public office "forever" any state officer who helped enforce the Fugitive Slave Law. Even the courts became involved: the Wisconsin supreme court held the law unconstitutional—and was reversed by the same United States Supreme Court which handed down the Dred Scott decision.

A significant element in resistance was the role of black Americans. While thousands fled to Canada, most remained and of these many were determined to fight the law, preferably in company with white abolitionists. Black communities held public meetings which pledged aid to fugitives, denounced the law, and endorsed forcible resistance. Blacks revitalized their vigilance committees or joined white groups with the same purposes: to alert the community to the presence of slave catchers, to protect fugitives, and to speed them on their way to freedom.

Blacks backed their words with deeds. In 1851 a Maryland planter, leading an armed party, tried to seize his escaped slaves living with blacks in Christiana, Pennsylvania. In the ensuing battle he was killed and his son wounded. U.S. Marines were dispatched to restore order while police rounded up suspects—38 in all, three of them white. When two trials failed to bring convictions the charges were dropped. That same year Boston blacks invaded the courthouse, seized a fugitive and sent him off to Canada. Arrests followed, but no convictions. Numerous other such incidents testified to the fact that for the first time in their history Northern blacks were carrying out organized resistance to an unjust law, and being supported by whites who felt like them. Behind them both was a growing body of white sentiment which made it almost impossible to convict offenders. This attitude was reflected in the popularity of Harriet Beecher Stowe's *Uncle Tom's Cabin*, published in 1852, which, by reducing slavery to simple human terms, helped to intensify anti-slavery feeling. That the book struck home was evidenced by the repeated Southern efforts to discredit and outlaw it.

What was the Southern response to the resistance? Actually, to the South, the Fugitive Slave Law was of more importance symbolically than practically. Few slaves escaped from the Deep South, and the cost of reclaiming slaves from the Upper South (from which most escaped) was often more than their value. But when it was proposed in 1852 that the law be repealed, a Mississippi senator replied that repeal "would be an act of bad faith" which would bring on disunion—an assertion echoed by other Southerners. Although the law was not in fact repealed until 1864, open and successful defiance in the North helped revive talk of secession. Southerners did not appreciate the irony in some Western abolitionists' justification of resistance on the grounds of the Virginia and Kentucky resolutions and on the nullification arguments of South Carolina.

The mounting sectional tensions were soon expressed in political action. In the elections of 1852 Whigs suffered such disaster that they were destroyed as a national political force. Western and Eastern voters were offended by the party's call for strict enforcement of the Fugitive Slave Law and an end to "all further agitation of the question." Many Southern Whigs bolted because they resented the candidate, General Winfield Scott, as the choice of Northern Free-Soilers. As a result, the Whigs carried no Western state, only two in the East and two in the South.

Dissension plagued the Democrats, too, but it did not rend the party until 1854, when tensions broke over the Kansas-Nebraska Bill and the Ostend Manifesto.

The bill, as sponsored by Senator Stephen A. Douglas of Illinois, and amended to meet Southern criticism, represented an effort to meet two pressing Northern demands—more land and a northern route for the projected transcontinental railroad—and the Southern demand for legal expansion of slavery. Should these demands be met, Douglas believed, the continuing agitation over slavery would be muted and sectional reconciliation firmly founded on the basis of mutual self-interest. Organization of the as yet unsettled lands of the Louisiana Purchase, extending from the borders of Iowa and Missouri to the Rockies, would provide millions of acres of virgin soil to land-hungry Westerners. Such organization would also be the preliminary step for building a railroad linking the Pacific with Chicago.

Since this required the South to yield its hope for a southern railroad route, it would receive in return repeal of the Missouri Compromise, thus throwing open the public lands of the United States to slavery and conceding the principle, long sought by the South, of federal nonintervention in the expansion of slavery. Further, since the area was to be organized in two territories—Kansas and Nebraska—the South could expect that Kansas, bordering on slave Missouri, would become slave, while Nebraska, to the north, would be free. In short, there was something in this for everybody, providing he were white. With passage of the Bill, Douglas took pride in pointing out that once again, as in 1850, he had helped to unify the nation by reducing the slavery issue from intractable moral terms to traditional practical politics.

Douglas' practicality turned out to be the sheerest romanticism. Abolitionists, of course, were furious. More significant, that great body of mildly anti-slavery Northerners which had been profoundly touched by *Uncle Tom's Cabin*, was angered that a Northern man should lead in extending what they believed to be a moral evil. Those Westerners, who cared little about the moral issue but perceived that slavery and free farming were incompatible, and dreaded the advent of black men into the prairies, bitterly resented the sanctioning of slavery in a land they had come to look upon as their own. Free-Soil Democrats, in bolting their party, spoke for such opinion when they condemned the measures as "a gross violation of a sacred pledge [the Missouri Compromise]" and as "part and parcel of an atrocious plot to exclude from a vast unoccupied region immigrants from the Old World and free laborers from our own states, and convert it into a dreary region of despotism, inhabited by masters and slaves." This theme of a conspiracy of slaveowners and their Northern minions was sounded time and again in Congress and taken up by editors, preachers, and politicians throughout the North. It was all the more potent coming from Democrats —many Northern Whigs had been saying it for years!

The sectional division deepened as Southerners closed ranks behind the bill. Originally many of them had had as little use for Douglas' measure as did abolitionists, but in the face of mounting Northern attack they rallied behind it. The agitation against the bill they saw as yet another indication of a Northern abolitionist conspiracy to subvert Southern social institutions and to deprive the South of its basic constitutional rights. Thus the bill became a symbol of Southern rights and an assurance that the federal government would respect them. The debates became increasingly bitter, and in the process what remained of the national Whig Party collapsed. Northern "Conscience Whigs" fought the measure, while Southern "Cotton Whigs" made common cause with the hated Democrats—a step toward the final absorption of Southern Whiggery into the Democratic Party. Thus, one of the two major national parties had split irrevocably, and the other was rent with schisms and feuds, many of them imbedded in conflicting sectional interests.

Where were the "Conscience Whigs" to go? Some drifted into the new "American" Party, which, with its bigoted appeals to Americanism seemed to offer a national cause transcending sectional divisions. Many joined with Free-Soil Democrats and various anti-slavery groups in the new Republican parties springing up in the West, dedicated to halting the expansion of slavery—parties which soon coalesced into a major party, which attracted to itself the anti-slavery elements of the "Americans" when that party split over slavery. While this basic political realignment was taking place, free farmers and upholders of slavery entered the territory of Kansas, setting the stage for the armed battles which transformed it into "Bleeding Kansas." Douglas' practical scheme for sectional amity proved to be the signal for sectional bloodshed.

The Ostend Manifesto further deepened sectional suspicion. Drawn up by the pro-slavery United States ambassadors to Britain, France and Spain—James Buchanan, John Y. Mason, and Pierre Soulé respectively—it reflected the designs on Cuba of Southern planters and their merchant allies in the North. The document bluntly called for annexation of the island, preferably through purchase from Spain. Should Spain refuse, then the United States, "by every law, human and divine," had the right to take it. Among the reasons given was that a possible slave revolt in Cuba might spread to the mainland. We cannot, said the ambassadors, "permit Cuba to be Africanized and become a second Santo Domingo, with all its attendant horrors to the white race, and suffer the flames to extend to our own neighboring shores." In short, Cuba must be obtained to protect slavery in the United States.

Coming fast on the heels of the Kansas-Nebraska Bill, it was seen by anti-slavery men, despite the Manifesto's repudiation by the Pierce Administration, as yet another indication of a slave power conspiracy—this time a bald bid to seize a foreign land and add it to the Union in the form of several slave states.

Such suspicions of Southern motives nurtured the success of Northern political groupings bent on curbing Southern expansion at home and abroad. By 1856 it was possible for them to form a political conglomerate, a national Republican Party, including traditional free-soilers, political abolitionists, Independent Democrats, Conscience Whigs, and dissident "Americans." The new party was not abolitionist, and as if to emphasize this, chose a slaveholder, Francis P. Blair, Sr., of Maryland, to preside over the opening session of its founding convention. Its members were far from united on such economic issues as tariffs and banking, and they differed on social issues, such as the places of native blacks and foreign immigrants in American society. The basic bond which held them together was opposition to slavery *in the territories*. On this minimum program the party offered a prospective road to success to radicals like Joshua Giddings and Thaddeus Stevens, cautious conservatives such as Abraham Lincoln and William H. Seward, and shrewd bosses like Thurlow Weed of New York and Simon Cameron of Pennsylvania. Its very diversity was a source of strength, for it thus appealed to numerous segments of Northern society.

For example, the party provided the only political expression for the growing anti-slavery movements of the North. Followers of Garrison still decried using political means, but more and more black and white abolitionists were seeking their ends through such action. Since it was obvious that no redress was to be had through Whigs, Democrats, or "Americans," the Republican Party offered the only hope, despite its weaknesses. Blacks pointed out that the party endorsed a constitution for Kansas which barred the entry of free blacks and that the party press consistently ignored black activities. Nevertheless, most supported the Republicans—like white abolitionists, they had no place else to go.

But abolitionism, while growing in numbers and respectability, did not provide the foundation necessary for a successful political party. Such was provided by numerous groups which had plenty of political "clout." Westerners were alarmed not only by the repeal of the Missouri Compromise but also by the shift in Southern policy which now found expression in opposition to free land. In 1854, the South fought vigorously but unsuccessfully against a bill reducing prices on some public lands. It thus appeared that the South was bent both on opening the West to slavery and to closing it to free farmers. Urban Westerners were no less disgruntled because successive Democratic administrations showed little interest in developing Western rivers and harbors.

Manufacturers in both East and West were now disillusioned about the Compromise of 1850: their support of that measure had not brought them the tariff benefits they had confidently expected. Promoters, bankers, contractors, and Westerners were intrigued by the Republican call for a transcontinental railroad with a northern route. Many Northerners, too, for a variety of reasons, wanted no annexation of Cuba, so ardently advocated by Northern as well as Southern Democrats. In short, the Republicans made appeal to many segments of Northern opinion which were far removed from abolitionism.

Nevertheless, permeating such considerations was a growing sentiment that slavery per se was a moral evil, a blot on the American record. *Uncle Tom's Cabin* sold more than a million copies in a year—astonishing in the pre-Civil War era—and its dramatization soon won sell-out audiences. Here was a vast public, prepared by the earlier work of Frederick Douglass and Williams Wells Brown, black men who testified firsthand to the evils of slavery—men whose testimony had been assiduously spread by abolitionist societies. Now their cries, as well as those of Mrs. Stowe, resounded from a thousand pulpits which had previously been mute or hostile. To give point to their claims, there was the Anthony Burns incident in Boston in 1854, when the power of the federal government was mobilized to return a fugitive slave to bondage. How could America be a moral nation when such an event could occur?

To such a question there was but one answer, and that answer was now provided by a legitimate political party committed to ending the evil, even if only gradually. The Republican Party, whatever its failings, was seen as the party of freedom. Intellectuals flocked to it—Emerson, Longfellow, Washington Irving, and Benjamin Silliman of Yale, perhaps the most notable American scientist of the time. Protestant preachers made Republicanism almost synonymous with Christianity, while Henry Ward Beecher, the most influential preacher of the day, used his organ, *The Independent*, to mobilize support for the party. The party in turn made a deliberate turn to the young, enlisting many of them in what was an idealistic crusade. The candidate enhanced such an appeal—John C. Fremont, the young "Pathfinder" of the Far West, the astronaut of his day, hero of a romantic marriage to Jessie Benton, daughter of the doughty old free-soil Senator from Missouri.

To practical party managers, Fremont had another asset: his political record was so slight as to be invulnerable to Democratic attack. Besides, the platform was such as to command support in the North: ban slavery in the territories, admit Kansas as a free state while keeping free blacks out, halt Southern expansionism as represented in the Ostend Manifesto, provide federal aid for building a transcontinental railroad, and enlarge federal spending for rivers, harbors, and roads. With such a program they enjoyed the support of the major Northern newspapers.

The Republicans were aided also by their enemies. In May of the election year, pro-slavery forces in Kansas, including recruits from as far away as Georgia and South Carolina, sacked the town of Lawrence, center of free state influence. Almost simultaneously, Representative Preston Brooks of South Carolina clubbed anti-slavery Senator Charles Sumner of Massachusetts into unconsciousness in the Senate chamber itself. To many Northerners, it now appeared that the South was moving beyond debate to violence, a belief enhanced by the leading role of pro-slavery Senator David R. Atchison of Missouri in the Kansas raid, and the honors bestowed on Brooks by Southerners. So suspicious was Northern opinion by this time that it placed little credence in reports from Kansas that soon after the Lawrence raid John Brown and his sons massacred five pro-slavery men.

If the anti-slavery North rallied to the Republicans in 1856, the slave South had ample reason to back the Democrats. Their platform denied the right of Congress to interfere with slavery anywhere and pledged the party to "resist all attempts at renewing, in Congress or out of it, the agitation of the slavery question." Perhaps even more pleasing to the South was the candidate: James Buchanan of Pennsylvania, a Northern politician who had long since won Southern support by his loyal adherence to the slavery cause. Their enthusiasm was not dimmed by his pledge to settle the slavery issue in terms satisfactory to the South. If he could do this, and "then add Cuba to the Union," he would be content to resign the presidency, he said. As Senator Albert G. Brown of Mississippi commented, Buchanan was as worthy of "Southern votes as Calhoun ever was."

But could the South alone carry the election? Obviously not, for it was a minority in both popular and electoral votes. Even with the support of Northern Democrats the issue was in doubt, for it was clear that the Republicans were gaining strength and it was indeed possible that they might win. What then? Once again prospects of a race war were envisioned and threats of secession raised. Out of these fears and anxieties came the great slave insurrection panic of 1856. From Texas to Virginia hysteria produced "slave plots" linked to fears of a Republican victory. Scores of unfortunate blacks were executed and many more flogged after they "confessed" to participation. To Southern whites, the link was clear: Republicans *were* in league with blacks to overthrow white supremacy in the South. Some of the plots were genuine—slaves had been plotting against their masters for a long time—but others were products of white imagination, assiduously cultivated by secessionists who saw political profit in the hysteria.

Beneath the hysteria, however, was a sober understanding that in Democratic victory rested the South's last hope of entrenching slavery within the Union. If through legislation and court decisions—the Dred Scott case was already being argued in the Supreme Court—the expansion of slavery could be given legal sanction, then responsibility for the consequences of annulling that sanction would rest squarely on the Republican North.

The South got its chance. Although Buchanan won only a plurality in the popular vote—the Republicans and "Americans" between them rolled up 2,212,000 votes to the Democrats' 1,833,000—he did win an electoral college majority. But the evidence of polarization was plain: Republican strength was concentrated in the North, while Buchanan's victory rested on a solid Southern and Border States (except Maryland) vote. True, Buchanan carried five Northern states, but there his margin was small and his triumph attributable to the "spoiler" role of the "American" Party in relation to the Republicans. Given Democratic victory, it was urgent now for Southerners to press for providing safeguards for the expansion of slavery. On the other side, Republicans, with their vote of 1,340,000, could look forward with confidence to 1860. For a party less than two years old they had made an auspicious beginning.

In such a clouded atmosphere came the Dred Scott decision. To understand the impact of that decision we must realize that it was an attempt not only to settle the issue of slavery but also to define the status of the free black. Scott, a slave, sued for his freedom on the grounds that since he had been taken into free territory he was therefore free—a stand previously upheld by the state courts of Missouri, in which he first brought suit. Now the state supreme court reversed its own precedents, and Scott's appeal to the United States Supreme Court was argued in the election year of 1856. So important did the case appear to Buchanan that after his election victory he intervened, persuading his political crony, Justice Robert Grier of Pennsylvania, to align himself with the Southern majority so that the sectional taint might be removed from what Buchanan knew was going to be a pro-slavery decision. Chief Justice Roger Taney was aware of Buchanan's intervention and sympathized with his aim to have the court reach a decision which would settle the slavery issue once and for all.

A major question before the Court was whether Scott could lawfully bring suit, and this it answered in the negative, holding that blacks were not citizens, either of individual states or of the United States. When the Constitution was adopted, said Taney, blacks were "regarded as being of an inferior order, and altogether unfit to associate with the white race, . . .

and so far inferior, that they had no rights which a white man was bound to respect." Obviously, the founding fathers never intended blacks to be American citizens. Further, although states bestowed state citizenship and it was a general rule that national citizenship derived from state citizenship, here too blacks were excluded, for states could not grant citizenship to persons "who were not intended to be embraced" within the Union. In short, racist views imputed to the Constitutional Convention were now held to be fundamental law. Thus, free blacks were stripped of such political rights as they possessed: they were reduced from second-class citizenship to no citizenship at all.

The court then asked whether Scott's claim to freedom because he had lived in free territory was valid, and again the answer was negative. Slaves were property, and property was given specific protection in the Fifth Amendment. Congress could not prohibit slavery in the territories, for that was an infringement on property rights, and so the Missouri Compromise was legally void. On the contrary, Congress' only power, "coupled with duty," was to protect slaveowners in their property rights.[4]

Understandably, the decision was greeted with approbation in the South, while in the North it was widely denounced as an act of a partisan, sectional court which held no moral sanction. To many Northerners it represented an ominous development—the South had moved from denying the right of Congress to regulate slavery in the territories to insisting that Congress had a positive duty to protect slavery there. And this new Southern position had the force of law! Republicans, who would have been condemned to innocuousness had they accepted the decision, made it plain they would annul it when they came to power. Northern Democrats were in a dilemma, for the decision had, in effect, nullified "popular sovereignty," their panacea for settling the slavery issue. But they could not openly attack the Court without grave political risks.

Blacks noted that Northern indignation was directed almost entirely at the territorial decision; little was said of the degraded status assigned to blacks. As much as whites, blacks appreciated the significance of the extension of slavery, but they also perceived—which few whites did—the dangers of depriving blacks of citizenship. Mass meetings throughout the North expressed black anger at the decision, and a new note of militancy was sounded. Charles L. Remond, a noted black abolitionist, urged moves to

---

[4] There was no one Dred Scott decision in the sense of a majority decision agreed upon by the Justices. The Court split seven to two—but so tangled were the issues that each Justice wrote his own opinion. The majority opinions, while varying in their reasoning, upheld the conclusions of Chief Justice Taney, cited above. These, of course, were repudiated by the dissenters, John McLean of Ohio and Benjamin Curtis of Massachusetts. For a brief review of the decisions see Allan Nevins, *The Emergence of Lincoln* (New York: Charles Scribner's Sons, 1950), I, chap. 4.

promote slave rebellion, and William H. Day, another black spokesman, called for armed resistance. Such appeals were voted down, but enthusiastic approval met the speeches of Frederick Douglass, who termed the decision "judicial incarnation of wolfishness" and Robert Purvis, a wealthy black leader of Philadelphia, who declared that he owed no allegiance to a government which denied him citizenship. Northern blacks now held out to their children the examples of Toussaint L'Ouverture, the liberator of Haiti, Nat Turner, and Crispus Attucks, first man to die in the Boston Massacre of 1770—all figures of black militancy.

For the moment, Northern white resentment was contained. Most people were doing well, thanks to the economy's recovery from the depression of the "Hungry Forties" and the shot in the arm from the gold in California. Railroads were being built, land passed from owner to owner in a fever of speculation, prosperity was reaching new heights. Under these circumstances moral fervor could go only so far. Then, in August, 1857, five months after the Dred Scott decision, the exuberant prosperity of the North vanished almost overnight in an economic collapse—merchants, banks, railroads, manufacturers went bankrupt and thousands of unemployed began to eke out a wretched existence on charity. Many explanations were offered, but a widely accepted one struck at the heart of sectional division: the collapse was due to the low tariff policies pursued by pro-Southern administrations, and in particular to the tariff adopted in March of 1857 which lowered import duties still further. How could Northern manufacturers remain in business when the American market was flooded with British imports, deliberately encouraged by Southern men who dominated the government? In short, the South was willing to sell out the North for its own interests.

The South retorted that the shoe was on the other foot. Tariffs were simply a means to impose upon the agricultural peoples of the South and West a tax to benefit a small group of Northern industrialists. If such men could not compete, then they were no more worthy of governmental subsidy than planters and farmers. And, speaking of subsidies, Southerners pointed to federal appropriations for fishing bounties, for development of rivers and harbors and railroads—which benefited the South little. Not only was the South plundered through the government, but also its wealth was drained away through Northern-controlled shipping, warehousing, and financing. The South did the work and the North took the profit. This familiar line of argument was the more galling to the North because Southerners pointed out that the South had proved almost immune to the depression and concluded that George Fitzhugh and other Southern spokesmen were right when they asserted that Southern society was indeed superior to that of the North.

Encouraged by the dissension generated in the North by the economic depression and the Dred Scott decision, and supported by Southerners who dominated the Buchanan Administration, pro-slavery forces moved to make Kansas a slave state. Their vehicle was the Lecompton Constitution, drafted by a pro-slavery convention, and submitted to Congress without a vote of the settlers—except for an article which gave voters a "choice" on slavery. They could accept the constitution with or without slavery—but in any case the constitution would be sent to Congress and existing slave property would be legal. A first election, characterized by widespread fraud, was for slavery; in the second, and honest, election, slavery was swamped. Despite this clear evidence of Kansas sentiment, the Buchanan Administration massed all its forces to force the Lecompton Constitution through Congress. Douglas and his followers, faced with this utter repudiation of "popular sovereignty," revolted. Now, Northern Democrats often found themselves in company with Republicans. The measure passed the Senate, but in the House it was amended to require an election on the constitution as a whole. Neither House would compromise. Out of this deadlock came the English bill, designed to "settle" the Kansas issue and hold the dividing Democrats together.

The measure called for submission of the entire Kansas constitution to the voters. To induce acceptance, Kansans were promised four million acres in public land grants and a small share in the income from the sale of another two million acres of public lands in the immediate future. If they did not accept, Kansans would be denied admission to the Union until they more than doubled their population—a curious requirement in light of the fact that Kansas, as a slave state, had been deemed worthy of admission on the basis of its existing population. Again the administration mobilized its efforts for the bill—this time successfully, although Douglas eventually came out in opposition. The Kansas settlers themselves decided the issue in August, 1858: they voted down the constitution, 11,800 to 1,900. Territorial status with freedom was preferable to statehood with slavery.

Why did the South make such an issue of Kansas, where there were few slaves and where it was obvious that slavery as such had no future? Several explanations have been offered, but perhaps the basic one was suggested by Jefferson Davis himself. Why, he asked, should Southerners care whether slaves went into the territories? And he answered: "Simply because of the war that is made against our institutions; simply because of *the want of security* which results from the action of our opponents in the Northern states." (Italics supplied.) Thus, the endangered Southern white minority must protect itself by providing on its borders friendly governments which would insulate the slave South from Northern subversion.[5]

The passions generated by Kansas carried over to the elections of 1858, intensified in the North by the belief that the continuing depression was the result of Southern tariff policy. In the South, Democratic anger at Douglas for his Kansas stand was not diminished when he avoided endorsement of the Dred Scott decision in his debates with Lincoln. The decision was irrelevant, he said, for slavery could not exist without slave codes, and white settlers would decide that question. With Kansas fresh in mind, Southerners found Douglas' position far from satisfactory. "Popular sovereignty," which seemed to promise so much in 1850, now appeared to be just another phrase for containment of slavery, and containment meant its ultimate extinction, as Republicans emphasized. So far as the slave South was concerned, Douglas Democrats and Republicans simply offered a choice of poisons.

Douglas sought to appease the unappeasable by advocating expansion into the Caribbean and Central America on the one hand, and on the other charging Republicans with belief in racial equality. Republicans hotly denied it, pointing with pride to their voting for the free state Kansas constitution which barred the entry of free blacks. Lincoln, while affirming the right of states to make blacks citizens, did not think that his own state, Illinois, should do so. Further, he did not favor "in any way" bringing about social and political equality of the races. Indeed, there were physical differences between them which would "forever forbid the two races living together on terms of social and political equality."

Quite a different Republican answer was given in the East. William H. Seward, making a bid for the labor vote, warned that the existence of slave labor not only degraded all labor but also threatened free white labor. Without naming Fitzhugh and others who said that slavery was the natural condition of all labor, Seward declared that free labor could not be secure in the face of such Southern beliefs. Thus there was an "irrepressible conflict" between the systems which could be settled only when the nation was either entirely free or entirely slave. Seward denounced the anti-black legislation passed in the North and demanded that just as all men were equal in the eyes of God so must they be equal in the eyes of the law.

The speech caused an uproar in the South, although the idea of sectional conflict had long been the stock in trade of Southern politicians and was at that moment a major issue in the Democratic campaign. Seward's speech, however, helped further persuade many Southerners that the

[5] Eugene D. Genovese, *The Political Economy of Slavery* (New York: Vintage Books, 1967), pp. 248–49.

Republican Party was indeed a Black Republican Party, bent on inciting slave revolts. The speech also stirred consternation among some Republicans, aware of Northern hostility to free blacks and anxious not to alienate voters who were responding to the party's appeal. Seward himself backed away from his temporary radicalism, but these developments demonstrated that while Republicans were generally conservative they had within them a pro-abolitionist following which could not be ignored. Seward might discard the mantle of radicalism, but there were many to pick it up and wear it proudly.

The election returns showed Republicans had little to worry about. Hammering at slavery as a wrong but insisting they opposed only its extension, the Republicans also bid for votes in the West by calling for a free land (homestead) policy and in the East by espousing a protective tariff. They swept the Northern elections; the offices they failed to win went largely to Douglas Democrats. In effect, the North repudiated the Southern policies of the Buchanan Administration.

The repudiation of the administration strengthened the hand of Southern extremists. Triumphant Republicanism, they averred, meant destruction of Southern society, bloody race war, subjection of Southern whites to savage blacks and their Black Republican allies, in addition to continued economic exploitation of the South by the North. Nor were Northern Democrats to be relied on—they were as hostile to the South as Republicans. There was only one answer: secession. A network of secessionist societies was developed. For the short run, they made a major issue of the new Southern demand: a federal slave code for the territories. No one expected that a Congress dominated by Republicans and Douglas Democrats would ever grant such approval. But failure to obtain such a code would supply still further evidence that only through secession could Southerners protect themselves.

A major problem for secessionists were those ardent defenders of Southern rights who dreaded leaving the Union. In less than a year after Republican victory at the polls, the secession cause was made more persuasive. John Brown, the militant abolitionist, seized the United States arsenal at Harper's Ferry as the first step in a project to penetrate the South and liberate slaves. Brown was speedily subdued, tried, and executed—but the fact that an armed attack on slavery had been attempted convinced Southerners of all shades of opinion that they were indeed in danger. True, Brown might be a fanatic, but behind him were the abolitionists who supplied his money and arms, and behind them were the Republicans, all the more menacing now because of their growing power.

The feelings of the South found swift expression. Travellers and businessmen from the North found their safety so threatened that they fled. Boycotts of Northern business enterprises were organized. Southerners who did not publicly avow the blessings of slavery were denounced. Slave codes were tightened and the limited rights of free blacks further restricted. Some states even provided for enslaving free blacks. State after Southern state pledged support to Virginia, on whose soil the raid had taken place. States which could find little or no money for public schools discovered ample funds to expand their militias. Alabama and Florida decreed that election of a Republican president would constitute legitimate grounds for secession, while South Carolina and Mississippi called for a convention to defend Southern rights amidst talk of a new "Southern Confederacy." The call for a convention failed—testimony to the continuing reluctance of many Southern whites to disrupt the Union—but now secessionists held the initiative. If white people were to be saved from the horrors of slave insurrection, armed and backed by Northern Republicans, what course other than secession was possible?

The Northern response was milder and mixed. Douglas Democrats, still seeking rapprochement with their Southern brethren, echoed the Southern charge that the Brown raid was the natural result of Republican agitation of the slavery question. Indeed, they charged that Seward and other leading Republicans had been privy to Brown's plans. Republicans disproved any such connection and condemned the raid, but, with an eye to their abolitionist wing, refrained from condemnation of Brown himself. It was obvious that in many Northern minds Brown was already a hero-martyr—his deed might deserve censure, but it had been done in a noble cause. If he employed violence, why should the South complain? It had not scrupled to use violence against free farmers in Kansas. And there were others, like Horace Greeley, who predicted that while the raid would hurt the Republicans temporarily, its ultimate effect would be good. It would "drive on the slave power to new outrages" which would so antagonize the North that the end of slavery was "ten years nearer than it seemed a few weeks ago." Actually, voters showed little response to the Democratic charges. The elections held during the height of the Brown hysteria showed only minor Republican losses—a significant indication of Northern feeling.

Black Americans felt no apologies were needed for Brown. On the contrary, they were as proud of him as they were of their own rebel, Nat Turner. Their only regret was that Brown's plan failed. Frederick Douglass, who had resisted Brown's entreaties to join the expedition—he thought the scheme impractical—nevertheless thought it a "sublimely disinterested effort to emancipate the slaves," led by a "noble and heroic" man. On Martyr Day, when Brown was executed, black businesses closed and thousands thronged to churches and meeting halls to pay their last respects to a fallen leader. Poverty-stricken though many of them were, they raised funds for the support of Brown's widow and widows of other members of his party. To many, Brown's death was not an end, but a beginning: the dramatic assault on the citadel of slavery augured, in the words of New York black women, "the unexpected realization of some of our seemingly vain hopes." And blacks did not fail to note that the first to die when federal troops stormed the arsenal was Dangerfield Newby, a free black. Ironically, the first resident of Harper's Ferry killed by Brown's men was a free black railroad porter.

As to the significance of Brown's raid, perhaps the most succinct appraisal was made by Brown himself before he set out for Harper's Ferry: "I expect to effect a mighty conquest, *even though it be like the last victory of Samson.*" (Italics supplied.) He did indeed give a mighty wrench to the pillars of the American temple. It is ironic that to bring freedom to the slave he had to menace a temple dedicated to liberty! As in a lightning flash, he revealed the basic issue which divided the nation, and while sober men in both sections recoiled from the revelation they sensed that somehow an unresolved question had been given new dimensions—a question vital to the meaning of American democracy. As the wounded Brown told Senator James M. Mason of Virginia: "You may dispose of me very easily . . . but this question is still to be settled—this Negro question, I mean; the end of that is not yet."

Such was the atmosphere in which the nation moved toward the fateful election of 1860—tense, foreboding, shot through with mounting feelings of frustration. If the North found it difficult to condemn Brown, it was not because it endorsed his act, nor because his behavior after capture elicited admiration, but also because he symbolized the feelings of all kinds of Northerners thwarted by Southern control of the federal government.

Western farmers were exasperated by Buchanan's veto of recent homestead legislation. Western businessmen were fuming bcause funds were denied for promoting navigation on Western rivers and the Great Lakes. Eastern and Western manufacturers were angered over the tariff reduction of 1857 and Southern indifference to the depression which followed. Bankers, speculators, contractors, and Western farmers were up in arms over Southern blocking of a transcontinental railroad route which favored the North. And the North was aroused more immediately in 1860 by the Southern-provoked deadlock in the House over the speakership, which tied up the business of Congress for eight weeks until a compromise candidate, backed by Republicans, was chosen. Contributing to the Northern mood was adoption by the Senate of Jefferson Davis' resolutions upholding the Southern position on slavery, including endorsement of a federal slave code for the territories.

It was thus easy for Northerners to believe that a slave power conspiracy threatened the progress of the whole country. This was all the more intolerable to them in that the progress of a free people was impeded by a backward minority section based on human slavery. Material and moral concerns thus fused in a powerful, dynamic sentiment determined at the very least to end Southern control of the federal government by halting the expansion of slavery.

To Southerners, the reverse was true: *they* were victims of Northern designs. Northerners not only sought to keep slavery out of the territories but also blocked Southern expansion into Cuba and Central America. Northern influence stopped a projected transcontinental railroad with a Southern route. Yankee shippers and bankers battened off financing and moving the cotton crop, while merchants profited handsomely in supplying the Southern market. The Northern drive for high tariffs was simply another move to colonialize the South. Harper's Ferry demonstrated how far the North was willing to go, and while the Yankees made public profession of condemning the raid their real feelings were shown by their failure to help in bringing the backers of Brown to justice. As for homesteads and public works in the North—why should the South give aid and comfort to its enemies?

To the South, it was clear that the North, enjoying superiority in numbers, wealth, and resources, was bent on subjecting the South—even at the cost of race war and the overthrow of white supremacy—which stood for the sanctity of white womanhood, a pure Christianity, and the values of Anglo-Saxon civilization. In the South, as in the North, material and moral concerns fused into a passionate appeal: the rights of the Southern minority must be respected—if not inside the Union, then outside of it.

That Southern Democratic leaders thought little could be gained inside the Union was obvious when they rejected the party nominee, Stephen A. Douglas, in 1860 and put up their own candidate, John C. Breckinridge of Tennessee. Douglas, backed by a united party, might well have won, but Democratic division all but assured the election of the Republican Lincoln. This, of course, suited secessionists—it provided ample ground for leaving the Union.

For their part, Republican leaders, scenting victory, took pains to assure it. Knowing they had the anti-slavery vote in their pockets, they muted the idealistic notes of earlier Republican campaigns and concentrated on bread-and-butter promises to attract the widest possible variety of voters: free farms in the West; protective tariffs in the East and West; unlimited immigration, a lure to both immigrant votes and the interests of industrialists; extensive public works, long demanded by Western businessmen; and a northern-route transcontinental railroad, with its wide appeal to nearly all Northern interests.

Apart from their reiterated opposition to the expansion of slavery, the Republicans had little to say of concern to the black man. Yet the black man had little choice. As Frederick Douglass observed: "as between the hosts of Slavery propagandism and the Republican Party—incomplete as is its platform . . . our preferences cannot hesitate." Some did not accept that logic. H. Ford Douglass, a black abolitionist leader in Illinois, pointed out that he could not vote in that state, nor could he send his children to public schools although blacks paid school taxes. Nor could he testify in court against whites—and when Douglass sought to enlist Republican support for allowing such testimony, he was turned down—by Abraham Lincoln, among others! So far as Douglass was concerned, all of the parties were "barren and unfruitful" when it came to lifting the Negro "out of his fetters."

To many whites in the Border States, and to oldtimers in all sections, the prospect of disunion was intolerable. In desperation they rallied to the ephemeral Constitution Union Party, with its vague platform of support for the Union and the Constitution, and silence on slavery. Even so, the party carried three Border States and polled nearly 590,000 votes.

The election of Lincoln compelled some answer to a question which had long divided secessionists. Should one state act on its own, or should no state act until there could be common action on the part of the South— or at least of the Deep South? The latter course meant delay, and many Southerners backed it, hoping against hope that somehow in the interim Southern rights could be preserved within the Union. Others supported it in the belief that faced with a unified South the North would make sufficient concessions to make possible reconstruction of the Union on a basis satisfactory to the South; that is, secession was to be temporary. Such views were anathema to those who looked toward an independent Southern Confederacy such as William L. Yancey of Alabama and Edmund Ruffin of Virginia—and they took the lead. With South Carolina in the vanguard, they swept the Deep South swiftly into secession. Within eight weeks after that state seceded they were able to take the next step of establishing the Confederate States of America. Naturally, such haste ruled out referring so momentous an issue to the people, and the question arises: Why the haste?

There were many reasons. In the first place, revolution is not a leisurely business, and many secessionists took pride in acknowledging that revolution *was* their business. They must strike when circumstances were ripe for success, and guard against any chance which might imperil that success. Thus, secessionists were enabled to take advantage of President Buchanan's curious policy of denouncing secession on the one hand while on the other insisting he could do nothing about it. This in turn meant that when Lincoln took office in March he was faced with an accomplished fact—not only was there an independent government established in Montgomery, but also federal forts, post-offices, custom-houses, and the mint at New Orleans were in Southern hands.

Second, submission of the secession issue to voters meant not only delay—but also the result would be a gamble which few secessionists were willing to take. Even among ardent Southern rights men there was reluctance to put the Union down, and some even declared publicly that Lincoln really was not to be feared, and that if he were, he could do little faced with a Senate and Supreme Court dominated by Democrats. Such men, of course, could be dismissed as old-line Southern Whigs, out of touch with the times, but beyond them was the ominous mass of poorer whites—yeoman farmers, mechanics, and mountaineers, typified by Andrew Johnson of Tennessee—who, for all their awe of the planting aristocracy, hated it as the source of their woes. Between them such forces had been potent enough in the 1860 elections to provide a majority in the South against Breckinridge, and even he had thought it expedient to disavow any intention of secession!

Given such conditions, it was not impossible (or so thought the extreme secessionists) that a compromise might be worked out—and such a compromise would have the backing of the Upper South, already strongly influenced by Northern trade and ideas and appalled at the prospect of serving as a battleground of warring governments. Without the Upper South, or at the least, without Virginia, it was doubtful whether an independent Confederacy could survive: the human and natural resources of the Upper South, to say nothing of the prestige of the Old Dominion, were essential to Confederate success. Speed, then, was essential to confront the North with a unified Deep South, to persuade or coerce unwilling Southerners to take a course from which there could be no turning back, and to strengthen the elements in the Upper South working to bring about secession.[6]

To Southerners who objected that secession meant war, there were soothing reassurances:

First, there would be no war, for the North *would* not fight. For all their talk, Northerners were more concerned about their skins and dollars than about an abstraction called the Union. Did anyone seriously think that the exploited textile workers of New England and the coal and iron miners of Pennsylvania would rally to the cause of a government dominated

[6] For a recent discussion of secessionist tactics in one state, see Charles B. Dew, "Who Won the Secessionist Election in Louisiana?" *Journal of Southern History*, XXXVI, No. 1 (February, 1970), 18–32.

by their bosses? Was it reasonable to believe that Northern bankers and merchants engaged in trade with the South would endanger the $200,000,000 owed to them by Southerners? Would these people really want to disrupt the traditional patterns which had prospered them? And then there were the Northern Democrats—was it credible that they would make war on their Southern brethren?

Second, the North *could* not fight. Too many of them were the "white slaves" of the factory system to make good soldiers. Indeed, the whole bent of Northern society toward moneymaking meant cultivation of wile and cunning rather than the martial virtues of courage and sacrifice. In addition, the North was not a united section but a disunited conglomerate. All along the Ohio Valley from Pittsburgh to Cairo, Illinois, were large groups of settlers of Southern origin who still felt loyalty to their homeland. Western farmers and Eastern bankers were in conflict, and labor and capital were at almost incessant war. If German immigrants tended to be Republican, the Irish were almost certain to be Democratic. Sectional animosities were so strong that should the issue of war arise, the Mississippi Valley states and the Far West would form confederacies of their own. Even within the Republican Party there was division. Had not Horace Greeley argued that the South had a right to secede? Beyond that, had not the arch-fiend, William Lloyd Garrison, endorsed secession? To secessionists it was obvious that Northern society was so constituted and so divided that it could not possibly wage war.

But, asked skeptics (and there were many), supposing war does come—then what? Here again the answers were reassuring. The debilitated employees of banks, mills, and factories were no match for Southern men, accustomed to life in the field and by temperament better suited for war than for the counting house. Northern soldiers would have nothing to fight for, while Southerners would be fighting for all they held dear: homes, wives, children, honor, and white civilization. The war would be short. The South would be fighting on internal lines of communication and supply which the invaders would have to extend themselves to penetrate. Before the North, with its undoubted superiority of resources, could accomplish this, the Confederacy would have struck such grievous blows that the North would sue for peace. Further, the South had one resource the North lacked: proved military leadership. Few in the North had distinguished military records, while the South could boast of Jefferson Davis, P.G.T. Beauregard, Thomas J. (later "Stonewall") Jackson, Albert Sidney Johnston, and others —and if Virginia seceded, surely she could count on Colonel Robert E. Lee, the soldier who had quelled Brown's "insurrection" at Harper's Ferry. Finally, the South had powerful friends. Britain and France were so dependent on Southern cotton that the Confederacy could assume their backing, even to the point of intervention, should that prove necessary.

In any case, argued the secessionists, there was really no alternative. It had proved impossible to protect Southern rights within the Union, and with each passing year the South grew weaker in relation to a North waxing strong in population, industry, wealth, and political power. Should the South pass up this opportunity to win her independence, it would be impossible to do so later. Then the North would first subvert and then overwhelm the Anglo-Saxon South and its way of life. Slavery would go, and with it, white supremacy. As Calhoun had predicted, blacks would be given equality with whites, and then blacks and "their Northern allies would be the masters, and we the slaves." This, as secessionists well knew, was *the* argument to rally whites to the Confederate banner, no matter what other issues might divide them.

The Confederates meant what they said. They did indeed found a government based on racism. Slavery was guaranteed in their constitution, and Alexander H. Stephens, the Confederate vice-president, emphasized the implication: "Our new government is founded upon . . . the great truth that the Negro is not equal to the white man; that slavery—subordination to the superior race—is his natural and normal condition." And, he added proudly, "Our new government is the first in the history of the world, based upon this great . . . truth." Once the argument for secession was placed on this level, there was no room for a Southerner to dissent.

While Deep South secessionists scored their triumphs, Upper South men frantically sought ways out of the impending crisis. Senator John J. Crittenden of Kentucky proposed extension of the old Missouri Compromise line to the California border, a plan which won the endorsement of the realistic Republican boss of New York, Thurlow Weed. But more realistic Republicans, such as Lincoln, noted that the proposal limited freedom to north of the 36/30 line while the slave states were free to expand southward into Central America, as slaveowners had avowed to do time and again. Also, the proposal made mockery of Republican pledges to contain slavery. Lincoln's arguments prevailed, and the consequent failure of the "Crittenden Compromise" was followed by still another attempt at compromise, this time from Virginia. That state sponsored a convention in February, 1861, to frame constitutional amendments which would satisfy the South and thus restore the Union—a hope that died aborning when Jefferson Davis declared that the Confederacy would not be party to any scheme for restoration of the Union.

Democrats and Republicans were both involved in these moves, signifying how far some Republicans were willing to go to appease Southern opinion. Some anti-slavery men in the party, such as Henry Ward Beecher and Horace Greeley, were willing to let the seceding states go in peace. In Congress, Republican votes helped carry a measure asking Northern states to repeal their Personal Liberty Laws, so hateful to slave catchers, and in response several states did repeal their laws or drastically modified them. Republican Congressmen voted to organize the territories of Colorado, New Mexico, and Dakota with no prohibition of slavery. As Stephen A. Douglas could not help noting, vast stretches of United States territories were now open to slavery—with Republican consent. Republicans backed a proposed 13th amendment to guarantee slavery in states where it existed and to forbid any future constitutional amendment giving Congress the power to outlaw slavery. This measure, which might have fastened slavery on the United States forever, actually passed both House and Senate and was ratified by three states before the fall of Fort Sumter.

The Republican strategy had three purposes: to neutralize the pro-Southern elements in southern Ohio, Indiana, and Illinois; to hold in line the crucially important Border States; and to isolate the fire-eating secessionists from the mass of Southerners by demonstrating the sincerity of Republican pledges not to interfere with slavery. When the Southern masses were so assured, many Republicans thought, the secession movement would lose momentum and the Union would be reconstructed without bloodshed.

The Republican policy was pursued after Lincoln took office. His inaugural address, while stating his own position firmly, carefully avoided giving offense to Southerners. His strict enforcement of the Fugitive Slave Law, so abominated by anti-slavery men, won the praise of Stephen A. Douglas. The new administration made no effort to regain federal installations seized in the South, nor did it take any step to put the nation on a war footing. Secretary of State William H. Seward, now that his rhetorical prediction of an "irrepressible conflict" had been vindicated, was frightened by the prospect of actual disunion. He met indirectly with representatives of the Confederacy—from which talks they believed they had a Union pledge to evacuate Fort Sumter. Seward also proposed that Lincoln provoke an international crisis to reunite the country! Lincoln rejected that, and he had no intention of surrendering the fort. But when the issue of the fort could no longer be avoided, Lincoln personally guaranteed to the governor of South Carolina that only supplies would be sent to sustain the men stationed there—not reinforcements. Lincoln also pledged that no reinforcements would be sent in the future without prior notification to the governer, unless the fort were first attacked.

The Republican strategy worked insofar as it demonstrated to white Northerners and Border State voters that the government was bending over backward to preserve the peace and the Union. To blacks it was cause for apprehension, for it smacked of an appeasement which, if successful, would, in the words of Frederick Douglass, "grant a new lease on life to slavery." And he bitterly put his finger on the basis of the appeasement: "Our rulers were ready enough to sacrifice the Negro to the Union so long as there was any hope of saving the Union by that means." Fortunately, by attacking Fort Sumter, "The slaveholders themselves have saved our cause from ruin!"

In the South, the Republicans failed dismally: quite simply, the South did not believe them. Besides, the tide of secession was running so swiftly that no appeasement on immediate issues could stem it, and belying Republican hopes, Southern Unionists were too weak and divided to check the trend. In any case, whatever illusions Republicans may have had about saving the Union peacefully were dispelled by Fort Sumter. The attack was more than an incident: it was a political act of the highest importance. It dramatically proclaimed Confederate sovereignty; it made irreparable the breach between the Confederacy and the United States; it compelled Southern dissidents to choose between disloyalty or rallying to the cause of their country; and by compelling forceful Union response, the attack brought into the Confederacy Virginia, North Carolina, Tennessee, and Arkansas, just as secessionists had hoped.

Why did Lincoln make an issue of secession? Readers today may find the question baffling: surely it was obvious he had no choice. At the time, however, some leading men in both major parties as well as pacifist abolitionists advised that the seceding states be allowed to depart in peace— often on the ground that once out of the Union the Confederacy would find the going so rough that she would be glad to return. Lincoln instead, chose to fight. Why? Partly because he believed there was no justification for legal secession; as he put it, "no government proper ever had a provision in its organic law for its own termination." Partly because the Republican Party could not afford to preside over the dissolution of the Union which it had sworn to uphold. But there were other, more basic considerations which made maintenance of the Union imperative.

First, neither East nor West thought it could prosper without the South. Eastern industry and Western agriculture were developing so rapidly that they needed not simply a national market but an expanding market— and an essential part of such a market was the South. Here was a thriving agrarian society, made up of nearly 12 million people, which absorbed vast quantities of goods from Northern factories as well as foodstuffs from the West. An independent South would mean in any event a restricted Southern market, and if it established direct free trade relations with Britain while erecting tariffs against the United States, what market would be left for Northern manufacturers?

Further, expansion in the North was based in large part on foreign investment and foreign imports. How were these to be paid for if not with cotton, which counted for more than half the value of United States exports in 1860? Farther afield, American interests in China were just beginning to benefit from the favorable treaties wrung from the Empire in the 1840s and 1850s, and Perry's opening of Japan presaged penetration of still another market. How could a crippled nation compete in Asia with such energetic giants as Britain, France, and Russia? As to Latin America, which had long beckoned to Yankee businessmen, how much hope was there if the gateway to trade, New Orleans, was in the hands of a hostile government? In short, the logic of economic expansion demanded a unified nation.

The logic was expressed no better than by Lincoln himself after the war began, in pointing out to Westerners their stake in preserving the Union. Noting that the section was cut off from direct access to the oceans and thus dependent on seaports elsewhere, he emphasized the link between economic growth and Union:

> As part of one nation, its people now find . . . their way to Europe by New York, to South America and Africa by New Orleans, and to Asia by San Francisco; but separate our common country into two nations . . . , and every man of this great interior region is thereby cut off from some one or more of these outlets, not perhaps by a physical barrier, but by embarrassing and onerous trade regulations. . . . These outlets, east, west and south, are indispensable to the well-being of the people inhabiting this . . . region. All . . . of right belong to that people and to their successors forever. True to themselves, they will not ask *where* a line of separation shall be, but will vow rather that there shall be no such line.

There were other economic factors making for keeping the Union intact. The manufacture of cotton goods—New England's principal industry—depended on the free flow of Southern cotton. Northerners were also heavily involved in financing and transporting the cotton crop on the one hand while handling Southern imports on the other. An independent South could mean the loss of much of this lucrative trade, and some feared, the payment of existing debts in a depreciated Confederate currency. (Such fears, contradictorily, help explain the pro-Confederate stand of many New York merchants—they hoped by appeasement to maintain trade ties with the South.) And there were bankers and other holders of United States government bonds and securities who thought a disrupted Union would surely mean a decided fall in the value of their holdings, as well as a drop in the value of the dollar. Such elements had hoped for compromise, and they had backed the Republican policy of placating the South, but when it became apparent that the South was not going to respond, they had no alternative save to back the Union.

Then there were questions of national survival. If the Confederacy were permitted to go, could the East, the West, and the Far West survive as one viable nation? Or would sectional interests fragment it also, as so many Southerners suggested? To many in the North what would happen was as clear as it was to a Philadelphia editor: the United States, "strong only in union, would dwindle into insignificant states, more contemptible than those of Germany or of Central America," keeping up "a petty show of distinct sovereignties, continually warring against each other, or adopting . . . restrictions to check each other's progress." Citizens, having no strong government to protect them, "would be secure in no part of the globe."

There were other questions to which the editor did not refer. If the United States were fragmented, would not each new government be dominated by a united South? And perhaps more ominously, would not a divided continent invite the unwelcome attention of European powers? Russia and Britain were already in North America, and Britain and France were active in Mexico. The unhappy history of that country, marked by almost constant interference in its internal affairs by the United States, Britain, and France, boded ill for any series of small republics carved out of the United States. Union was strength—and only strength commanded respect in the jungle world of international politics. Without it, America would be lost.

Without the Union, Northerners would be lost in yet other ways. To them, Union meant homeland, with all the subtle associations of feelings, beliefs, values, and attitudes which the word embraces. It gave them identity as Americans. It afforded them the psychological security which a sense of identity brings. Its open society held out limitless vistas of progress for them and their children. Moreover, they were proud of being Americans. Was not their country the hope and refuge of the poor and oppressed everywhere? Was it not, as Lincoln said later, "the last best hope on earth" for the common people? If American blacks and Indians fell outside this sense of mission, it bothered Northerners little, for they prided themselves rather that their society was free while that of the South was slave. All of this sense of security, mission, and moral superiority was threatened by secession. If, as Eugene Genovese has argued, planters were fighting for their lives in the fullest sense of the term, it is equally true that Northerners were fighting for theirs.[7] If Southerners could not conceive of living without slavery, Northerners could not imagine existence without the established Union.

[7] Genovese, *Political Economy of Slavery*, p. 270.

**The American Eagle Surprises Jeff Davis
in His Attempt to Rob Her Nest.**
Harper's Weekly. June 22, 1861.

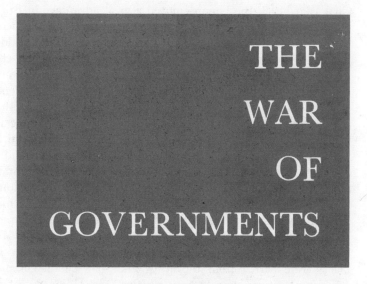

CHAPTER III

THE
WAR
OF
GOVERNMENTS

When the war came, neither Union nor Confederate governments were prepared for it—and most leaders on both sides assumed it would be short.
Thus, both sides were slow to make the adjustments necessary to wage a
protracted conflict. Even then, neither government demonstrated full understanding of the problems the war presented—not surprising in view of
the fact that generations had passed since the American people had been
involved in a major struggle and had never experienced total war. All that
can be said is that the Confederacy proved less capable than the Union
in dealing with its problems. And this, not because the Confederacy lacked
leaders of courage, experience, and intellect, but because the leaders did
not comprehend the realities of the world in which they functioned. This
will become apparent as we discuss the diplomatic, military, and internal
issues confronting both sides.

Union diplomacy had two major aims: to prevent foreign recognition of the Confederacy, and to fend off efforts of major powers to use America's distress for their own ends. In this, the role of Britain was crucial. As *the* world leader, her stance would be adopted by France and other powers— with the exception of Russia, still smarting from her defeat at the hands of Britain and France in the Crimean War just five years before. When the Civil War began the Union enjoyed a great advantage in British opinion. Workers viewed the United States as demonstrating the benefits of the kind of political democracy they were seeking at home. Middle class free traders looked upon the developing economic relations between the countries as vindication of their principles. Imbuing these Britons as well as countless others was the belief that Union victory meant an end to slavery, a sentiment strong among religious Britons. For spokesmen they had such men as John Bright and Richard Cobden, the redoubtable industrialists who had led the successful campaign for repeal of the Corn Laws in the 1840s; John Stuart Mill, the eminent social philosopher; and Robert and Elizabeth Browning. Throughout the country numerous editors, preachers, and politicians took up the Union cause as the cause of freedom.

They soon received a rude shock. American officials made it plain that slavery was *not* an issue, that the Union was pledged to protect slavery where it existed, and that the Union had only one war aim: reunification. Union supporters in Britain were further dismayed as news came that free blacks were barred from the army, and that Union commanders were returning fugitive slaves to their masters. The Union defeat at Bull Run in the summer of 1861 added to their discomfiture, but not as much as the continued silence of the Lincoln Administration on slavery. Men like Bright and Mill never lost hope, but many others came to feel that if the war were simply a question of who ruled whom it was of little concern to liberal Britons. Some indeed felt that if slavery were not an issue then the moral advantage lay with the Confederacy, which was fighting for national liberation, however misguided it might be. And some ardent anti-slavery men, like John E. Cairnes, the noted economist, felt it would be wise to end the war by containing slavery within an independent Confederacy.

Washington, bent on appeasing the Border States and anti-black sentiment in the North by eliminating slavery as a war issue, failed to perceive the dangers in the drift of British liberal opinion—namely, that sympathizers with the South would capitalize on it to bring about a shift in British policy favorable to the Confederacy. Who were these sympathizers? Largely members of the landed gentry and the upper middle class, who felt some class affinity for Southern aristocrats (both had an ingrained contempt for "trade") but even more deeply feared that a Union victory would stimulate the British movement for democratic parliamentary reform and would encourage the growth of labor unions, just embarked on a new period of growth after aborted efforts of the 1840s. As Charles Francis Adams, the American ambassador noted, such Englishmen dreaded "the growth of liberal opinions and . . . habitually regard America as the nursery of them." They were joined by shippers resentful of Yankee competition and those business interests which saw in an independent Confederacy opportunities for profitable trade, free of tariff barriers, in which raw cotton would be traded for British manufactures. Speaking for Southern sympathizers were the powerful London *Times*, literary men such as Thomas Carlyle and Sir Edward Bulwer-Lytton, and historians of repute like Edward A. Freeman and George Grote.

That both points of view were articulated in the cabinet of Lord Palmerston presented both dangers and opportunities to the Union. As in public opinion, the opportunities were not exploited, again largely because of Washington's failure to take an anti-slavery stand, and that fact, combined with Union military reverses, encouraged the advocates of intervention to speak out. Palmerston, an old-line English Whig aristocrat with a profound distrust of democracy, had no high regard for the United States, and was particularly irked by the shut-off of cotton and the Morrill tariff. But he was cautious, preferring to await the trend of public opinion at home and the turn of events in America before formulating a long-term policy. In the meantime, he adopted neutrality. Ironically, his first move in a neutral direction provoked a storm of protest in the United States, which in turn set the stage for a succession of crises which nearly disrupted relations between the two countries.

As soon as news of Lincoln's order to blockade Confederate ports reached London in May, 1861, the British government, without waiting for formal notification, proclaimed neutrality and recognized both the blockade and Confederate belligerency. This was a boon to the Union, for it denied the Confederacy easy access to war supplies. But Northern opinion, which expected nothing less than outright support for the Union, was outraged. The significance of British observance of the blockade was ignored, while the recognition of Confederate belligerency (which Lincoln had already accorded through his proclamation of blockade) was seen as a devious step toward recognition of Southern independence. The long-held popular suspicions of British government actions, intensified by the animosity of more than a million Irishmen who had fled their devastated land as a result of the famines of the 1840s, found outlet in furious speeches and editorials. Even *Harper's Weekly*, which took a moderate position in the controversy, urged that if the British persisted in being unfriendly the United States should embargo all trade with Britain, a step which "would very quickly bring John Bull to his senses."

Northern feeling flared again after the humiliating Union defeat at Bull Run in July, 1861. With the North reeling from the shock and Union sympathizers in Britain dismayed, pro-Southern British newspapers and politicians complacently concluded that the Confederacy could not be conquered and counselled separation. More ominous was a speech made in October by Earl Russell, the foreign secretary. Since slavery was not an issue of the war, he declared, the only question was between empire and independence, and the only answer was permanent separation. Privately he urged upon Palmerston Anglo-French mediation, with the threat of hostility if the Union did not accept. The prime minister was not persuaded. The public expressions enraged the North. Typical was a *Harper's Weekly* editorial: "No spark of generosity, or sympathy, or kindly interest in other people's welfare ever illumines British foreign policy, or the foreign articles of the leading British journals."

Such feeling was still simmering when the impetuous act of an American naval commander seemed to bring Britain and the United States close to war. In November, 1861, Captain Charles Wilkes fired on a British mail ship, the *Trent*, and removed from it two Confederate commissioners bound for Europe, James M. Mason and John Slidell. This was not only a violation of international law—taking persons from a neutral ship bound for a neutral port—but a direct challenge to the British government. To make matters worse, Wilkes was hailed as a hero at home. He was thanked by the House of Representatives, congratulated by Secretary of the Navy Gideon Welles, applauded by the press, and wined and dined by exuberant citizens, eager to celebrate any kind of "victory" to compensate for the lack of any real military success. Even within his own cabinet Lincoln was almost alone in feeling that Mason and Slidell would prove to be "white elephants." So intense was public feeling that the administration could formulate no immediate response to the British demands for an apology and restoration of the prisoners.

The affair provided an opening for Confederate sympathizers in Britain. Led by the London *Times* they whipped up a war hysteria while the British government alerted the fleet and dispatched troops to Canada. But war feeling subsided in both countries as weeks passed with no new incident to inflame the crisis, and of perhaps more importance, neither government was anxious for war. In December the British government was privately informed that Wilkes had acted without authority, and the rise in the London stock market when the news leaked out gave indication of how the business community felt about an American war. In Washington, Lincoln and others were familiar with the letters of Cobden and Bright to Senator Charles Sumner, telling of division both in public opinion and in the cabinet, and advising that American action would prove decisive in whether the advocates of war or the men of peace would get the upper hand. Accommodation, wrote Bright, would baffle "the menaces of the English oligarchy."

Accommodation it was. Seward believed the United States had a poor case, and Lincoln thought it enough to be involved in "one war at a time." Besides, European governments counselled concessions to the British. A somewhat reluctant cabinet fell in line. Mason and Slidell were turned over to the British—which the latter accepted also as an apology—while Seward sent a note more designed to appease Northern opinion than to justify the needs of the case: he was gratified that at long last the British accepted the doctrines of maritime rights so long held by the United States.

A new crisis soon appeared, this time provoked by Britons. Taking advantage of a loophole in the British neutrality law, shipbuilders provided war vessels for the Confederacy but carefully avoided arming them, which was specifically forbidden by law. This was done in locations outside the United Kingdom, usually supervised by British firms. Repeated protests by Adams proved of no avail, until the flagrant circumstances of the building of the notorious *Alabama* eventually produced an order for its seizure in July, 1862. But the ship slipped away, and although it was still in British waters no effort was made to take it. The North believed that the British government connived at its escape, and feelings mounted as the British-built vessels plundered and sank American merchant shipping. So successful were they that American shippers quit the business, selling out to foreign, largely British, interests. This was a bitter pill to swallow for a people who since colonial days had boasted of their merchant marine.

Even more dangerous during the summer and fall of 1862 were projected moves toward British intervention. Taking advantage of Union setbacks, climaxed with another defeat at Bull Run, which further demoralized Union supporters in Britain, Confederate sympathizers in Parliament openly proposed mediation. Palmerston, while heading off the move, himself thought the time ripe for Anglo-French intervention, looking toward separation of the sections. Russell agreed, advising that if the Union rejected mediation the Confederacy should be recognized. The prime minister then held off, awaiting news of Lee's invasion of Maryland; should the Union be defeated, he wrote, "the iron should be struck while it is hot." The iron was cold: Lee fled after the bloody engagement at Antietam, and Lincoln, who had long awaited such a victory, took advantage of it to issue the preliminary Emancipation Proclamation.

From then on the danger of intervention receded. Friends of the Union took new heart as the war now assumed a clear moral dimension, while friends of the Confederacy, such as the London *Times*, discredited themselves by suddenly reversing their long standing hostility to slavery, denouncing the Emancipation Proclamation as an incitement to slave rebellion and finding unsuspected virtues in the South's "peculiar institution." In the meantime it was made known that the Union would look upon mediation as an unfriendly act and recognition of the Confederacy as an act of war. Neither Palmerston nor Russell wanted war with the United States—particularly since the war was now a war of abolition. When in October Napoleon III of France revived once again his scheme of inter-' vention, Russell turned him down. The Russian government, also approached by Napoleon, not only rejected his proposal but read him a lecture obviously designed for British as well as French eyes. Foreign governments, it said, should avoid "the appearance of any pressure whatsoever of a nature to wound public opinion in the United States, and to excite susceptibilities very easily aroused at the bare idea of foreign intervention."

When Lincoln issued his final Emancipation Proclamation on January 1, 1863, the massive tide of Union sentiment beached what was left of British interventionism. Mass meetings throughout the country not only hailed Lincoln and his policy but also condemned intervention and the building of war vessels for the Confederacy. John Bright noted the "considerable change" in public opinion, while Henry Adams, with youthful exaggeration, wrote joyfully of the "almost convulsive reaction in our favor." The government got the message. In April, despite the dubious legality of the move, Russell seized a Confederate warship, the *Alexandra*. In the summer came news of Gettysburg and Vicksburg—and a new issue, the building of ironclads designed to break the Union blockade. So fearful was Adams of the potential of the new ships that he warned Russell that if they sailed, "this is war." In fact, two days before Adams penned his note Russell had ordered detention of the ships and extraordinary measures to prevent their escape, although title to the vessels was technically held by a French firm. The era of confrontation was over. Palmerston's cautious "wait and see" policy had paid off for the Union—partly because of Union military success, partly because Lincoln had made emancipation a war aim. In international as well as in national affairs the black American role proved important.

If the Union had long failed to appreciate the diplomatic importance of Emancipation, the Confederacy had long underrated the value of diplomacy, primarily because it believed the need for cotton would compel international recognition of the South. The British cotton textile industry, based on American raw material, was the country's biggest, employing a million workers directly while three million other people earned their livelihood from it indirectly. Southerners agreed with Senator James Hammond of South Carolina when he said in 1858, that without Southern cotton, "old England would topple headlong and carry the whole civilized world with her." For much of the war this view shaped Confederate policy. In the words of William H. Russell, the war correspondent for the London *Times*, "Liverpool and Manchester [major cotton production centers] have obscured all Great Britain to the Southern eye." It was a long time before it dawned on Confederates that Britain had interests other than cotton, and that the war provided an opportunity to end its dangerous dependence on the American supply.

So little was diplomacy regarded in the Confederacy that no secretary of state served more than a few months until Judah P. Benjamin took over in February, 1862, and held the office through the defeat at Appomattox. The Confederacy's case was simple: it had peacefully established a government with the consent of the people, and that government was in full control of the territory to which it laid claim. According to accepted standards of international law that government was entitled to formal recognition. So, in the weeks before Fort Sumter, it sent to Europe three commissioners to gain recognition, treaties of commerce—and after war broke out—defiance of the Union blockade. None of the commissioners was "well fitted" for the job, according to E. Merton Coulter, the noted Southern historian.[1] Earl Russell received them informally and made no commitments. Napoleon III gave warm promises of support, provided Britain acted first. Disgusted, one of the commissioners resigned his post and returned to tell the South that international recognition would be gained only when it was won by force of arms.

The British government, of course, had no intention of getting involved at that time. It avoided recognition while at the same time conceding belligerency to the Confederacy and observance of the blockade to the Union. The same policy, as well as long standing naval considerations, led Britain shortly to close her ports to privateers of both sides. But since the Union had commissioned none, the ban did not affect it, while the closure frustrated Confederate plans to turn privateers loose on Yankee shipping and take their prizes to British ports. The obvious failure of its diplomacy prompted the Confederacy to dispatch two new agents, Mason and Slidell, to England and France respectively. The crisis which arose from their arrest buoyed Southern hopes, but the Union backdown prevented the Confederacy from reaping much advantage from the affair.

Nor did their reception in England augur well for Confederate hopes. The London *Times*, which had done so much to foment war hysteria over the *Trent* affair, now advised Britons to give the commissioners a cool welcome, for they were "blind and habitual haters and revilers of this country." It characterized them as "about the most worthless booty it would be possible to extract from the jaws of the American lion." American aboli-

---

[1] E. Merton Coulter, *The Confederate States of America, 1861–1865* (Baton Rouge: Louisiana State University Press, 1950), p. 186.

tionists lost no time reminding their British friends that Mason had drafted the infamous Fugitive Slave Law of 1850 and that Slidell was an unscrupulous politician whose unsavory machinations as the emissary of President Polk had helped bring on the Mexican War. Slidell soon departed for France, where he quickly became a friend of Napoleon and almost as quickly won the distrust of other Confederate agents in Europe. Mason stayed in London, helping develop pro-Confederate sentiment, but pointedly ignored by the government. When in the summer of 1862 he requested an interview with Earl Russell to discuss recognition, Russell turned him down. The Confederacy, wrote the Foreign Secretary, had still to demonstrate "promise of stability and permanence," and thus the time for recognition had not yet arrived.

Continued British observance of the ever more effective blockade, the seizure of Confederate warships built in England, and the failure of Britain to recognize Confederate independence—all soured Southern feelings toward a country from which they had expected so much. In addition, Britain was blamed for frustration of the French attempts at mediation. And there were sources of friction within the Confederacy itself. British consuls interfered with drafting of British subjects into the army, and they conducted their affairs through the British ambassador in Washington. How could one do business with men who reported to an official accredited to an enemy government? Southern bitterness found expression in editorial comment to the effect that the Confederacy had "no worse enemies . . . than the British government and the majority of the British nation."

The Confederate government ostensibly yielded to the popular clamor, but it was in fact embarking on a new policy arising out of its diplomatic failures. The new policy was equally unrealistic: by a show of firmness the Confederacy would compel foreign powers to reassess their attitudes. Early in 1863 the Senate voted to confirm new diplomatic appointments only to governments which recognized the Confederacy. To give force to this move, an envoy en route to Russia was refused approval and had to return home. Later, the Mason mission to London was formally ended and all British consuls expelled from the Confederacy. In December, Davis in his message to Congress excoriated the British as the authors of Confederate misfortunes abroad, charging them with a hypocritical policy "which under professions of neutrality had become subservient to the designs of our enemy." The new policy produced no better results than the old. After Gettysburg and Vicksburg what power was going to risk recognizing the Confederacy?

Whatever diplomatic illusions the Confederacy entertained were largely dissipated with the fall of Atlanta and Sherman's March to the Sea in 1864. In desperation, the Confederacy played its last card: emancipation. Secret instructions were sent Mason to offer abolition in return for British recognition, and Mason, back in London, obtained an interview with Lord Palmerston himself. The Confederate envoy played this last card poorly. Afraid that an open proposal would leak to the enemy, and "if not accepted the mischief resulting would be incalculable," he wrote that he made "no distinct proposal" but confined himself to allusions which he felt sure the prime minister could not "misunderstand." For the record, Mason sought to impress upon the sophisticated Palmerston that the Confederate military situation was really "encouraging," that the North was ready for peace, that Britain was in grave danger should the peace take place, and that France was ready to follow Britain's lead. Understandably, Palmerston was not persuaded, and Mason reported that even the "most ample concessions" on slavery would not now change British policy.

Nevertheless, Mason persisted. Perhaps doubtful that his "allusions" were clear he met with the Earl of Donoughmore, a power in the parliamentary opposition and a "fast and consistent friend" of the Confederacy. Supposing, Mason asked, he were to meet with Palmerston again and openly propose abolition in exchange for recognition, "Would your government then recognize us?" The Earl replied that "the time had gone by now, especially that our fortunes seemed more adverse than ever."

(Confederate diplomacy was shortsighted not just in letting time pass it by but also in failing to reckon with Britain's world interests and the complexities of domestic British politics. Southern expectations mounted with the successive crises in Anglo-American relations, but Southerners became embittered when the British government responded to them purely in light of British interests. In pursuit of these interests, Britain wanted no war with the United States. This was in line with Palmerston's general policy: nonintervention in potentially dangerous situations while energetically promoting British interests in Asia, where it was safe and profitable to take an aggressive stance. The policy was well summarized in a letter from Richard Cobden to Senator Sumner at the height of the *Trent* crisis: "although Palmerston is fond of hot water, he boasts that he never got us into a serious war. As for his colleagues, they are all . . . peaceable men."

Thus, despite much brash rhetoric from Palmerston and others, Britain did not get involved in the Italian War of 1859, nor the Polish Rebellion of 1863, nor the war over Schleswig-Holstein in 1864. Neither did the government allow its reaction to the American crises to get out of control.

The explanation partly lies in considerations of empire. Nonintervention, so long as British security was not endangered, facilitated expansion in Asia. But in 1857 British authority in India—by far the most profitable British possession—was challenged by a widespread rebellion which was not finally crushed until 1859. All during the American Civil War the British were preoccupied with restoring their rule over peoples who failed to appreciate the benefits of Anglo-Saxon civilization. The British were also teaching the Chinese lessons. In 1860 British and French armies crushed Chinese resistance to their continued incursions. British military and naval forces were essential to exploit the opportunities thus opened in addition to those necessary to "pacify" India.

With British power spread so thin, Canada was vulnerable. Its three-thousand mile frontier was poorly defended, and its internal strife between English and French so bitter that by 1864 government activity was virtually paralyzed. British Columbia, in the Far West, was already economically a satellite of San Francisco, separated from its Canadian neighbors by a thousand miles of wilderness, and while talk of annexation to the United States was muted during the war, it had not died out. In the United States the long-held prospect of annexation was revived by Senator Sumner when he proposed such a step as payment for the depredations of the *Alabama* and other Confederate raiders on American shipping. The temporary American abrogation of the Rush-Bagot Agreement of 1818, banning warships on the Great Lakes, emphasized such an approach. The danger of an American takeover helps explain the British North America Act of 1867, which established the Canadian Confederation, as it helps explain British caution in dealing with the United States.

And off stage, but threatening, was Russia. Defeated by Britain and France in the Crimean War just five years before Fort Sumter, she had made it plain that when the international situation changed she would nullify the treaty imposed on her in 1856. In the New World this meant supporting the United States as a counterweight to Britain. So, Russia vetoed the mediation proposals of Britain and France, and when it appeared that Britain might intervene in the Polish Rebellion, Russia dispatched fleets to New York and San Francisco, with promises to aid the Union should the occasion demand. Under these circumstances Britain had to move cautiously, lest war with the United States free Russia to move in the Middle East (the issue of the Crimean War) as a step toward invasion of India, a bugaboo of British policy since the Napoleonic wars.

Domestic considerations, too, argued against aggressive action. The Crimean War was still a live and bitter memory with the British public, and Palmerston was well aware that much of his current popularity stemmed from his role in ending what had become an unpopular war. Besides, he was operating in a politically transitional period, when the old Whig and Tory Parties were in dissolution and the later Conservative and Liberal Parties were still crystallizing. His cabinet was made up of men representing both tendencies, which in itself made for cautious policy, while the divisions on the American issue were so deep that they became public.

In October, 1862, the chancellor of the exchequer, William E. Gladstone (later a famous Liberal prime minister), made a speech praising Jefferson Davis, seeming to presage Confederate recognition. A week later the secretary for war, Sir G. Cornewall Lewis, a friend of the Union, retorted publicly that the government had no such intention. For his part, Palmerston was impressed with the indignation aroused by Gladstone's speech—and Gladstone himself backed off, explaining that his speech had been misunderstood.

Political decisions reflected influences operating upon the government. The cotton crisis—upon which the Confederacy had counted to win recognition—did not appear until late 1862, and until then the lack of fresh raw cotton worked few hardships. Taking advantage of the bumper crop of 1860 British merchants and manufacturers had stockpiled cotton and that lasted a long time, thanks to a slump in the market for finished cotton goods. When markets revived and supplies dwindled, holders of raw cotton prospered mightily. Few merchants or manufacturers were in a mood for war. Also, the threat of a cotton shortage worked in a way unforeseen by Confederate strategists: it provided a powerful new stimulus to the movement to promote alternate sources of supply, such as Egypt and India. When Southern planters came back into the market after the war they found that their erstwhile dominance was gone.

While British dependence on Southern cotton was reduced, the importance of Northern wheat was increased. The flood of American grain during the critical years of 1861 and 1862 emphasized the fact that when Britain's European suppliers had bad crop years she was dependent on American supplies for food. Further, the American supplies kept food prices and wages low, and thus contributed to the competitive advantage of British industry. In addition, grain imports helped to pay for the vast outpouring of civilian and military goods to America during the war.

Which brings us to another reason for British nonintervention: neutrality was profitable. With Yankees driven from the sea, British shippers no longer had much quarrel with the Union. On the contrary, because they were making fabulous profits from the trans-Atlantic trade they wanted nothing to disturb it. They were particularly fearful of any British move which would provoke Americans into executing their threat of authorizing privateers—which would, of course, be directed against British trade everywhere. Other British interests were equally adamant about neutrality. Woolen goods manufacturers, iron and steel producers, coal mine owners— all were prospering from the war and British neutrality. Naturally, they wanted no change. More aggressively pro-Union were those members of the British public who had invested in United States enterprises, and as Henry Blumenthal has noted, "British investments in United States railroads, banks, and mining and land companies, . . . exceeded those in the English cotton industry." [2] Nor could the government ignore the fact that the United States was the single biggest customer of Britain.

Neither could British labor be overlooked. The articulate, skilled workers were demanding the right to vote, and among their spokesmen were Cobden and Bright, who identified the cause of democracy in Britain with that of the Union in America. Such workers were also struggling to win recognition of their craft unions—eminently conservative pragmatic organizations of the type later seen in the American Federation of Labor in the United States. These new unions were growing in numbers, wealth, and influence and enjoyed considerable middle-class support. That working-class opinion was significant is attested to by the Confederates' purchase of *Reynold's Weekly Newspaper*, a journal with large readership among workers and their families.

The Confederate campaign to enlist labor support met with more success than we originally thought, especially in the cotton districts of Lancashire, where the widespread unemployment and distress were blamed on the Union blockade rather than on the glut of finished goods on the market. It is not surprising, then, that hungry workers supported proposals for British intervention to end the blockade. For various reasons some labor leaders elsewhere were sympathetic to the Confederacy. [3]

Nevertheless, there were also workingmen, especially among the younger leaders, who perceived the link between labor's future at home and the fate of the Union. In their view, defeat of the Union would strengthen the enemies of labor and democracy at home. Such feelings were expressed in greetings sent to Lincoln by Manchester workers on the eve of Emancipation. "Our interests . . . are identified with yours," they said, pointing out that the British enemies of the Union were "chiefly those who oppose liberty at home." Palmerston, of course, was not about to give workers the vote. Neither was he going to inflame the issue by involvement in America, unless such involvement was fool proof.

Intervention might be fool proof if the Union suffered a series of military debacles, which presumably would make it receptive to offers of mediation. No such situation developed. If Union forces received repeated setbacks in the East, troops in the West won decisive victories—a fact duly noted in London.

How *did* Union military victory come about? Superiority in resources is only part of the explanation; resources, to be effective, must be intelli-

---

[2] Henry Blumenthal, "Confederate Diplomacy: Popular Notions and International Realities," *Journal of Southern History*, XXXII, No. 2(May, 1966), 167.

[3] Joseph M. Hernon, Jr., "British Sympathies in the American Civil War: A Reconsideration," *Journal of Southern History*, XXXIII, No. 3 (August, 1967), 356–67.

gently applied. The Union problem was to find generals who knew how to exploit its wealth in men and materiel; the Confederate problem was how to take advantage of its internal lines of communication and how best to use the resources it had. In short, questions of strategy. The basic issues were long in coming to the fore, for both sides shared the initial belief that the war would be short, settled by a decisive battle or two. The first Battle of Bull Run was significant in this respect. It forced the Union to re-think the war as a long term affair requiring some notions of strategy, while it persuaded Confederates that they were invincible and that an immediate march on Washington would end the war—a project vetoed by General Joseph E. Johnston, who realized that his celebrating troops were in no condition to cope with fresh Union forces lying between them and the capital. But even when the war settled down to a long contest, neither side fully appreciated the need for implementing strategy. Not until 1864 did the Union produce the rudiments of a general staff system to manage and coordinate its far-flung armies. The Confederate army produced none; indeed, there was no unified overall command until February, 1865, when Lee was made general of all the armies.

The basic Confederate strategy was defensive. By simply protecting its own territory the Confederacy would at once assure foreign powers that it had no aggressive designs and wear down Union sentiment so that a negotiated peace would result. Given the divisions in Northern opinion and in the Border States, as well as the moods of war weariness which swept the North as late as 1864, the view was not so unrealistic as it appeared to those Southerners who pressed for offensive action. Such action, as Jefferson Davis pointed out, would be folly: the Confederacy had neither the manpower nor the material resources to sustain a Northern invasion. When, due to diplomatic and domestic political pressures, such invasions were undertaken, they failed. Lee was checked at Antietam, and later crushed at Gettysburg. In the West, when Braxton Bragg tried to reach the Ohio River through Kentucky and round out the natural frontier of the Confederacy, he was forced to retreat to Confederate territory.

The Union strategy had to be offensive: Confederate territory had to be brought back into the Union. This called for movements in Virginia, and for others down the Mississippi, to sever the Confederacy, while the Union naval blockade would cut off supplies for the rebels. Thus, the Confederacy would be steadily constricted until it could no longer resist. This was the strategy, but despite the obvious importance of the Western theater it was neglected in both policy and public opinion—a myopic view shared by the Confederacy. For most of the war, on both sides, there were two fields of battle: that in Virginia, and that in the West. And the war in Virginia seemed the more important.

The Confederate strategy worked well in Virginia. Until 1864 a succession of Union generals suffered such grievous defeats as to occasion despair in Lincoln: Irvin McDowell at the first Bull Run, July 1861; George B. McClellan, in the Seven Days' Battles, July, 1862; John Pope, second Bull Run, August, 1862; Ambrose Burnside, Fredericksburg, December, 1862; and Joseph Hooker, Chancellorsville, May, 1863. The tide was not turned until Grant was called from the West in 1864, and even then the Union attained its objectives only at what was then considered an unacceptable price in human life.

Apart from questions of personality and personal feuds—which were by no means inconsequential—the basic weakness of Union generals in Virginia was their failure to understand the kind of war they were fighting. In conditions of total war they fought a traditional war of limited objectives, the kind Lee and Stonewall Jackson knew how to fight much better than their opponents. The Eastern outlook was symbolized by McClellan. An able training commander, he saw his role of combat commander as that of inflicting such injury on the enemy as to persuade him of the error of his ways without doing such damage as to embitter him. When the war threatened to go beyond such a limited objective, as with full emancipation, McClellan became openly insubordinate.

In the West, the Confederate strategy failed. The war was less than a year old when Grant took Fort Donelson, a key post on the Cumberland River in Tennessee. A few weeks later he and William T. Sherman inflicted a stunning defeat on the Confederates at Shiloh, Tennessee, in a battle so bloody it shocked and dismayed the South while it aroused clamor in the North for Grant's removal. Shortly thereafter, Union troops, convoyed by the Navy, occupied New Orleans, the major port and banking center of the Confederacy. By midsummer of 1862 Nashville and Memphis, important trading and transportation centers, were in Union hands. The full significance of these events was less appreciated in Washington and Richmond than in London. When Mason pressed for recognition, he was reminded that while Union forces made no headway in Virginia, "the capture of New Orleans, the advance of the Federals . . . to Memphis, and the banks of the Mississippi as far as Vicksburg," made the issue uncertain. Thus, the British government was "still determined to wait." It was still waiting when Mason was ordered by the Confederacy to close down his mission in September, 1863.

The fall of Vicksburg on July 4, 1863, in effect gave the Union control of the great inland waterway, the Mississippi. For the Confederacy, it was a major disaster: an army of 30,000 men under General Kirby Smith was now isolated in Texas; supplies from Mexico and Texas were cut off; and Union troops were now free to penetrate the Deep South, the heart of the Confederacy. And penetrate they did, despite reverses, as at Chickamauga, where in September, 1863, Bragg forced withdrawal of Union

forces to Chattanooga and then laid seige to the city. By the end of November the Confederates were in retreat, battered and dispirited after their
losses at Lookout Mountain and Missionary Ridge. Now the way was clear
for invasion of Georgia, and for the larger objective of cutting the Confederacy horizontally, to supplement the vertical cleavage accomplished on
the Mississippi.

By September, Atlanta, a Confederate arsenal and major railroad center, had fallen to Sherman, and from there he set out on his famous March
to the Sea. With little opposition, moving on a front 60 miles wide, living
off the country and destroying anything of possible value to the enemy, he
reached Savannah, Georgia, early in December and shortly received its surrender. For all practical purposes, the war was over. The Confederacy was
now severed both at the Mississippi and along Sherman's line of march.
Cut off from western supplies and from the Deep South, the Confederacy's
ability to wage war was tremendously reduced. Only in Virginia was there
a semblance of a fighting force left, and it was deprived of its food by Sheridan's destruction of the Shenandoah Valley in September, 1864. Then,
early in 1865 Sherman moved north from Savannah, planning to trap remaining Confederate forces in a pincers move between his forces and
Grant's. Lee's surrender at Appomattox in April simply recognized the inevitable.

Union success in the West was partly attributable to fortuitous circumstances. Just as Lincoln was vexed by quarrels between his generals in
Virginia, so Davis was confronted with feuds among his Western commanders, culminating in almost open mutiny among the officers of Braxton
Bragg's command. Davis' long support of Bragg simply made the situation
worse. Further, Confederate preoccupation with the East precluded dispatch of reinforcements to the West at critical moments. Thus, Lee's
Gettysburg campaign meant no troops were sent to relieve Vicksburg.
Basically, however, the Union cause triumphed because it had in Grant
and Sherman, not only two generals who worked well with each other, but
also men who grasped the total nature of the war and acted on that understanding. Not only must Confederate armies be defeated. Not only must
the enemy's ability to wage war be destroyed. But also the Southern will to
resist must be crushed. To Southerners, all this smacked of barbarism; to
the Union generals it was simply application of a military doctrine suited
to the situation. The essential difference between the Eastern and Western
theaters was put succinctly by Lincoln when he was pressed to remove
Grant after the bloodletting at Shiloh: "I can't spare this man; he fights."

The gulf between conventional and total war was further exemplified
at Fort Donelson, when the Confederate general, Simon Buckner, asked for
terms of surrender. In his famous response, Grant said, "No terms except an
unconditional and immediate surrender . . . I propose to move immedi-

ately upon your works." Buckner replied that he had no alternative but to accept such "ungenerous and unchivalrous terms." Chivalry? When peoples and governments were locked in combat to the death?

Sherman's rationale was set forth when officials of Atlanta protested his order to evacuate the city prior to its destruction, a step Sherman deemed necessary before he set out for Savannah. He would not revoke his orders, he said, "because they were not designed to meet the humanities of the case, . . . We must have peace, . . . To secure this, we must stop the war . . . To stop war we must defeat the rebel armies . . . To defeat these armies we must prepare the way to reach them in their recesses." Since Atlanta might become a focal point of future Confederate efforts, it must be denied them. That this would mean hardship for civilians was true, but Atlantans must remember that they had sent troops and war supplies to "carry war into Kentucky and Tennessee." Southerners had started the war, and they must take responsibility for the consequences; they "might as well appeal against the thunderstorm as against these terrible hardships of war. They are inevitable." The Union wanted no Southern possessions, "but we do want and will have a just obedience to the laws of the United States. That we will have, and if it involves the destruction of your improvements, we cannot help it." Among the possessions named by Sherman which the Union did not want, he included "your Negroes." Surely a strange statement to make nine months after the Emancipation Proclamation! Nevertheless, it is clear that Grant and Sherman were fighting a new kind of war, and the test of their doctrine was that they were winning! And winning not only campaigns in a purely military sense. Southerners agreed that no single event of the war so undermined their will as Sherman's March to the Sea.

Second only to establishing its independence, the basic problem confronting the Confederacy was who should govern whom. Planters quickly moved to take control. The permanent Constitution was written by the provisional Congress, a one-house body chosen by secession conventions. It was ratified by such bodies, with no submission to a popular vote. This was due both to the haste necessary to establish a government before Lincoln was inaugurated, and to distrust of majority rule, to which planters ascribed all their ills in the Union and all their problems in Southern states where democratic reforms had made headway. As former United States Senator James H. Hammond of South Carolina said, believers in annual elections and universal suffrage "must be kept from putting their hands upon our Constitution." Sharing Alexander Hamilton's belief that government properly belonged to "the rich, the well-born, and the educated"—but not his faith in a strong central government—they took the

United States Constitution as their basis, modifying it to protect minority rights to an even greater extent than had the original.

Thus the emphasis on states' rights. Planters could do little about democracy within some individual states, but they could make sure that their interests would not be sacrificed to majority rule in the Confederacy as a whole. The new Constitution, then, derived its authority from the people—but only through "sovereign and independent states." Significantly, there was no obligation of the new government to "promote the general welfare," as the United States Constitution prescribed. More specifically, planters continued inclusion of three-fifths of slaves as a basis for Congressional representation, providing themselves with a political advantage over the mass of Southerners who owned no slaves. They kept a check on Congressional policy itself by requiring that all appropriations must receive a two-thirds vote in both House and Senate. The rise of potentially dangerous commercial and industrial interests was guarded against by prohibiting Congress from financing any but minimal public works and from passing any tariff designed to "promote or foster any branch of industry." On the right of secession the Constitution was silent—but does any government anywhere provide for its own dissolution?

While entrenching their political power, the planters also acted to protect their property. The old fifth amendment guaranty of private property against central government seizure was retained in the new Constitution. State action was likewise restrained, despite the states' rights doctrine. As in the old Constitution, no state could coin money or impair the obligation of contracts, thus protecting the wealthy against the poor, who traditionally had sought to save themselves through state issue of paper money and laws postponing execution of contracts, such as foreclosures. Slave property received special attention. No state could pass any law "denying or impairing the right of property in Negro slaves." In territories not yet states, "the institution of Negro slavery . . . shall be recognized and protected by Congress and by the territorial government." Importation of foreign slaves was banned, a provision which benefited great planters by helping to keep slave prices high, while at the same time it outraged small planters who hoped to benefit from low prices resulting from reopening of the African slave trade.

Would this minority government work? It did, early into the war. Repeated Union setbacks in the East, faith in the power of "King Cotton" to bring foreign intervention, and belief that dissension in the North was a sign of early Union concession of Southern independence—all these contributed to a mood of euphoria which united Southerners while it glossed over sources of discord. When it became apparent that the war was going to be long, that foreign recognition was not forthcoming, and that Confederate armies in the West were in almost constant retreat, the deep fissures of Southern society revealed themselves again. The poor began to rebel. Business interests took issue with planters. Old-line conservative Whigs asserted themselves against Democrats. Democrats divided among themselves.

There were issues aplenty. The conscription law alienated the poor, and some of the wealthiest planters, such as Howell Cobb of Georgia, opposed it. The impressment of farm supplies angered yeoman farmers and planters alike. Suspension of the writ of habeas corpus was viewed as a step toward a Davis dictatorship. Taxes on profits alienated business-men, and workers resented Confederate strike-breaking. Above all, the galloping inflation, which the government seemed unable to control, pro-duced a mood of discontent and bitterness. All these· tensions found expression in the confused politics of the Confederacy.

Here the doctrine of state sovereignty came home to plague the Con-federacy. Claiming that troops were necessary for state defense, the governors of Louisiana, Mississippi, and Georgia kept state militia units out of Confederate service. The governor of Georgia, Joseph E. Brown, went even further. He practically nullified the conscription law within his state, and then, during the critical month of September, 1864, when Atlanta fell, he gave a month's furlough to the state militia of 10,000 men which he had permitted to be made part of the Confederate army. Governor Zebulon Vance of North Carolina commandeered the output of woolen and cotton textiles in his state for exclusive use by North Carolinians while Confederate soldiers from other states lacked clothing. That state and South Carolina both on occasion banned out-of-state shipment of foodstuffs. When it was legal to do so, state judges freed conscripts on writs of habeas corpus, a practice followed also by some Confederate judges. Since there was no Confederate Supreme Court to pass on the issues, decisions of the lower courts stood. Thanks to the states' rights doctrine, as well as to resentment of Davis and suspicion that he might appoint Judah Benjamin as a Justice, Congress never established a Supreme Court to interpret law for the Confederacy.

The planter aristocracy itself did not remain united. In South Carolina planters, angered both by impressment of slaves for army service and by impressment of their crops, brought about dissolution of the secession convention and a state executive council, both of which had prosecuted a vigorous pro-Confederate war policy. In 1864 they helped elect a governor opposed to the Davis Administration. Aristocrats who failed to gain desired appointment retired to devote their efforts to discrediting the government. Robert Toombs, a wealthy planter of Georgia, resigned from the army when he was denied promotion to major-general, refused to plant food crops instead of cotton, and when given a command of Georgia troops in 1863 admonished them not to "mutiny, unless it should be necessary in defense of constitutional rights"—after he had just listed all the ways in which their rights were being violated! Robert Barnwell Rhett went back to South Carolina after he failed to be appointed an official of the Confederacy and used his Charleston *Mercury* to attack the Davis government. In Richmond itself Whig planter-oriented newspapers carried on incessant psychological warfare against the administration.[4]

(Apart from such issues as inflation, conscription and impressment, a major source of planter discontent was the defensive military strategy, proved again a failure by the fall of Atlanta.) The resulting clamor for aggressive action provided Davis an opportunity to relieve the bleak military picture and strengthen the position of the government. The idea was suggested by General John B. Hood, an impetuous veteran who had lost both an arm and a leg in Confederate service—and who also lost Atlanta. Enjoying Davis' admiration, Hood persuaded the president to approve a daring plan. The general would go north to Tennessee from Georgia, pulling Sherman, fearful for his supply line, after him, thus sparing the South from further invasion. With the initiative in his hands, Hood would recapture Nashville and then move north to the Ohio River.

The plan miscarried. Sherman refused to take the bait, preferring to march to the sea with no supply line, living off the country as he went. And Union armies were waiting for Hood as he pressed northward. At Franklin, Tennessee, Confederate troops suffered appalling losses, including the loss of twelve generals. As the victorious Union troops retreated to Nashville, eighteen miles away, the weakened Hood pursued them, moving into a trap. It was sprung on December 15, when General George H. Thomas struck the Confederates, shattering them in what the eminent Southern historian, Clement Eaton, called "the most complete victory of a Union army during the war." [5] In short, there was no hope for the Confederacy in either a defensive or an offensive strategy—except perhaps in the East, where Lee still held out.

A growing realization of this prospect helps explain the disintegration of the one-party system in the Confederacy. (The Democratic Party split into two major blocs: one in support of the Davis Administration, one in opposition. Basically it was a struggle between those who wanted war to the bitter end and those who saw that some kind of accommodation must be reached with the Union.) Many of the latter were old-line Whigs who had never felt at home with Democrats, had been less than enthusiastic about secession, and now were alarmed that their worst fears might be

---

[4] For a summary discussion of the Confederate press as a whole, see J. Cutler Andrews, "The Confederate Press and Public Morale," *Journal of Southern History*, XXXII, No. 3 (November, 1966), 445–65.

[5] Clement Eaton, *A History of the Southern Confederacy* (New York: The Free Press, 1954), p. 281.

realized. Naturally, they turned against the men who led them into disaster. This was true also of many traditional Democrats, who blamed Davis—and Benjamin—for the turn the war was taking.

The Confederate war effort then met with increasingly powerful resistance from within. Vice-president Alexander H. Stephens, an old-line Whig and lukewarm secessionist, rarely went to Richmond, and when he did it was to lead opposition to Davis. Congressmen harrassed Cabinet appointees, forcing out Judah Benjamin as Secretary of War, and a successor, James A. Seddon. Christian Memminger, Secretary of the Treasury, resigned when Congress rejected his proposals for financial reorganization. When Davis in 1862 sought to extend suspension of the writ of habeas corpus throughout the Confederacy to replace its suspension in areas threatened by invasion, Congress refused. Not until February, 1864, did Congress authorize general suspension of the writ, and then only under restricted conditions. Meanwhile, Davis lost control of Congress as a result of the elections of 1863. The tension between Congress and Davis is illustrated by his vetoing 39 acts of Congress, and his strength is shown by the fact that only once was a veto overridden.

Given this situation, the Southern people needed a rallying point. There was none. The logical person was Davis, but he was cold and austere in public, however warm he was in private. Distrustful of the common people, he could not bring himself to arouse their support until it was too late to make much difference. The cause was sufficient in itself to warrant loyalty and enthusiasm, he believed. Indeed, on occasion he alienated potential support, as when on legalistic grounds he vetoed a bill to provide widows and orphans of soldiers with the pay and allowances due their deceased husbands and fathers. He felt this was a responsibility of the states, and cited as support for his opinion, of all things, the laws of the United States in effect when the men enlisted! [6] Nor did Davis try hard to mollify his critics in and out of Congress; on the contrary, he seemed to take a perverse pleasure in provoking them. When Congressional pressure forced him to remove Benjamin as Secretary of War he promoted Benjamin to the top cabinet post of Secretary of State. Yielding to the clamor for Bragg's dismissal after the disaster at Missionary Ridge, he brought the discredited commander to Richmond to replace Robert E. Lee as presidential military advisor. Not much wonder the South was both astounded and dismayed.

Congress itself provided little to inspire the confidence and respect of the people. Its sessions were often secret, and no official record of its debates was kept. Not so secret was the fact that its deliberations were frequently marked by drunkenness. Violence and threats of violence punc-

[6] James D. Richardson, ed., *The Messages and Papers of Jefferson Davis and the Confederacy* (New York: Chelsea House—Robert Hector, 1966), I, 216–17.

tuated the sessions. An Alabama representative tried to assassinate Henry S. Foote of Tennessee, and Foote himself took a shot at another Tennessean who opposed him. In the Senate, Benjamin H. Hill of Georgia threw an inkstand at William L. Yancey of Alabama, hitting him in the face with such force as to draw blood. Yancey's followers' claim that the incident resulted in Yancey's death shortly thereafter, unfounded though it was, did little to enhance the standing of Congress in public esteem.

Nor were there voluntary agencies to help keep up the morale of a war-weary people. There was nothing in the Confederacy comparable to the United States Sanitary Commission, which, with its popular fairs throughout the North, did so much both to raise funds to aid the troops and to bolster homefront morale. The charitable work undertaken by Southern women was largely an upper-class affair. Charity was dispensed to soldiers and their families, but little sense of community was generated. The war, after all, was a planters' war.

All of this, together with repeated military setbacks, nurtured the growth of peace movements. These, as we shall see, grew out of the anger and despair of poorer whites, but eventually they enlisted more widespread support. The election campaign of W. W. Holden in North Carolina in 1864 indicated how far peace sentiment had developed, but even earlier that year the governor and legislature of Georgia had endorsed resolutions ominous for the Confederate future. The resolutions interpreted state sovereignty in such a way that Georgia could decide for itself its "future connection" and "future allies." This development, as well as Governor Brown's removal of the state militia from Confederate forces after the fall of Atlanta, prompted Sherman to invite Brown and the Confederate Vice-president, Alexander H. Stephens (who had a hand in the resolutions), to discuss peace terms. They declined, but it was clear that the Confederate front was cracking. Representative W. W. Boyce of South Carolina, one of the few Congressmen to serve all during the war, became openly defeatist, and Representative Foote of Tennessee advocated peace proposals. In Alabama, conditions were such in 1864, wrote Walter L. Fleming, the Southern historian, that had the war continued until the 1865 elections, "there is no doubt that an administration would have been elected which would have refused further support to the Confederacy." [7]

Many peace advocates pinned their hopes on a Democratic victory in the Northern elections of 1864, believing that a compromise peace could thus be obtained. When that proved illusory, some reverted to earlier "hawkish" positions, while others, like former United States Supreme Court Justice John A. Campbell, thought the time ripe for negotiations with the

[7] Walter L. Fleming, *Civil War and Reconstruction in Alabama* (New York: Columbia University Press, 1905), p. 137.

victorious Lincoln Administration. So strong was peace sentiment that Davis, who never faltered in his determination to win Southern independence, felt constrained to show that he, too, wanted peace. The way was opened to him through a Northern proposal. Francis P. Blair, Sr., a staunch Unionist who enjoyed Lincoln's respect, got the President's permission to see Davis with proposals for ending the war. Lincoln, however, refused to hear the proposals, obviously looking upon the mission as a means of sounding out the enemy, without committing himself. Also, no less than Davis could he disregard the war weariness of his people.

Blair's project was naive: an armistice, preparatory to joint action against the French in Mexico. Out of such collaboration, he believed, would come reunion on terms acceptable to both sides. Davis, realizing that such an agreement would be tacit recognition of Southern independence, accepted negotiations between "the two countries." Lincoln agreed to a meeting looking toward peace for "the people of our one common country." Given such basically different outlooks it is not surprising that the consequent Hampton Roads Conference in February, 1865, was a failure.

Davis had shrewdly appointed two peace men to the commission— Alexander H. Stephens and John A. Campbell, as well as a firm Virginia Confederate, R. M. T. Hunter. Thus, if the conference failed, Davis could hope to rally the whole country behind him. Such hopes as the commissioners entertained for an armistice were speedily dashed. Lincoln made it plain that he knew nothing of the nature of Blair's proposals and that an armistice was out of the question. Peace, however, could be attained immediately upon the disbandment of the Confederate army and Southern acceptance of Emancipation. In return, Lincoln pledged himself to use his influence for a generous policy of Reconstruction. Further, while he would give no assurances on the subject, Lincoln thought it possible for slaveowners to be compensated, citing Northerners who were willing to appropriate $400 million for the purpose.

Lincoln's terms were, of course, rejected. Confederate leaders could not bring themselves to confess to their people that nearly four years of bloodshed and destruction had been in vain—and some, including Davis, still hoped for some kind of military miracle which would bring victory. This at a time when Sherman was marching north from Savannah and Grant was moving against Richmond!

The discussion so far helps explain Confederate defeat. How are we to explain the Confederacy's holding out for four long years in the face of overwhelming odds? Part of the explanation lies with events in the North. The Union was slow to utilize all the psychological and material resources at its command; it devoted too much attention to the stalemated war in Virginia while neglecting the more important Western theater; and it had difficulty finding competent generals in the East. Further, the work of the pro-Confederate antiwar underground as well as the public activities of the Peace Democrats, coupled with the recurrent moods of war weariness in the North, encouraged Southern hopes for a peace recognizing their independence.

Southern factors were perhaps even more important. While "hawkish" planters held firm control of the government, their opponents were divided and scattered, ranging from dissident planters to antiwar poor whites. The peace movements were only locally organized, often operating underground with all the limitations and hazards associated with secret organizations. Lacking national organization they possessed neither outstanding leadership nor the benefits of a coordinated nationwide association. Above all, they offered no social or political program which might have attracted mass support in opposition to the planters.

Why? Largely because Southern whites—even those opposed to the war—could not conceive of a biracial society in which black people would be free. To them, conditioned by generations of contempt and dislike for blacks, this meant not simply black equality, unacceptable in itself, but also black domination, which was intolerable. Black domination would be enforced by Yankee rule—and Yankee rule was an abomination. With a sure grasp of Southern white psychology Davis rallied his people for a last stand after the failure of the Hampton Roads Conference. The South, he said, would never "consent to purchase at the cost of degradation and slavery permission to live in a country garrisoned by their own Negroes and governed by officers sent by the conqueror to rule over them." Thus, war to the end.

While the Confederacy tried in vain to grapple with the problems of a great war, the Union government slowly and pragmatically adjusted to the crisis. This entailed great and permanent enlargement of federal power. Right at the start, Lincoln, in an unprecedented exercise of presidential authority, suspended the writ of habeas corpus on the Eastern seaboard from Washington to Philadelphia, expanded the regular army, and transferred $2,000,000 in public funds to three trusted individuals to be spent by them for war purposes. All these measures, of dubious legality, were later approved by Congress. As the war went on the federal government took over entire responsibility for supplying the army and later enforced a national manpower policy through the draft.

Nor was the new authority restricted to purely military measures. As we shall see, Washington actively intervened in the economy through the protective tariff, the issuance of greenbacks as legal tender, and the promotion of a national bank system which involved driving state bank notes out of circulation. State governments became federal clients to share in the land grants offered by the Morrill Act. The transcontinental railroad was a national project, backed by federal funds. Perhaps most revolutionary in terms of federal-state relations was adoption of the thirteenth amendment. Even some of its leading supporters doubted that it was "constitutional." Slavery and emancipation, they felt, were matters for state, not federal, action. They swallowed their doubts and accepted Lincoln's unorthodox move as part of the necessities of war.

Adoption of the amendment symbolized the decline of the states' rights doctrine in the North. Such sentiment was there, of course, but most of its proponents were willing to yield sufficiently to enable the Union to survive. Governor Seymour of New York was loud in asserting his rights, but his obstructionism fell far short of that of such Confederate governors as Vance and Brown. Most governors looked to Washington for guidance and support; such discontent as arose came from a feeling, typified by Governor Andrew of Massachusetts, that Lincoln was not pressing the war vigorously enough. So, the states generally acquiesced in Washington's expansion of power, and when draft resistance developed they did not hesitate to ask federal troops for aid.

The new relationship between the states and Washington was dramatically illustrated in the case of Indiana. A legislature dominated by Peace Democrats tried to cripple the war effort by stripping the Republican governor, Oliver P. Morton, of his military authority. The move was frustrated by Republican members who boycotted the session, and thus prevented a quorum. The gleeful Democrats then adjourned, with no appropriations voted for operating the state government. Morton then turned to Washington for $250,000 to carry him over the emergency. He got $2,000,000. From then on Indiana was safe in Union hands.

Who were the Peace Democrats? They were the minority of their party who held that the war was illegal and unjust and that peace should be brought about as quickly as possible on the basis of "the Constitution as it is and the Union as it was." How they expected to persuade the Davis government to give up Southern independence was never made clear. Formally the Peace Democrats were careful to stay within the limits of the law, using their public position to arouse opinion against the Lincoln Administration and to obstruct the war effort while avowing their loyalty to the Union. They were frankly racist: when Emancipation became national policy they inflamed white feelings by conjuring up nightmares in which Southern blacks would sweep into the North and take over white neighborhoods, white jobs, and white women after massacring Southern whites.

They had able and influential spokesmen, such as Governor Horatio Seymour of New York, and Congressmen Daniel Voorhees of Indiana and

Clement L. Vallandigham of Ohio. In Chicago, Wilbur F. Storey used his newspaper, the *Times,* to sow doubt and dissension among the masses attracted by his sensational journalism, while in New York the corrupt former mayor, Fernando Wood, who had urged the city's secession after Lincoln's election, tried to undermine popular confidence in the government through the *Daily News,* owned by his brother, Congressman Benjamin Wood. Samuel F. B. Morse, the Catholic-baiting inventor of the telegraph, headed a Peace Democrat propaganda organization, the Society for the Diffusion of Political Knowledge. Not so well known at the time was an Illinois Peace Democrat, Melville Fuller, who later as Supreme Court Justice upheld black segregation in the classic case, *Plessy v. Ferguson.*

The tone and content of the Peace Democrat position is typified in Vallandigham's farewell speech to Congress in January, 1863. Lincoln, he said, had set himself up as a bloody dictator, suppressing the liberties of the Northern people while he vainly sought to crush the South. Now, in desperation the President, through the Emancipation Proclamation, threatened Southern whites with "servile insurrection with all its horrors." The war must be stopped, he said. How? Let the soldiers quit fighting, fraternize, and return home. Let all sections resume their former intercourse. "Let slavery alone. Hold elections at the appointed times. Let us choose a new President in sixty-four." In this way the Union would be restored naturally and the welfare "of the African will have been best secured."

The strength of the Peace Democrats lay in their varied and widespread constituencies: New York merchants yearning for restoration of profitable Southern markets; Southerners settled along the Ohio River in Ohio, Illinois, and Indiana; workers and poorer farmers trapped in inflation and threatened by the draft; whites fearful of a black influx to the North; Northerners who sympathized with the Confederacy; and, at times, a general public weary of a bloody war which seemed endless. Indicative of the success of their appeal is the fact that for a time the legislatures of both Illinois and Indiana were controlled by Peace Democrats.

But behind the public activities of the peace men was something more ominous: a network of secret organizations, known variously as the Knights of the Golden Circle, the Order of American Knights, and the Sons of Liberty. The link between public and underground movements against the war was symbolized in 1864 when Vallandigham became supreme commander of the Sons of Liberty. Such organizations were not content with mere advocacy of their views. They discouraged enlistments, encouraged and protected deserters, and helped organize violent resistance to the draft, including beating and killing draft officials. Members engaged in outright sabotage of bridges, railways, and telegraphs. Loyal Union people came to look upon all Peace Democrats as venomous snakes that struck without warning—(Copperheads.) — *Peace (Democrats) — a against the war.*

The Peace Democrats presented Lincoln with a thorny problem. On the one hand he had no desire to curb free expression of opinion, but on the other he could not permit the growth of potentially dangerous subversion. Early in the war, faced with a threatened secessionist takeover of Maryland which would have isolated Washington in enemy country, he had suspended the writ of habeas corpus between Washington and Philadelphia—an exercise of power later ratified by Congress. Hundreds of suspects were rounded up and held without trial. When the threat passed, an outraged public opinion compelled release of many prisoners and formation of a commission to inquire into the cases of those still held. This the Administration was the more ready to do because early in 1862 it shared General McClellan's optimism that come spring he would take Richmond and end the war.

By September it was obvious that the war was not going to end quickly and that the preliminary Emancipation Proclamation had afforded Peace Democrats a keen weapon with which to slash at the government. Lincoln then suspended habeas corpus throughout the entire country, giving military commanders wide latitude in all cases involving disruption of the war effort. Prisoners so held were subject to trial before military tribunals. Did he have authority to do so? Yes, said the President, on the grounds of a national emergency and the power of the executive to put down insurrection. No, claimed the Peace Democrats, alleging this as further proof of Lincoln's dictatorial bent. But many loyal to the Union cause questioned whether the right of suspension belonged to the President or to Congress— the right to suspend habeas corpus is in the Constitutional article relating to Congress—and whether military tribunals could lawfully try civilians in areas where the courts were open. Finally, in March, 1863, Congress authorized the President to suspend the writ throughout the country and extended the protection of the federal government to civilians and army officers who executed the President's orders. With this backing, Lincoln proclaimed a further suspension of the writ in September, 1863. In the meantime, federal and state agents infiltrated the secret organizations, providing leads for the arrest of active Copperheads.

No one knows how many were swept up in the dragnets of military commanders—certainly more than the 13,000 reported by the army, for state as well as other federal agencies engaged in the practice. Figures are even more deficient in distinguishing between those picked up for desertion, bounty-jumping, sabotage and other purely military offenses, those charged with seditious utterances, and others rounded up purely on suspicion. The last provided a field day for informers, motivated by patriotic zeal, or the pay, or a desire to satisfy personal grudges. Doubtless, also, many gullible men went to prison for unlawful acts committed at the instigation of secret police agents. Lincoln himself upheld arrests on suspicion, asserting that under the necessities of war arrests were made "not so much for what has been done, as for what probably would be done." As for seditious utterances, asked the President, "Must I shoot a simple-minded soldier boy who deserts, while I must not touch a hair of a wily agitator who induces him to desert? . . . I think that in such a case, to silence the agitator, and save the boy, is not only constitutional, but withal, a great mercy."

However persuasive the President might be, the heavy-handed way in which generals executed his orders contributed to the very dissension he sought to quiet. Even good Republicans were aroused by reports of aged and respected citizens hustled from their beds in the early morning hours and hauled off to prison, while Peace Democrats found a new and popular issue with which to attack the government. There were other cases, of course, in which the government had some grounds for action, and of these the most famous was that of Vallandigham. The Ohio politician was already notorious as a Copperhead when he deliberately challenged suspension of the writ of habeas corpus in Ohio. In a carefully prepared speech on May Day, 1863, he excoriated the whole war policy of the administration, with special denunciation of the draft and of Emancipation. Then, shrewdly setting the ground for a constitutional argument, he advised his aroused listeners to confine themselves to action at the ballot-box, where an outraged citizenry would drive out "King Lincoln." Vallandigham was speedily arrested and sentenced by a military commission to close confinement for the duration of the war. A federal court turned down his application for a writ of habeas corpus and his lawyers appealed.

Lincoln was shaken by the uproar in the North over the arrest of a Peace Democrat for speaking his mind. He had no stomach for suppressing dissent, and he had no intention of providing the Copperheads with a martyr. On the other hand, his preference for suspending habeas corpus over resorting to judicial process was based on his belief that the latter was too slow and cumbersome to meet the exigencies of war. Nor, at this particular time, could he afford to show signs of weakness, for the Northern public was still dazed by the Union catastrophe at Chancellorsville a few days after Vallandigham's speech. Nor could he affront Union soldiers, to many of whom Vallandigham was the personification of home front treachery.

Lincoln's solution was ironic: release the prisoner, thus avoiding possible complications in the courts, while attaching to him the stigma of treason. Vallandigham was exiled to the Confederacy, where perplexed Confederates treated him courteously but without enthusiasm while they arranged for his speedy departure. Ironically, one reason for Southern coolness was Vallandigham's insistence that he was a United States citizen, a mere prisoner of war, thus precluding any attempt to enlist him in the Confederate cause.[8] In the North, his case finally reached the Supreme Court in 1864, the Justices holding that their power of review did not extend to military commissions—in effect upholding Lincoln's proclamations. In this, as in other cases, the wartime court gave a liberal interpretation to the war powers of the federal government.

Copperhead politicians presented one problem; newspapers presented another. The issue came to a head when General Ambrose Burnside, who had arrested Vallandigham, closed down the *Chicago Times*. Clamorous protests from Peace Democrats, War Democrats, and Republicans brought about Lincoln's revocation of the general's order—and Storey continued to revile the administration with impunity. However, in Indiana, Maryland, Missouri, and Kentucky, some Copperhead journals were suppressed with no great outcry. The last major issue arose in 1864, when two New York Copperhead newspapers published a fake presidential proclamation calling for 400,000 new troops, foisted upon them by an adventurer hoping to benefit from stock market manipulation when the hoped-for panic developed. The editors were released shortly after being arrested and the papers resumed publication after two days of suspension.

Did the Copperheads really present a clear and present danger to the Union? Lincoln thought so. The Union was endangered, he said, by "a most efficient corps of spies, informers, suppliers, and aiders and abettors" of the Confederacy. Most scholars think this an exaggeration. The Peace Democrats were a powerful irritant, perhaps potentially dangerous, but certainly not so in the circumstances. They capitalized on the grievances of many people, ranging from New York merchants to Illinois coal miners—many of whom did indeed look to the ballot-box for redress. Such people wanted no part of conspiracies against the government. Such men as did engage in subversive action were speedily ferreted out by the agents of the Provost Marshal, General James B. Fry. Indeed, on the one occasion when Copperheads might have made their weight felt, their rhetoric proved to have little substance. In July, 1863, Confederate General John Hunt Morgan and his cavalry swept into a section of southern Ohio supposedly seething with Copperhead sentiment. Fully expecting aid, he was quickly disillusioned: Copperheads joined with Unionists in resistance. The Copperheads, wrote one of his disgusted officers, "fought harder than the others."

Granting Lincoln's belief that the government was faced with a dangerous internal conspiracy, the abrogation of civil liberties was relatively mild, especially in view of the fact that a major war was being fought on American soil and in light of federal practice in later major wars. Few

---

[8] Frank L. Klement, "Clement L. Vallandigham's Exile in the Confederacy, May 25–June 17, 1863," *Journal of Southern History*, XXXI, No. 2 (May, 1965), 149–63.

prisoners other than those convicted of serious crimes, such as sabotage, were confined for long, and few seem to have suffered from the calculated brutality which marked the treatment of war objectors in federal prisons during World War I. And, of course, there was nothing to compare with the prison camps for Japanese-Americans in World War II. Copperhead newspapers generally published with little interference, and Copperhead politicians enjoyed their liberties to the fullest—even, in the case of Ohio Peace Democrats who demanded that Lincoln free Vallandigham forthwith! In short, Lincoln was not about to allow an abuse of liberty to destroy a Union dedicated to liberty—but neither was he going to permit the pretext of public safety to be used to destroy liberty.

The Copperhead problem was handled with relative ease through the pressures of loyalist public opinion and use of the coercive power of government. More serious, because it went to the heart of the administration's outlook and conduct of the war, was the deepening split in the Republican Party. The division, which had its origins in pre-war party politics, was essentially between two wings which may be loosely described as Conservative and Radical. Aware of the danger so posed to his administration, Lincoln tried to embrace both wings in his cabinet, making Seward, the Conservative spokesman, Secretary of State, and Salmon P. Chase, a veteran Ohio abolitionist and Radical, Secretary of the Treasury. Neither group was a well-knit, cohesive faction, for they differed among themselves on such issues as homesteads, tariff, greenbacks, and national banks; but as the war went on their differences over war policy sharply differentiated them. The Conservative position, represented in the Senate by such outstanding men as Jacob Collamer of Vermont, James R. Doolittle of Wisconsin, and Preston King of New York, reflected the official line of the administration.

In this view, as we have seen, the war had a limited political objective: restoration of the Union as it was. Slavery, therefore, was not an issue. Since slavery was not an issue, it followed as a matter of principle—as well as a political tactic—that slaveowners in the Border States and in the South must be assured protection of their property rights. Further, to ensure maximum public support in the North for such a war, nothing must be done which might alienate large bodies of white opinion. Thus, no acceptance of black volunteers, no policy of Emancipation. The war was thus still further limited: it was to be a white man's war. How was it to be won? By sufficient exercise of federal authority to put down the insurrection and restore the Union with as little disruption as possible.

To Radicals this made little sense except as a futile exercise in nostalgia. Numbering among them such redoubtable party stalwarts as Thaddeus Stevens in the House and Benjamin Wade of Ohio, Zachariah Chandler of Michigan, and Charles Sumner of Massachusetts in the Senate, they derided Lincoln's official declaration that the war was the result of "discontented individuals" who had engaged in "combinations too powerful to be suppressed" by normal means. The Union faced, not combinations of malcontents, but an organized government with a successful army in the field, a government which might well win foreign recognition unless the Lincoln Administration perceived the war for what it was: revolution. So, revolutionary means must be used: slavery must go; black men, free and slave, must be armed as Union soldiers; the full war power of the government must be used to crush the planting aristocracy once and for all. The planters had thrown down the gauntlet. Let the Union pick it up, not to restore the Union as it was, but to usher in a new Union made up of truly free men, black and white, who, liberated from planter control of government, could each achieve his own individual destiny according to his character and abilities. The Radicals, in other words, were good nineteenth century Liberals!

Between the two extremes was a large moderate faction, typified by Senator Lyman Trumbull of Illinois, who originally supported the administration but increasingly tended to Radical positions. And then there were War Democrats, represented in the cabinet by Edwin B. Stanton, Secretary of War, and in the Senate by Andrew Johnson of Tennessee and John B. Henderson of Missouri. Generally sympathetic to the administration they divided on specific issues, but Johnson was as implacable a foe of Southern planters as was Thaddeus Stevens.

So long as there was hope for a short war with limited aims, the Radicals had few supporters. In July, 1861, for example, the House of Representatives, by a vote of 121 to 2, affirmed the Union war aim: "to defend and maintain the supremacy of the Constitution, and to preserve the Union with all the dignity, equality and rights of the several States unimpaired." Ruling out any significant change as a result of war, the resolution also disavowed any objective "of overthrowing or interfering with the rights or established institutions [i.e., slavery] of those States." But as the war went on, with victory proving elusive while casualty lists mounted, the Conservative position eroded. Moderates tended more and more to vote with Radicals, and eventually some Conservatives went over to an all-out war policy. The process began early. In December, 1861, the House, by a narrow vote, rejected reaffirmation of its July resolution, and that same month both House and Senate established a joint committee to inquire into the conduct of the war, an ominous sign of Congressional dissatisfaction with administration policies.

This meant increased tension between the Congress and the White House, for Lincoln was loath to give up the Conservative policy on which he had embarked. But he too was influenced by the exigencies of an unsuccessful war. Slowly and often reluctantly he adopted such Radical policies as he deemed advisable, while fashioning them in such a way as to make them his own (as in Emancipation). His progress was too slow for Radicals, who looked upon him as a weak man who dallied and vacillated while the Union's survival was at stake. And behind him, manipulating him and national policy, was the sinister figure of the astute Seward, who had no stomach for revolutionary war—or so believed the growing Republican opposition.

The first open clash came in July, 1862. A Congress disgruntled by repeated Union defeats in Virginia, passed a Confiscation act much more drastic than a similar law passed a year earlier. The new law, designed by Radicals to destroy planter power, ordered confiscation of all property of those "engaged in armed rebellion" or who aided and abetted it. The slaves of such Confederates were declared free forever. Lincoln threatened to veto the bill, on the grounds that confiscation worked forfeiture of property beyond the lives of guilty parties and therefore was unconstitutional. Congress yielded to the extent of an explanatory resolution limiting penalties to a Confederate's lifetime. Lincoln accepted both the bill and the resolution—and then took the extraordinary step of transmitting his proposed veto message together with the measures he had just signed! Naturally, this angered Radicals—but Lincoln had avoided a confrontation. They had their bill, and he had his interpretation of it.

That interpretation did little to enhance the President's popularity among those who wanted planter power destroyed. Enforcement was so lax that the law brought in less than $130,000 to the government. As Allan Nevins pointed out, "though many confiscation actions were begun, little property was taken. . . . Nobody was terrified, and almost nobody hurt." [9] The consequence was, as noted by Fawn Brodie, that despite their losses, the planting aristocracy after the war remained "a powerful political force." [10] Wade Hampton, one of the greatest of the planters, used that power with telling effect years later to overthrow the Reconstruction government in South Carolina, as Mississippi planters had done earlier. [11]

The feud between White House and Radicals was still simmering when in December another Democratic general, Ambrose Burnside, sacri-

[9] Allan Nevins, *The War for the Union* (New York: Charles Scribner's Sons, 1960), II, 204.

[10] Fawn M. Brodie, *Thaddeus Stevens: Scourge of the South* (New York: W. W. Norton & Company, Inc., 1959), p. 167.

[11] Robert Cruden, *The Negro in Reconstruction* (Englewood Cliffs, N.J.: Prentice-Hall, Inc., 1969), Chapter 6.

ficed more than 12,000 men at Fredericksburg in futile assaults against entrenched Confederates. The North was shocked, not only by the losses but also by the outcome, which suggested that perhaps the Confederacy could not be conquered. Even the usually sanguine editor of the *Chicago Tribune*, Joseph Medill, privately despaired that the war could be won. Radicals now determined that the time had come to turn the war around, to embark on policies which could bring victory. The first step was to get Seward out of the cabinet, for he was held responsible for the war failures. Senator Chandler even believed Seward was a traitor.

Within three days of the Fredericksburg battles Republican Senators met in secret caucus to consider strategy. Before them was a dispatch sent by Seward to Ambassador Adams in London in July, at the very time when Lincoln was suggesting Emancipation. The letter indicated that the secretary was opposed to Emancipation, and blamed abolitionists equally with slaveowners for the slave insurrection which must result. The pertinent paragraph read: "It seems as if the extreme advocates of African slavery and its most vehement opponents were acting in concert together to precipitate a servile war—like the former by making the most desperate attempts to overthrow the Federal Union, the latter by demanding an edict of universal Emancipation as a lawful and necessary, if not, as they say, the only legitimate way of saving the Union." To Radicals, here was direct proof of Seward's hostility to all-out war, as well as disloyalty to national policy on Emancipation.

The Senators decided to send a committee to the President to urge upon him such partial reconstruction of the cabinet as would bring about a united and vigorous war effort. Senator Collamer, no Radical, was chosen to present the caucus position: the war must be fought through to victory; to this end, the President must involve the cabinet in decision-making; the cabinet must be made up only of men pledged to full prosecution of the war; army commands should be entrusted only to generals fully committed to defeating the Confederacy. The caucus action was unanimous, except for Preston King of New York, who immediately informed Seward and Lincoln.

Seward, no stranger to pressure politics, made a ploy of his own. He resigned, hoping the President would turn him down. Instead, Lincoln asked him privately to withdraw the resignation. Seward refused. This meant a crisis, as Lincoln well knew. He could afford no sign of public disunity within the cabinet, for such would be interpreted at home, abroad, and Richmond as indication of internal weakness. Neither could he give the impression that Congressional pressure dictated cabinet appointments. But neither could he ignore the near-unanimous vote of the Republican caucus. It caused him more distress than "any event of my life," he told a visitor.

Caught between Seward and the caucus, Lincoln temporized. He took no action on Seward's resignation. He met with the committee, discussed the issues, and arranged a joint meeting between it and the cabinet, with Seward absent. At that meeting Chase, the source of reports on cabinet discord, was maneuvered into denying any real disunity. Radicals, who had long believed him, were furious—and a discomfited Chase submitted his resignation. Lincoln then rejected both his and Seward's, keeping both wings of the party within the cabinet and asserting his control over his official family. This demonstration of political finesse solved the immediate crisis. It did little to abate Radical suspicions—for Seward was still in the cabinet. But he carefully confined himself to foreign policy thereafter, and Radical discontent focused on the President.

This erupted a year later when Lincoln undertook to fashion an overall Reconstruction policy to replace the makeshift governments already established, as in Louisiana and Tennessee. Since the states had never legally been out of the Union, in Lincoln's view, all that was necessary was to restore state control to loyal citizens—and such a step was within his power as President. Besides, a demonstration to the South that peace meant control of the South by white Southerners might help undermine the dogged Confederate resistance that was prolonging the war—a resistance based in large part on Southern fear that defeat meant Yankee rule enforced by vengeful blacks.

Lincoln's view was anathema to Radicals, and to many other Republicans as well. Their position was that the seceding states had forfeited their status. Such states were in fact now analogous to territories, subject to rule by Congress, and their eventual admission as states purely a Congressional function. Behind the tedious debates over constitutional interpretation lay a real issue: the nature of the reconstructed South. Anti-Lincoln Republicans wanted a South dedicated like the rest of the nation to free enterprise, individual initiative, and expansion—in short, freedom for all, as nineteenth century Liberals understood the phrase. To accomplish this, the power of the planters must be destroyed. Lincoln simply wanted the Union restored—and for this, Emancipation was essential. Further he would not go.

The issue emerged when, in December, 1863, the President proclaimed a sweeping amnesty, with some few exceptions, for Confederates who took an oath of allegiance. Then, he stated that when 10 percent of the voters eligible under 1860 laws took the oath in any state, they could establish a government which "shall be recognized as the true government of the state." Blacks were thus excluded from politics, although Lincoln later privately suggested that the franchise be extended to black Union war veterans and those of property and intelligence. In another step to appease Southern white racial fears, he declared in the proclamation that while such new state governments must accept Emancipation, laws "which may yet be consistent as a temporary arrangement with their [freedmen's] present condition as a laboring, landless and homeless class, will not be objected to by National Executive." Had Lincoln lived, he would have seen how planters used such terms to justify a modified form of slavery under the notorious Black Codes of the Andrew Johnson Administration. At the time, Lincoln had a more pressing problem: to protect himself against the attack he knew would come from Congress, he tactfully noted that while his policy was the best he thought possible, "it must not be understood that no other mode would be acceptable."

Congressional Republicans did come up with another policy. In July, 1864, Congress passed the Wade-Davis Bill. Like Lincoln's measure it was lily-white; in all other respects it was tough and punitive. When a *majority* of white male citizens took an "ironclad" oath of allegiance, they were empowered to elect a convention to "re-establish" a state government, voting for such to be restricted to whites. Confederate officeholders, and soldiers who served "voluntarily," could neither vote nor serve in the conventions. Constitutions adopted by such conventions must prohibit slavery; repudiate war debts, both state and Confederate; and bar Confederate officials from voting and holding office. The measure also stripped such officials of their United States citizenship, and, in a direct assertion of Congressional power, enacted universal Emancipation without compensation and prescribed criminal penalties for violators.

Here was indeed a challenge to the President. He had long held that Congress had no power over slavery within the states—at the time he was laboring to obtain an amendment to the Constitution which would outlaw slavery. Likewise, the consistent legal position of the administration was that the war was the work of combinations of malcontents. This stand avoided what Lincoln thought the "metaphysical question" of whether the states were or were not out of the Union. The Wade-Davis Bill assumed they were out, and as Lincoln told his cabinet, "We cannot survive this admission," by which he meant that there was no Union if it were conceded that states could voluntarily quit the Union. Further, Lincoln intended to keep Reconstruction in his own hands, if only because Confederate resistance would be stiffened by such Congressional action.

But, as with the Confiscation Act and the cabinet crisis, Lincoln had no desire to antagonize a powerful group of Republican leaders. He let the bill die, neither signing nor vetoing it—a course open to him because Congress had already adjourned. Then he took the unusual step of proclaiming his objections to the measure while also advising that for such states as wished to adopt it the bill was "a very proper plan." While thus avoiding an open challenge to Congress, he was also engaged in psychological warfare with the Confederacy. In effect, he told the South it had two alternatives on Reconstruction, and suggested the wisdom of accepting his while there was yet time. The difficulty was that Southerners thought there was yet a third possibility: they expected a Democratic election victory and much better terms from the next administration.

Radicals were not impressed with Lincoln's gesture, either. Wade and Davis retorted with a bitter manifesto accusing the President of a "studied outrage on the legislative authority of the people." Then came a threat: "our support is of a cause, and not of a man; . . . the authority of Congress is paramount and must be respected; . . . and if he [Lincoln] wishes our support he must confine himself to his executive duties." In the gloomy summer of 1864 such words were not to be taken lightly.

Why the gloom? Because the war's end seemed as far away as ever. Grant, from whom so much had been expected, had still not broken Lee's army, and while he was grinding forward it was at a cost in human life that the North found insupportable. Nor was there compensating news from the West, where Sherman was pushing toward Atlanta—again at great cost in casualties. As if to emphasize Confederate resilience, General Jubal Early swept into Maryland and Pennsylvania in July, levying tribute on townspeople, burning, looting, and destroying as he went, until he was within sight of Washington itself. Two divisions were detached from Grant's forces to help drive him back! Measuring the lack of Northern confidence, the greenback dollar fell to its lowest point in the war—35 cents in terms of gold. Thurlow Weed, the powerful New York Republican supporter of the administration, wrote in August, "The people are wild for peace." This was an exaggeration, of course—but there was more than a grain of truth in it.

Democrats appealed to such sentiment as they met in Chicago late in August, when Union morale was at its lowest. The war plank of the platform was written by none other than Vallandigham, whose return to the country had been winked at by federal authorities. The plank declared that "after four years of failure to restore the Union by . . . war," the time had come to end it. Hostilities should cease and a convention called quickly to restore the Union "on the basis of the Federal Union of the States." Significantly, slavery was not mentioned, although delegates made plain their opposition to Emancipation. The candidate was General McClellan.

Democrats were confident of success. They had a platform and ticket to appeal to a war-weary public, and the opposition was rent with increasing dissension. Lincoln, of course, had been renominated unanimously by the Union Party, a combination of Republicans and War Democrats, but behind that facade was deep division. Early in the year Senator S.C. Pomeroy of Kansas had urged Republicans to unite behind Chase because Lincoln could not be re-elected. Then in May extreme abolitionists, led by Wendell Phillips and B. Gratz Brown of Missouri, bolted the party, choosing a ticket headed by General Fremont. The general's following was not large, but it was large enough to tip the balance in doubtful states. Just as the tiny Liberty Party helped bring Polk into the White House in 1844, so might these bolters aid the Democrats in 1864.

Even more ominous was the "secret" movement to dump Lincoln as a candidate. It included such powerful politicians as Senator Ben Wade of Ohio and Massachusetts Governor John Andrew, and influential editors like Horace Greeley of the *New York Tribune* and Theodore Tilton of *The Independent*. Lincoln could not be re-elected, they held, and the Republican Party would be pulled down with him. Thus, they called for a new convention in September, "to concentrate the Union strength on some one candidate who commands the confidence of the country, even by a new nomination if necessary." Lincoln's friends clamored that he take some dramatic step to refute the widely-made charge that he was indifferent to peace proposals made by Confederates, and so was responsible for prolonging the war.

Lincoln was not given to dramatics, but he did authorize informal contacts with Confederates. One such, involving Horace Greeley, revealed that the Confederate agents had no authority to act and that their real objective was not peace but Democratic election propaganda. Lincoln seized the opportunity to tell the public he was ready to discuss authorized Confederate peace proposals, embracing restoration of the Union and Emancipation. Should such come, he promised "liberal terms" on related issues, by which he meant Reconstruction and compensation to slaveowners. Another such informal mission met with Jefferson Davis, and got from him a statement which played into Lincoln's hands. Noting that Emancipation was already in progress, Davis said, "We are not fighting for slavery. We are fighting for independence, and that, or extermination, we *will* have." The President saw to it that this report received the widest and most potent publicity. Even so, the general gloom was so pervasive that in August Lincoln himself despaired of his re-election.

Then, almost immediately on the heels of the Democratic convention, came reports that Atlanta had fallen. Almost overnight Northern opinion switched from despair to exultation—a feeling enhanced by Sheridan's sweep of the Shenandoah Valley soon after. At long last victory and an end to the war were in sight! Politicians quickly adjusted to the new mood. McClellan belatedly accepted his nomination but repudiated his party's peace plank, vowing to continue the war until the Union was restored. Republicans who planned for a new convention and a new nominee quietly dropped the project. Fremont quit the race, endorsing Lincoln. Whether a bargain was involved is still not clear, but it seems significant that within a day of Fremont's announcement Lincoln obtained the resignation of Montgomery Blair, who as postmaster general had incurred the enmity of Radicals. The reunited Union Party swept the elections. Only three states—New Jersey, Delaware, and Kentucky—went for McClellan, although the popular vote was not that lop-sided: Lincoln, 2,200,000; McClellan, 1,800,000. Impressive and significant was the shift in votes for the House. Prior to the elections, the Unionist majority was 27; now it was 107!

    That the Union government fared as well as it did was due in considerable degree to Lincoln's leadership style. Where Davis was austere, inflexible, indifferent to public opinion and quarrelsome with his Congress, Lincoln was affable, accessible, getting his way through political dexterity, avoiding open confrontation with Congressional opposition whenever possible. He was open-minded to a degree rare in Chief Executives, adopting the policies of his critics when finally persuaded of their wisdom, as in Emancipation and enlistment of black soldiers. So, he was able to hold together for the duration of the war a fractious, feuding coalition, while imposing upon it his own leadership. Whether that leadership could have survived without the fall of Atlanta at a critical moment is a question one cannot answer. It should be noted, however, that Sherman's triumph was no accident—it was the result of long planning in which the administration was involved.
    For all his flexibility, Lincoln could be as adamant as Davis on issues in which he felt principles were involved. Believing that neither he nor Congress could lawfully decree permanent and universal abolition he fought for Congressional approval of a thirteenth amendment which would lawfully do so. Frustrated in one attempt, he returned to the fray, using all the influence of the White House, including some means so devious that Thaddeus Stevens remarked that while the amendment was "the greatest measure of the nineteenth century," it was passed "by corruption, aided and abetted by the purest man in America." As for Reconstruction, the President was firm against destroying the planter class. He would not strip them of their property, save for slaves, and even there he favored compensation. His influence is seen in what might have been an epoch-making Freedmen's Bureau Bill of March, 1865. The measure promised 40 acres of land each to former slaves, but "subject to such title thereto as the United States can convey." Since this meant, under the joint resolution accompanying the Confiscation Act of 1862, that confiscated lands were forfeit only through the lifetime of a Confederate owner, title would revert to his heirs on his death. In any case, since the provision was little implemented by Lincoln's successor, Andrew Johnson, the promise remained just that—a promise never fulfilled.
    Lincoln, then, was more adroit as a politician than Davis, but he also realized, as Davis rarely did, that beyond the politicians were the people, that he must not get too far ahead of them, and that he must keep them

informed. Abolitionists pressing him on enlisting blacks and adopting Emancipation reported time and again that he would not act until the public was ready. His various messages to Congress were really addressed to the public, stating his policy in simple, understandable language. When he sent his projected veto message of the Confiscation Act, and issued his curious proclamation on the Wade-Davis Bill, he was not only appealing to the opposition, he was also talking to the voters.

Consequently, there was little of that persistent credibility gap which undermined confidence in Davis and has plagued some other presidents since. Voters thought Lincoln was wrong at times, but they had an impregnable belief in his honesty that exasperated such Radical opponents as Wendell Phillips, who said that the President was only "Kentucky honest." When Radicals and Copperheads alike charged that Lincoln behaved like a dictator, voters simply did not believe them. *Harper's Weekly* expressed popular feeling when the uproar over the Wade-Davis Bill was at its height: "To charge him with extraordinary and dangerous assumption of power, is childish. . . . It is simply impossible to make the American people believe that the President is a wily despot or a political gambler." Despite earlier reservations, blacks came to share this belief in Lincoln. Frederick Douglass, addressing an abolitionist convention in 1863, said that Lincoln impressed him as ". . . an honest man. I never met with a man who . . . impressed me more entirely with his sincerity, with his devotion to his country, and with his determination to save it at all hazards."

The widespread belief in the President's integrity was sustained by Lincoln's practice of keeping in touch with the public through every means at hand, one notable means being "public letters" to his critics. Out of many, two examples must suffice. Peace Democrats in New York denounced the arrest of Vallandigham and suspension of habeas corpus. Lincoln responded, not in legalistic phraseology but in simple human terms designed to win public approval. Must he shoot a deserter while the man who induced him to desert must be untouched? He gently ridiculed the claim that wartime curbs on civil liberties meant their permanent suppression. He could no more believe that, wrote Lincoln, than he could believe that "a man could contract so strong an appetite for emetics during temporary illness as to persist in feeding upon them during the remainder of his healthful life." To the man in the street, this had the ring of sound common sense.

The other example stems from an invitation extended to Lincoln to address Union supporters in Springfield, Illinois, in 1863. Lincoln sent a letter instead, important, among other things, because it boldly confronted the race issue. Aiming at the Copperhead opposition, Lincoln wrote: "You are dissatisfied with me about the Negro. . . . I certainly wish that all men could be free, while I suppose you do not. . . . I suggested compensated emancipation, to which you replied you wished not to be taxed to buy Negroes. . . . You dislike the Emancipation Proclamation, . . . You say it is unconstitutional. I think differently." (In a deleted portion of the public message, which was sent privately, Lincoln cited military authorities as believing that "emancipation . . . and the use of colored troops constitute the heaviest blow yet dealt to the rebellion.")

Then came a passage pregnant with significance: "You say you will not fight to free Negroes. Some of them seem willing to fight for you; but no matter. Fight you, then, exclusively to save the Union. . . . But Negroes, like other people, act upon motives. Why should they do anything for us if we will do nothing for them? If they stake their lives for us they must be prompted by the strongest motive, even the promise of freedom. And that promise, being made, must be kept." Noting that Union victories were "jotted down in black and white," Lincoln predicted an early peace. "And then there will be some black men who can remember that with silent tongue, and clenched teeth, and steady eye, and well-poised bayonet, they have helped mankind on to this great consummation [of a truly democratic republic], while . . . there will be some white ones unable to forget that with malignant heart and deceitful speech they strove to hinder it."

In short, Lincoln was asking his people to share the perception which had come to him only slowly and painfully: the future of the Union as a democratic republic was inseparably intertwined with that of black Americans.

Seeking for the Wounded, by Torch-light after the Battle. *Harper's Weekly. March 8, 1862.*

CHAPTER IV

THE
SOLDIER'S
WAR

The failure of governments to anticipate and plan for a long war meant hardship and tragedy for soldiers. For long there were no plans for care of sick and wounded soldiers, no provisions for prison camps, and no preparations for supply of such elementary military needs as food, clothing, weapons, and ammunition. Since each government relied on volunteers, little thought was given to problems of conscription, should a need for such a system arise. Each side learned by doing, stumbling from one makeshift solution to another as problems arose, until eventually a pattern of order and planning developed. For all this bungling, vacillation, and incompetence, and the corruption which accompanied it, there was a price, of course. Soldiers paid for the mistakes of statesmen and generals.

Lincoln's initial call for 75,000 militiamen for three months' service was received with such enthusiasm by young men on farms and in factories that the states could have filled their quotas many times over. However, the Union defeat at Bull Run in July, 1861, ended the delusion of a short war and diminished that enthusiasm. Even so, there was sufficient response to the calls for men that by December, 1861, more than 640,000 volunteers were in the Union army, compared to 20,000 in the regular army—and many of the volunteers had signed up, not for three months, but for three years! The response in itself presented a problem, for it was the responsibility of the states not only to meet the manpower quotas assigned by Washington but also to provide food, clothing, equipment, and training until such time as the men were mustered into federal service.

As a consequence, the individual states and the federal government were all in the market at the same time bidding for the same goods—an ideal situation for enterprising businessmen at home and abroad, however discomforting or dangerous it might prove to soldiers. Uniforms differed from regiment to regiment and from state to state, which in combat made it difficult to distinguish friend from foe—with, of course, disastrous consequences. The uniforms and blankets supplied were all too often made of "shoddy," the refuse of woolen mills, which literally came apart in heavy rain. Many a Union soldier mounted guard in underwear, without pants or overcoat, even in freezing weather. The supply of shoes was no better. Some lasted less than a day and few lasted more than a month. Since the supply of even these was inadequate, many volunteers went barefoot or made-do by binding raw-hide to their feet. Food was good so long as the soldiers were in small camps in their home states. As Fred A. Shannon commented, if local farmers and businessmen "demanded their pound of flesh, at least they gave flesh in return." [1] Once in federal service, the men were at the mercy of unscrupulous contractors, whom the ardently pro-war *New York Tribune* denounced for foisting off on the government "putrid pork" and the "fag ends" of cattle rejected for civilian consumption.

The issue of weapons was chaotic. Some troops were equipped with new model Springfield rifles, said to be among the best in the world at the time. Others got smooth-bore muskets, of a type dating back to the Revolutionary War. Even more unfortunate were those who received what the Count of Paris, a French volunteer in the Union army, called the "refuse of all Europe." These were weapons bought abroad by state and federal agents to meet the urgent need for arms. In many, the barrels were so brittle that they broke easily, to say nothing of the fact that the barrels were crooked to begin with! Some were so slow to fire that they presented hazards to the user. After a while soldiers conveniently "lost" such guns, in the hope of getting something better. But nearly all the muskets and rifles issued were muzzleloaders, which in combat proved useless in the hands of some troops. In the heat of battle, the men, failing to notice that an initial charge had

---

[1] Fred A. Shannon, *The Organization and Administration of the Union Army, 1861–1865* (Cleveland, Ohio: The Arthur H. Clark Company, 1928), I, 77.

not fired, rammed in another, and so jammed the gun. The plight of such troops needs no elaboration!

That this was no way to win a war was clear to Edwin Stanton when he took over the War Department in January, 1862, and steps were quickly taken to remedy some of the worst weaknesses. States were forbidden to compete with the federal government for supplies; from then on all supplies must be obtained through Washington. Contracts were thrown open to competitive bidding, eliminating some of the abuses which characterized the widespread practice of private contracts. Inspectors went into factories to insure compliance with government specifications. Uniforms were standardized and their quality improved. A measure of order was introduced into the issue of weapons, as up-to-date products of government arsenals and private firms became available. Not until 1864, however, did the army adopt the Spencer breech-loading repeating rifle, which fired 14 rounds a minute, although the gun had been available even before war broke out. The improved morale of troops so armed was visible, as was the discouragement of Confederates confronted with a gun which, it was said, Yankees "loaded on Sundays and fired all the week."

Food continued to be a source of the soldiers' gripes, not so much on the score of quantity as on quality, lack of variety, and poor cooking. In permanent camps the rations were so generous as to warrant foreign comments that the Union army was the best fed in the world. But the diet was unbalanced. It was heavy on meat (especially salted), bread, beans, and coffee. Fresh fruits and vegetables rarely appeared, and then only to halt the spread of scurvy. On the march, men subsisted on "iron rations"— minimum amounts of salt pork, beans, coffee, and hardtack, a hard bread biscuit, usually carried in the dirty haversack of the individual. Often the men had to eat beans half-cooked, which, as one soldier recalled, caused "an almighty bellyache that would double a man up." The consequence, of course, was a high incidence of stomach troubles and the appearance of such deficiency diseases as scurvy. This illness plagued white troops at an average annual rate of 13 cases per thousand men. Indicative of an even poorer diet among blacks is the record of 88 cases per thousand.

The diet problem was compounded by poor cooking. Early in the war each soldier did his own cooking, with predictable results. When company cooking was established, it was done by men detailed to such duty, with equally predictable results. Eventually the army got around to employing full-time cooks in permanent camps, and it was even longer before combat troops enjoyed the benefits. In the meantime, men on the move made do with their "iron rations," cooked as the occasion allowed. It is not surprising that such troops scrounged the countryside for fruits, vegetables, and livestock, regardless of orders to the contrary.

If some of the widespread sickness in the army was due to poor diet, much arose from poor hygiene among the troops. Independent young men, freed for the first time in their lives from the restraints of home and community, barely tolerant of even the rudiments of military discipline, simply ignored the rules for personal and camp cleanliness—until they learned better from experience. Early in the war some camps did little digging of latrines—long slit trenches with earth piled alongside to be used to cover the waste. When they were dug, many men did not use them— partly because the ground around them became fouled and was never policed. Inevitably, water supplies were polluted and outbreaks of such diseases as typhoid fever resulted. A particularly noxious example received public attention early in 1863, nearly two years after the war began. In a camp of 7,000 convalescent soldiers, investigators found "an area of over three acres, encircling the camp as a broad belt, on which is deposited an almost perfect layer of human excrement." Rain run-off had carried the waste to the camp's water supply.

Lack of personal cleanliness added to the problem. Even in camp many men rarely bathed; one soldier noted that he never saw a cook with clean hands. Troops on the march went for weeks without bathing or getting out of their clothes. Lice, fleas, flies—and in some regions, malarial mosquitoes —abounded, spreading sickness while adding to the men's discomfort. Such conditions help explain the Union war death toll of 224,000 from disease and accident, compared to 140,000 killed or mortally wounded in battle. Untold thousands of men were discharged, their health weakened; sub- sequent deaths from poor health are not reflected in the war statistics. Significantly, it is estimated that 57,000 men died in service from dysentery and diarrhoea, both closely related to poor diet and poor hygiene.

Many of the deaths can also be attributed to poor medical care. In the rush to create an adequate medical staff from the 98 surgeons (headed by an 80-year-old veteran of the War of 1812) available when war began, almost anyone with a claim to medical knowledge was commissioned, particularly in the volunteer regiments raised by the states. Some, of course, had had sound professional training and experience, and worked conscientiously to improve the care of the ill and wounded. Others, however, had little training and less interest in their patients. Even with such lax requirements, the number of doctors proved inadequate and the army resorted to employing "contract doctors," civilians who worked temporarily caring for soldiers. Many of them were so incompetent that they could not prosper in private practice even during a war-time shortage of medical men. Surgeons were the most dreaded by the troops. Some were experts, but all too many learned by doing the amputations which became a horror story of the war.

But, as the better doctors pointed out, they worked under conditions less than ideal. Limited for a long time to a rank no higher than captain they found themselves at a disadvantage in dealing with colonels and generals. Thanks to the army's supply system they often found themselves dangerously short of instruments, medicines, drugs, and dressings after combat. The field hospitals to which ill and wounded soldiers were first brought were usually makeshift arrangements of huts and tents. When these were not available—and for a long time the supply of hospital tents was inadequate—the wounded were placed in nearby houses, barns, and chicken-coops. There the doctors had to work. In one such hospital a reporter found "the maimed, gashed, and dying . . . confusedly together;" the surgeon produced "a little heap of human fingers, feet, legs and arms" as wounded men looked on in horror.

Survivors unable to return to active duty were sent to general hospitals behind the lines. At first these were little better than field hospitals, housed in factories, warehouses, schools, and churches, often lacking medicines and bedding, and some "so badly managed as to defy comparison with any other hospitals 'in the civilized world.' " [2] Gradually, permanent institutions were built throughout the North, providing 136,000 beds by the end of the war. Fortunate was the soldier sent to one of the better of these, with its gardens, spaciousness, fresh air, cleanliness, well-prepared food, and conscientious care. Equally unfortunate was the trooper who landed in one of the others, with its dirt and squalor, corrupt staff who cheated on the patients' rations, and provided only a careless minimum of patient care.

But even the best hospitals were limited in what they could do. Congress, which otherwise spent money like water, looked with an austere eye on patients' rations: it kept them at 18 cents a day per man, although inflation was fast reducing that to 12 cents a day in terms of what it could buy. Plumbing, although much improved, continued to provide health hazards. Nursing remained at a low level, thanks largely to the hostility of the medical bureaucracy to employing women, even after they had proved their worth in service. Carefully recruited, the women nurses proved to be capable, honest, and concerned, much to the comfort of patients lucky enough to have them. Even so, they were never more than a minority—probably 20 percent—of the nursing staffs. Most nursing was done by men: fugitive slaves pressed into service, invalids barely able to care for themselves, and misfits whose army units gladly detailed them to hospital service. When such help proved insufficient, civilians were hired on contract. Many turned out to be petty thieves who robbed their patients. Some were drug pushers, exploiting a market encouraged by doctors who, following the practice of the day, prescribed liberal doses of opium and morphine for the wounded.

[2] George W. Adams, *Doctors in Blue: The Medical History of the Union Army in the Civil War* (New York: Henry Schuman, 1952), p. 149.

Nevertheless, despite all these shortcomings, the death rate from disease in the Civil War was lower than in previous American wars and far below that of the European armies in the Crimean War just a few years before. This can be explained in part by the fact that young Americans of the 60s were in basically better health than their ancestors and their European counterparts. Also, as the army progressively tightened up on its discipline it concentrated heavily on hygiene rules, and the enforcement of them was made easier by the growing understanding of doctors and soldiers that there was a link between health and cleanliness. The growth in authority of the medical department made it possible for doctors to get more appropriations for hospitals, to develop new techniques for surgery, and to cope with hostile generals.

The development of an army ambulance corps, pioneered by Dr. Jonathan Letterman, helped reduce the recurrence of such conditions as those present after the second battle of Bull Run in 1862, when many Union wounded lay on the field for days, without food or medical attention, although the victorious Confederates permitted the Union army to recover its wounded. Also, the organization and repeated inspections of general hospitals led to improvement in the care of sick and wounded. Perhaps most important was the work of the United States Sanitary Commission, a quasi-official body dominated by civilians. This organization worked doggedly and successfully to improve care of the ill and wounded, to upgrade hospitals, to get rid of incompetent doctors, and to pressure the army and its medical bureaucracy to reform their practices.

It should also be remembered that the war took place before the revolution in medical theory in the late nineteenth century transformed procedures and techniques. The germ theory of disease was still to come, and the importance of asepsis not yet understood. Anesthesia was known, but its application was so hazardous that it was somewhat feared. In short, much of the suffering and mortality of the war was due to man's inadequate knowledge and understanding of his own ecology.

Part of the health problem lay in the lax discipline which for long characterized the army. Men brought up in a tradition of individual independence were not about to yield to a military tradition which held obedience to be a prime virtue, and this was as true of foreign-born soldiers —Scots, Irish, Germans—as of native-born. Colonel Thomas Wentworth Higginson, the abolitionist commander of the black 1st South Carolina Volunteers, tried to alert the public to the serious nature of the problem: "An army is an aristocracy. . . . No mortal skill can make military power effective on democratic principles. . . . Personal independence in the soldier, like personal liberty in the civilian, must be waived for the preservation of the nation." [3]

The colonel spoke from experience but he made few converts. The Northern people and government alike were persuaded that if democracy worked well in civil life it should work equally well in the military. This explains the decisions early in the war which influenced discipline until its end. First, the regular army was kept intact, so that for a long time the services of trained officers and men were lost to the burgeoning volunteer army. Second, the volunteers were raised through the states and their organization based on the state militia system. This meant that noncommissioned and commissioned officers up to the grade of captain were elected by the soldiers, while higher ranking officers were usually appointed by state governors. Third, wealthy men were authorized to raise and equip regiments privately, and in return were commissioned colonels; they compensated their helpers with lesser offices. To further complicate the problem, most outfits were organized locally: whole companies might come from one town or neighborhood, to which all hoped to return.

One result of the system was a plethora of officers who owed their posts more to wealth, social standing, or political influence than to fitness for command. While some proved in time to be capable leaders, many were incompetent, or corrupt, or cowardly in battle. Obviously, such men inspired little respect among the troops, and discipline and morale suffered as a result. Another consequence was mutual suspicion between volunteer officers and West Pointers when the regular army eventually detached officers for service with volunteer regiments. The regulars tended to look down upon the volunteers as upstart incompetents, while the volunteers felt the West Pointers formed a clique which covered up each other's mistakes and sought to discredit the volunteers by failing to cooperate in combat operations. Naturally, the quarrels and suspicions of the officers filtered down to the troops, with ill effects on discipline. Indeed, so great was the problem that as late as January, 1863, Lincoln found it necessary to admonish General Joseph Hooker for undermining troop confidence in his predecessor, General Ambrose Burnside. Said the President: "Neither you nor Napoleon, if he were alive again, could get any good out of an army while such a spirit prevails in it."

It should be noted, however, that the very conditions of American life as well as the way in which the army was recruited militated against the type of discipline necessary to wage a major war. The rank and file felt strongly that officers were no better than they, and that when it came to war the officers were just as ignorant. If soldiers thought an order sensible,

---

[3] Thomas W. Higginson, "Regular and Volunteer Officers," *Atlantic Monthly*, XIV (September, 1864), 349.

they obeyed; if not, their compliance was apt to be casual. Thus, early in the war they did not use latrines; slept on guard duty; and disregarded injunctions to keep their weapons clean. Officers, in turn, failed to enforce their commands.

Contributing to this informal attitude was the local nature of the units involved. The lawyer who served as captain had as little incentive for antagonizing the sons of his clients as did the politician turned colonel for alienating voters back home. Besides, the men themselves could be nasty if their feelings were irritated too much. In October, 1861, a company of a privately-raised New York regiment were so aroused by the appointment of a captain they despised that they burned him in effigy and otherwise made life so unpleasant that he resigned. About the same time mutinies broke out in several other New York regiments among three-year men angered because three-month men were going home and because they lacked adequate clothing and other supplies. Even late in the war, when Union armies penetrated the South, soldiers printed their own papers on captured Confederate equipment, setting forth their grievances and pillorying unpopular officers.

Such demonstration of the American soldier's independent attitudes was not confined to enlisted men. One example has a curiously modern ring. In August, 1862, Captain Silas Canfield of the 21st Ohio Volunteers, then in Alabama, received an order to restore a fugitive slave to his master. Canfield refused, on the grounds that it was an unlawful order. (The Confiscation Act of July, 1862, declared free all slaves held by active Confederates.) No action was taken until Canfield moved to free runaway slaves held in the local jail. Then he was arrested and confined to quarters while charges were drawn up. Thereupon other officers preferred charges against the commander. The outcome: the slaves in jail were freed, Canfield was released, and the officers dropped their charges.

Steps to correct the worst abuses in discipline were taken after the Union defeat at Bull Run in July, 1861. Army camps were transformed into training centers. Panels were set up to examine officers, the mere threat of which brought a wave of resignations while the boards themselves weeded out the obviously unfit in the lower grades. Colonels and generals, however, were largely untouched. Replacement in the lower grades continued to be by election, but in time this process provided remedies for its evils. As the war went on it became apparent to soldiers that it was better to be led by a courageous disciplinarian than by a good guy who sneaked off for a drink when the fighting got hot. But the problem of leadership remained throughout the war, largely because of the practice of putting recruits in new regiments instead of sending them as replacements to veteran outfits. The result was a constant stream of raw recruits and untrained officers, with correspondingly poor discipline and high casualty rates.

Nevertheless, by the end of 1863 a general tightening of discipline was evident throughout the army, partly because veteran troops accepted it more readily, partly because of the improvement in the calibre of officers, partly because it was essential to cope with the crop of new men who preferred the bounties that went with volunteering to being caught in the federal draft that went into effect in March, 1863. Even so, the army remained far from a model of military order. Some officers continued to cheat soldiers out of their allowances, and some still skulked to the rear in combat. Some soldiers were little better. Once in the South they looted and pillaged, despite orders to the contrary. One officer wrote that they "even steal from the Negroes."

Discipline was closely associated with morale, and the morale of soldiers, like that of civilians, fluctuated with the fortunes of war. In the first, fine, careless rapture of patriotism after Fort Sumter there was no lack of enthusiastic volunteers, but when it became apparent that this was going to be a long and bloody war, enthusiasm waned. Many who first rallied to the flag left the cause to others when their three-month term was up, naturally arousing resentment among those enlisted for longer terms. Then the states and federal government successfully stimulated recruiting through bounties, until, in April, 1862, in unbelievable optimism, the federal government halted all recruiting. This lent substance to the belief, in and out of the army, that McClellan was about to take Richmond and end the war. Confederate victories ended the euphoria, and the backlash in sentiment was pronounced. Soldiers were soured and enlistments fell off. A now anxious administration forced the states to draft recruits, but the response was so disappointing that in March, 1863, a federal draft was ordered. While it produced few draftees it did provide a steady flow of "volunteers" who preferred to serve with a bounty rather than without it. Obviously, their attitudes left much to be desired.

As the war went on, evidence of poor morale was not hard to find. Drunkenness, which contributed to one of the mutinies early in the war, continued to be a problem to the end. Some generals sought to solve it by banning alcohol in their commands—action which simply provided a market for bootleggers. Others supplied modest whiskey rations—with equally little positive effect. It is true that in Civil War America hard drinking was looked upon (by men) as a sign of masculinity, but troops had little need to demonstrate their prowess. Rather, like the poor, soldiers found in getting drunk a way to survive miserable circumstances.

Another was sex. For soldiers with money, brothels were available in nearly every town, an accepted feature of urban life of the time. In the South, some soldiers "married" what one officer described as "simple country women" before they moved on and others patronized prostitutes who, Union and Confederate sources agree, were plentiful even in rural areas. Black women everywhere were regarded as fair prey. Inevitably, venereal disease became a problem: the average annual rate in the Union army was 8.2 percent among whites, 7.7 among blacks. These figures doubtless understate the situation, for they represent only those who sought treatment. That the army realized the seriousness of the problem is indicated by the eventual establishment of a hospital specifically devoted to care of venereal patients.

More significant was desertion. About 260,000 officers and men went AWOL during the war, of whom 60,000 returned to their outfits, leaving a total of 200,000 who left permanently, including 12,500 black soldiers. There were many reasons why men left, ranging from sheer cowardice to their being needed at home to feed their families. Even so, such a high figure argues that morale was far from high. The desertion of officers was a scandal of the time, calling forth invectives in Congress and angry editorials in the press. General Rosecrans was not the only commander who excoriated "desertion by officers of white liver, feeble constitution, and [Confederate] connections."

Even more ominous were signs of such disaffection as alluded to by Rosecrans. In February, 1863, officers of an Illinois regiment encouraged soldiers to stack their arms and cheer Jefferson Davis—an act for which 21 of them, including a colonel, were discharged. In the summer of 1864 a whole company deserted to the enemy in Arkansas, and in Washington 300 men deserted in a body, got civilian clothes and disappeared.[4] At the time it was habitual to ascribe such happenings to secret Confederate agents and to the subversive work of such underground pro-Confederate organizations as the Knights of the Golden Circle and the Sons of Liberty—and there was some truth in the allegations. But they ignored the fact that even among loyal men there were deep-seated grievances.

We have already indicated some of them: shoddy clothing and shoes, (shoes were of utmost importance to men who often had to march 20 miles at a stretch), poor diet, and inadequate medical care. Measures were taken to alleviate such conditions, as we have seen, but other sources of unrest were viewed with all too little concern.

First among these was pay. Early enlistees got $11 a month; in August, 1861, pay was increased to $13, and in 1864 to $16. The joker was that by 1864 inflation was such that the soldier could buy less with his pay than he could in April, 1861. In addition, combat troops never knew when they

---

[4] Ella Lonn, *Desertion During the Civil War* (Gloucester, Mass.: Peter Smith, reprint, 1966), pp. 148, 153.

would be paid. So long as soldiers were in camp they could count on pay every two months; once in the field they might not get paid for four, six, or even eight months. Families dependent on soldiers' pay suffered, even though charitable organizations and some local and state governments provided welfare for such families. In some places soldiers' families got little or nothing after the initial raptures of public-spirited citizens had evaporated—a fate they shared with families of black soldiers, who somehow were usually overlooked in the dispensation of beneficence, public or private.

The soldiers themselves were thus made prey for the loan sharks who lurked in every outfit, and for the sutlers. The sutler, said a veteran, was sure to be "on the make. . . . His sole motive was gain." He was a licensed army merchant who peddled to the troops, at exorbitant markups, such items as candy, fruit, butter, tobacco—and often whiskey on the side. Enjoying a monopoly on regimental trade, he extended credit generously, for the law permitted him a lien against soldiers' pay. When protests forced repeal of the law, the sutlers' lobby—with powerful connections in state politics—got another passed reinstating the liens but limiting them to one-sixth of a soldier's monthly pay.

The bounty system was another source of discord. Veterans who enlisted without such inducement, except for the $100 federal bounty paid on discharge, or who enlisted on small bounties, felt duped when later enlistees got as much as $350 in local and state bounties, and for a time, an additional $300 federal grant, all payable on enlistment. The bounties were said to help tide families of poor men over the early months of the war. Frequently most of the bounty money ended up in the pockets of bounty brokers, men who conducted a flourishing business in helping states meet their manpower quotas. Naturally, the "bounty men" were resentful.

The veterans' gripe was not simply about the money—it also stemmed from the fact that brokers often foisted off on the army men so unfit for service that they were speedily discharged, thus depriving the army of the manpower needed to win the war. Veterans especially resented the "bounty jumpers," petty criminals who enlisted again and again, pocketing a bounty each time, until the army caught up with them. Pressed into service they were sources of corruption, fled in combat, and deserted at the first opportunity. Nor were veterans happy over the evasion of military service sanctioned in the draft law: men who could afford it were permitted to hire substitutes or pay $300 to the federal government in commutation of service. To soldiers it was plain that in war all who were physically able should share the hazards; to businessmen it was evident that their work was so vital that they should be exempt from service.

Other factors help explain poor morale. The war seemed endless, at least until late in 1864. Union generals came and went, but Richmond stayed secure in Confederate hands. Grant took Vicksburg, and Meade turned back Lee at Gettysburg—but still the war went on, with its mounting toll of dead, wounded, and diseased. Back home the war seemed to lose support. Civilians resisted the draft with force: draft officials were killed and maimed and anti-draft riots broke out in scores of cities and towns. Nearly 160,000 drafted men simply did not appear for induction, having taken refuge in Canada and the Far West. The Democratic Party platform in 1864 declared the war a failure and there was clamor for a negotiated peace. If the people back home wanted such an end to the war, why should soldiers sacrifice themselves at the front? Mixed with these feelings was bitterness toward the peace advocates: such men strengthened Confederate morale and so prolonged the war.

Soldiers also felt considerable bitterness toward some commanders. All too aware that they might themselves be wounded, they learned that General Carlos Buell left much of his hospital equipment behind when he set off on a campaign in Kentucky; that Grant, in his Virginia operations, drastically reduced the number of his ambulances; and that farther South commanders requisitioned ambulance horses for the cavalry. Indeed, some generals seemed indifferent to soldiers' lives. Burnside sacrificed nearly 1300 dead and 9600 wounded in one day in repeated and futile attempts to capture Confederate positions at Fredericksburg, Virginia, in December, 1862. Less than two years later 12,000 men were killed or wounded in one day when Grant failed to dislodge Confederates at Cold Harbor, Virginia. Enlisted men could agree with the colonel who wrote home from the Cold Harbor front that they had been "foolishly and wantonly sacrificed."

Moreover, as the war intensified, not only death or injuries became more possible—but also the chances of capture. Early in the war this was no great problem in soldiers' eyes: they would be exchanged, or released on parole—which meant no more fighting! This arrangement broke down late in 1862. Thereafter captives faced the dread prospect of such infamous Confederate prison camps as Andersonville, where 13,000 prisoners died, the horrors of which lost nothing in the telling by Northern newspapers. Of a total of 195,000 Union prisoners, 30,000 died in various camps.

In addition to war weariness, soldiers suffered from sheer physical exhaustion. For much of the war little fighting went on during the winter, and soldiers could recuperate in camp. However, as Union armies penetrated the South they were in combat for longer periods of time. This often called for forced marches of 20 to 30 miles, with the object of engaging the enemy immediately upon contact. Loaded down with 50 pounds of arms, equipment, and woolen clothing, in hot sun and torrential rain, thirsty, dusty, rain-sodden, with blistered feet, the men went on, sometimes forbidden rest stops, while officers—contrary to regulations—rode comfortably on horseback. If contact was made, the troops had to fight; if not, they got a night's rest. John W. De Forest, the novelist, described the soldier's feelings from experience: "Compared with the incessant anguish of going, there was a keen luxury in throwing one's self at full length [on the ground] and remaining motionless. It was a beast's heaven; but it was better than a beast's hell—insupportable fatigue and pain." Some soldiers tried to ease their fatigue with whiskey. De Forest himself, during a day's sickness, made a long march only by dosing himself with opium.[5]

Are we to say then, in view of this discussion of soldiers' grievances and complaints, that the Union army was generally demoralized? Not at all. Signs of demoralization there were, as in the large number of desertions, and many indications of poor morale—but against them must be weighed the record of troops in combat, which is, after all, the basic test. Instances of cowardice, as at the Battle of the Crater, when white soldiers refused to attack, were relatively rare. The same men who cursed Burnside and Grant at Fredericksburg and Cold Harbor nevertheless obeyed the orders to attack, time after time, until they were called off. If General George H. Thomas earned the title of "the Rock of Chickamauga" it was largely because his men stood with him while other Union troops were swept from the field. That both sides fought doggedly in that battle is indicated by their losses: 16,000 Union men were killed, wounded, or missing; nearly 18,000 of the triumphant Confederates.

Nor should one underestimate the significance of the dramatic episode during the battle of Chattanooga, November, 1863. Union troops, ordered to confine themselves to securing the rifle pits at the base of Missionary Ridge, instead went through them, stormed up the hill under heavy rifle and cannon fire, and routed the entrenched enemy from the crest. When Grant demanded to know by whose order it was done, Thomas replied, "Their own, I fancy."

Nor were other expressions of good morale lacking. In March, 1863, the New Jersey legislature condemned the Emancipation Proclamation and called for an "honorable" end to an "unnecessary" war. In response, the 11th New Jersey Volunteers resolved to "put forth every effort, endure every fatigue, and shrink from no danger, until . . . every armed rebel shall be conquered, and traitors at home shall quake with fear." [6] That same year Ohio soldiers could vote in their gubernatorial election. There were two choices: John Brough, a Unionist committed to victory; and Clement Vallandigham, active exponent of a negotiated peace. The soldier vote was clear: nearly 40,000 for Brough; 2200 for Vallandigham. Similarly in the

[5] John W. De Forest, *A Volunteer's Adventures: A Union Captain's Record of the Civil War*, ed. James H. Croushore (New Haven: Yale University Press, 1946), pp. 94, 96. This series of letters and essays, written during and immediately after the war, is one of the most realistic accounts of the war.

[6] Henry Steele Commager, *Documents of American History*, 8th ed. (New York: Appleton-Century-Crofts, 1968), I, 428.

presidential election of 1864 the soldier vote helped carry key Northern states for Lincoln. In short, no matter how weary they were of war, no matter how justified their grievances, Union soldiers were determined to fight until they won.

In the same spirit, most Confederates fought to the end, as Grant's troops found to their cost during the year-long campaign in Virginia which ended the war. But good morale was harder to maintain in the Confederate army than in the Union, basically because the growing consciousness of defeat did little to lift men's spirits. Antietam, Gettysburg, Vicksburg, Atlanta, Chattanooga—these disasters had a cumulative effect, leading men to question risking their lives in an obviously losing cause.

Declining morale was reflected in many ways. Cases of drunkenness increased. There was more straggling—the practice through which soldiers sought surreptitiously to avoid combat. Even seasoned veterans now fell victim to panic, as at Missionary Ridge, where entrenched Confederates fled in disorder before the advancing Federals. More ominously, secret peace societies began to appear among the troops. In Georgia in 1864 one such group planned to desert and then attempt to win over other soldiers to do likewise in order to end the war. A more organized movement in Alabama planned to mutiny on Christmas Day, 1864, by laying down their arms and calling for peace.[7] Such moves were quickly suppressed; what could not be suppressed was desertion.

The incomplete Confederate records show 100,000 deserters, of whom more than a thousand were officers, but reports of government and military officials indicate that the problem was more serious than these figures suggest. As early as July, 1862, the Secretary of State declared that desertions and illegitimate absences had so weakened the army "that we are unable to reap the fruits of our victories." The fall of Atlanta two years later and Sherman's subsequent March to the Sea accelerated the trend. Reports in Richmond in February, 1865, had it that 72,000 men went AWOL in the preceding four months. Even Lee confessed he was unable to stop the drain; that same month he said, "Hundreds of men are deserting nightly and I cannot keep the army together unless examples are made of such cases." A new and ominous aspect of the situation was that, despite the widely-circulated stories of Northern prison-camp horrors, men were increasingly deserting to the enemy, although many still went home or fled to the mountains and swamps to join the armed bands of previous deserters and draft evaders who held sway there.

[7] Lonn, *Desertion During the Civil War* (Gloucester, Mass.: Peter Smith, 1966), pp. 27, 100.

The basic Confederate problems were similar to those of the Union army: weak discipline, low and irregular pay, poor diet, insufficient clothing and shoes, and inadequate medical care. Lee believed that "insufficiency of food and non-payment of the troops . . . have more to do with the dissatisfaction among the troops than anything else." But while the Union took some steps to remedy deficiencies, the Confederacy was increasingly unable to cope with the problems of its soldiers. In addition, the Confederacy had a built-in source of grievance in its conscription law, first passed in April, 1862, a year before that of the Union.

Unable to pay more than token bounties to volunteers, faced with a sharp drop in enlistment after the first war enthusiasm had worn off, and with the failure of a state draft, the Confederacy resorted to nationwide conscription, the first such law in North American history. Its numerous exemptions invited evasion. Lawyers early augmented their incomes by obtaining such exemptions—for fees as high as $500. Enterprising printers soon had fraudulent exemption papers for sale at $400 and up. The provision that drafted men could provide substitutes from non-conscript classes gave rise to a flourishing business in which brokers supplied substitutes for $500 and up.

Such practices meant that the conscription law discriminated against the poorer whites who could not afford such fees, and their anger was not lessened when the act was amended to exempt those managing at least 20 slaves. "A rich man's war and a poor man's fight" became the epigram in which the poorer whites expressed their bitterness—a feeling they carried with them into the army. Nor was the treatment accorded the poor conscript likely to improve his morale: volunteer soldiers and officers alike tended to regard him with dislike, even contempt. The substitute system was ended in December, 1863, but the poor man's bitterness was not assuaged—for the Confederacy extended the planter exemption to all managing 15 slaves! Actually, such exemptions were used by very few, but to poor men they embodied a planter class privilege which it was not willing to give up even in war.

Discipline in the Confederate army was even worse than in the Union, partly because the class structure of Southern society clashed openly with the democratic tradition that the South shared with the North. Class conscious planters who enlisted as privates—as many did—were openly insubordinate to officers who were "non-gentlemen." On occasion they physically assaulted officers who insisted on enforcing orders. This is a heinous crime in any army—but somehow such privates were rarely punished, a lesson not lost upon poorer common soldiers.

Discipline was made more difficult also by the way in which units were organized and officers chosen. As in the Union army, regiments were raised by the states and companies were likely to be composed of men from one neighborhood, resulting in a casual relationship between officers and men, although this relationship, as with Federals, was marked by resentment among the rank and file of the privileges that went with officer status. In addition, company officers were elected by their men, while higher officers were appointed by state governors, usually on the basis of social or political influence. Men of wealth who raised their own regiments were naturally rewarded with high rank. As the war went on, so many officers proved incompetent or cowardly that steps were taken to weed them out, but many slipped through the screening. Obviously such officers got little respect from their men. Like Yankees, Confederates obeyed orders only when they made sense, and this tendency was accentuated not only by the example of wealthy privates but also by that of feuding generals and of governors, such as Joseph E. Brown of Georgia and Zebulon B. Vance of North Carolina, who openly defied Confederate policies to which they objected.

The lack of discipline was manifested in many ways. Despite orders, troops, especially cavalry, plundered and pillaged—not only in forays into the North, but also in Confederate territory. When prostitutes were ordered out of camps, men contrived to keep them in. Bans against whiskey were flouted by officers and men alike. Regulations on personal and camp hygiene were largely ignored, with the same disastrous results to health as in Union camps—a situation emphasized by general infestation with lice and fleas. So widespread was this insubordinate attitude that courts-martial hesitated to impose severe punishments. Indeed, even for deserters the punishment was usually so slight that some men deserted again and again.

The pay of the common Confederate soldier was as meagre as was that of the Yankee. He could count on only $11 a month until 1864, when pay was raised to $18. But inflation in the South was much worse than in the North. In 1864 bacon sold for $9 a pound in Richmond, butter for $25 a pound, while a pair of shoes cost $125. Actually, the soldier could not count on his pay. Even early in the war pay might be two months late; by 1864 he might not get paid for more than a year. In South Carolina and Mississippi troops were in such straits that they refused to obey orders until they were paid.

How could a man take care of his family under such circumstances? Obviously he could not. As did the Union, the Confederacy made no provision for soldiers' families, and as in the North, the task was undertaken by private charities and local and state governments. Effective as such efforts were in many areas, they fell woefully short of the need, especially as inflation and the downward turn in the South's fortunes took their toll. True, in some states new laws protected the property of soldiers' families by putting off collection of debts until after the war, but in the immediate situation the issue was not alone property but also hunger and sickness.

Wives wrote to their husbands with such devastating effect that editors, preachers, and politicians pleaded with them to cease. The family man, forced to choose between loyalty to the Confederacy and loyalty to his family, often chose to go home to protect his family. Significantly, such deserters met with little disapprobation in the communities to which they returned.

If the diet of Union soldiers was bad, that of Confederates was wretched. Food shortages in the army appeared in 1862, and by the following year troops were reduced to a daily ration of hominy, a pound of corn bread, some rice, and a half pound of salt beef or pork. The meat was generally of poor quality, and often the measure included hunks of bone— and neither its taste nor food value was improved by the cooking, done usually by soldiers who took turns at the chore. The men were supposed to have coffee, but it vanished from their meals except when soldiers exchanged tobacco for coffee with fraternizing Yankees or when Confederate troops overran Union camps. Since few vegetables or fruits were provided, soldiers scrounged for them on farms. As the Union invasion spread, and sources of supply were cut off, even the usual scanty rations were reduced— or not issued at all. Troops often went for days without food; early in 1865 Lee reported that his men in battle had had no meat for three days and predicted "calamity" unless the men got more food quickly.

Actually, the South was not that short of food. Grant's troops in the West lived well on the supplies they found, as did Sherman's men on their March to the Sea. Why then was there a food shortage in the army? There are several explanations: the South lacked a sufficient supply of salt to preserve the meat that was available—it must be remembered that this was long before the day of refrigeration; the transportation system was slow, inefficient, and inadequate—food by the ton rotted at way stations and in freight cars; farmers were unwilling to sell produce to the government when they could get much higher prices trading with private businessmen.

The Confederacy tried to cope with the problem by bringing in food through the blockade, and, when persuasion failed, by compelling farmers to sell food and other supplies to the army at fixed prices, well below the mounting inflationary levels and payable, not in cash, but in bonds— promises to pay. Some food did come through the blockade, but the policy of impressment failed. Infuriated farmers and planters withdrew produce from market, and halted the law's enforcement in many areas, with the backing of state officials, while in its overall effect it reduced production at the very time the Confederacy needed all the food it could produce.

As for the troops, they were hungry. And, granting all the problems related here, they felt there were other reasons why they *were* hungry. Profit-minded speculators were hoarding food, hoping to take advantage of the rising market; and some equally profit-minded officers in the commissary department were withholding rations to sell on that rising market. Such developments naturally disgruntled the soldiers.

Besides, as time went on, the Union provided more and better clothing and shoes for its men, while the Confederate supply situation got worse. Early in the war the wool region of West Virginia was cut off, and the alternate source, Texas, was too far from railroad connections to be of much value. Even the stock of cotton was inadequate. In 1861 Confederates began burning cotton likely to fall into Union hands; more than 2,000,000 bales are said to have been so destroyed by the end of the war. Besides, in a campaign to promote food crops, states successfully limited cotton production. And, as Union invasion went on, less of that output reached the Confederacy. Year by year the Confederate cotton crop fell sharply.

Nor did Confederate policies encourage the best use of what was available. Manufacturers, resenting government imposed profit limits and the notorious slowness of the Confederacy in paying its bills, showed little interest in fulfilling war contracts. Those who were interested were frustrated by a conscription policy which drafted workers into the army. State sovereignty provided yet another obstacle. North Carolina, a key center of cotton textile production, reserved all its output for its own soldiers and civilians, indifferent to the needs of the Confederate army as a whole.

The result was that eventually many men were on duty without underwear, overcoats, or blankets. Union reports tell time and again of Confederate prisoners clad in rags; Lee complained repeatedly of his men's "scanty clothing." The supply of shoes was never sufficient: many a Confederate trooper marched and fought on bare feet, even in the snows of winter. One source of supply the men made for themselves: when a Union camp was taken, Confederates went after food and clothing. It was a measure of their desperation that they stripped Union dead of their shoes and uniforms. But as Confederate victories became rare, even this source was dried up.

Given these conditions it is not surprising that at least twice as many Confederate soldiers died from disease as from battle wounds, which claimed the lives of 94,000. As with Union troops, the major killers were diarrhoea, dysentery, and typhoid. But while the care of Union ill improved, that of Confederates declined. Medicines were in such short supply that doctors appealed to Southerners to grow plants and herbs, including the opium poppy, which could be used for medical purposes. The medical department of the army established laboratories to produce the more badly needed medicines and took over two distilleries to provide an adequate supply of medicinal whiskey. Such vital drugs as quinine, morphine, and opium had to be obtained through the blockade, smuggling, or trade with the North. The supply was never adequate for the need.

Neither was the supply of doctors. The Confederacy apparently never had more than 3400 in service, as compared with more than 11,000 in the Union army. Many of these, as in the North, were incompetent—volunteer regiments were even permitted to elect their own surgeons! Eventually, examining boards were set up to get rid of the quacks, but many remained. Soldiers complained that doctors were incompetent, brutal, indifferent, and often alcoholic—with good cause in many instances. This was even more true of the contract doctors hired in emergencies.

Army field hospitals were as crude as those of the Union, and equally dreaded by soldiers, for here were performed the amputations to which surgeons resorted as a matter of course. Whiskey or opium when available might calm the patient's pain for the time being, but given the shortage of dressings and bandaging, which often resulted in the wrapping of wounds in rags, as well as the surgeon's ignorance of asepsis, the result was frequently death from gangrene. Great general hospitals were organized in Virginia and Georgia, but even they often lacked what similar Union hospitals took for granted: fresh milk, fresh food, kitchen utensils, dishes, and spoons. Most nursing was done by untrained men, with the same consequences as in the North. The Confederacy, however, accorded more official recognition to its women than did the Union: one outstanding nurse was commissioned as a captain of cavalry!

Wounded men who fell into the hands of the enemy were in dire straits, whether Union or Confederate, for each side took care of its own first. If Union wounded at Chickamauga went without care for days, at Gettysburg, according to a nurse, surgeons spent nearly five days on amputations while "the rebels lay in a dying condition without their wounds being dressed or scarcely any food." As for ordinary prisoners, ragged and illnourished as they were, they were easy prey to the rigors of Northern winters and poorly organized prisoner camps. Of nearly 215,000 Confederate prisoners, about 26,000 died, or slightly more than 12 percent, compared to the Union death toll of 16 percent in Confederate camps.

For the soldier, Union or Confederate, the war was not entirely an unrelieved tale of grimness and terror. In camp there were alleviations: gambling, religious exercises, horseplay, organized amusements, letters to and from the folks back home, and, if one could afford it, visits to nearby towns, with their restaurants, theatres, saloons, and brothels. If Union and Confederates fought each other, it was also true that they often fraternized: exchanging newspapers (foreign observers were astounded at the avidity for reading among the troops), trading coffee for tobacco, even gambling together. All this familiarity, however, could not obscure to the men the fact that they *were* in a war, a war in which their lives were at stake. Whatever romantic notions they may have entertained had long since vanished in coping with filth, exhaustion, hunger, disease, and fear. There was simply a job to be done. They would see that it was done—but they wanted to be around when it was finished!

The debt owed the returning Union soldiers was a national debt that could never be paid—so declaimed a thousand preachers, politicians, and editors in the North. Veterans were soon disillusioned. The wounded were expected to get along on meagre pensions, and no provision had been made for their continued hospital care. Farmers went back to rundown properties, with no government aid in prospect at the very time markets were shrinking and prices falling. Their bitterness was not allayed by the evidences of the prosperity of neighbors who had stayed at home. Workers returned to towns where a postwar depression was beginning to take its toll of jobs. Many went West, hoping to take up homesteads or find jobs in such cities as San Francisco.

But to many the Northern cities and towns were their homes, and they had little intention of leaving. As the winter of 1865–1866 went on, newspapers in Northern centers reported thousands of former soldiers roaming the streets, begging and clamoring for relief. Cities and states which had raised millions to put men in uniform now insisted they had no obligation to help the men when they were out of uniform. Erstwhile patriotic employers now discovered that veterans were poor employment risks: army service, it was said, encouraged loose moral habits which made former soldiers unfit for civilian jobs! Jobless and hungry veterans responded with demonstrations, riots, and the forming of associations which eventually found voice in a national organization, the Grand Army of the Republic, a potent political force which won preferential treatment for veterans in public employment, improved pensions for the wounded and disabled, and hospitalization for ailing veterans.[8]

For Confederate veterans the prospect was even grimmer, for they had no claims on the federal government and were indeed regarded as rebels. Well or disabled, they had to make their own way in an impoverished South, unless some private charity came their way. Hungry, angry, embittered by the knowledge of defeat, by the presence of the hated Yankees as conquerors, by little hope for the future, they turned on the vulnerable symbol of all their frustrations: the now free blacks. Thus the Ku Klux Klan

---

[8] Mary R. Dearing, *Veterans in Politics: The Story of the G.A.R.* (Baton Rouge, La.: Louisiana State University Press, 1952).

and similar secret terrorist organizations sprang up. Shrewd planters and the "new men" of the South who emerged from the war turned such sentiments to their own account as they planned to overthrow the state governments of Congressional Reconstruction.

Robert Smalls, Captain of the Gun-Boat "Planter."
Harper's Weekly. June 14, 1862.

CHAPTER V

THE
BLACK
MAN'S
WAR

"God be praised! that it has come at last," wrote Frederick Douglass of Fort Sumter, confident in his perception that the war meant abolition. Eight months later he was in despair: "the friends of freedom [had been] basely betrayed" by politicians and generals alike. In 1863 he exulted over the Emancipation Proclamation, but in 1864 he brooded over talk, inside and outside the administration, of a compromise peace which would leave slavery untouched in a restored Union. Yet, whatever his responses to changing situations, Douglass held firm to a basic faith: no matter how much white politicians might deny it, the war *was* a war of black liberation; since it was such a war, blacks must fight, even if white men tried to keep them out of the army; through fighting, blacks would earn both freedom *and* equality. In this, Douglass mirrored the attitudes of most blacks, caught up in a war they knew to be of decisive importance to them, but a war in which decisions were made by white men. Some blacks accepted the dictum that it was indeed a white man's war, and concluded that no good could come from getting involved in white men's quarrels. As a Cincinnati black teacher put it: "It being their fight I assure you they are welcome to it."

Blacks had ample reason for skepticism. The President affirmed the Union's limited war aim: restoration of the Union as it was. This was re-affirmed by Congress, which also assured the public at home and abroad that there was no intention of "interfering" with slavery where it existed. This policy was reflected in action. Blacks who tried to enlist were sum-marily rejected. When they formed their own military companies they were told bluntly that their services were not wanted, and local police for-bade them from further drilling. Union generals returned to their masters fugitive slaves who sought refuge in Union camps. In the East, General Benjamin F. Butler offered use of his troops to Maryland in case of slave insurrection. In West Virginia General George B. McClellan assured slaveholders that he would put down slave rebellion with "an iron hand," and ordered his troops to protect all property—which, of course, included slaves.

Such actions went unrebuked by the administration, but when Gen-eral John C. Fremont in Missouri (August, 1861) and General David Hunter in South Carolina (May, 1862) freed slaves in their commands the orders were countermanded by Lincoln. Fremont was shortly thereafter relieved of his command and Hunter was compelled to disband a regiment he had raised among the slaves. The black men were not paid for their service. In similar fashion the Secretary of War, Simon Cameron, was packed off to Russia as an ambassador within weeks of his urging in his annual report the freeing and arming of slaves held by rebels—a suggestion ordered deleted from the records by Lincoln. To blacks, the inference was clear: acts on behalf of abolition brought swift reprisal. The intensity of black feeling was reflected in the verdict of J. P. Campbell, a leading black clergyman, that the countermanding of Fremont's proclamation demon-strated that the President "is not now, and never was, . . . an anti-slavery man."

Blacks were not persuaded by official explanations that the generals had far exceeded their authority and that Cameron had turned the War Department into a shambles. The credibility gap widened. Fremont was replaced by General Henry W. Halleck, who excluded fleeing slaves from his lines. McClellan, an avowed foe of Emancipation, was promoted to general-in-chief in November, 1861. As if to cap black frustrations, Lincoln ignored the whole issue of black freedom in his message to Congress a month later—but suggested that the race problems of the nation might be solved through colonization of free blacks abroad.

Apart from the larger implications of the Lincoln policy, militant blacks, such as Douglass, were also disturbed by its more immediate con-sequences. It stimulated already widespread black cynicism about the war, and thus inhibited struggle for black participation, which in turn endangered the goal of freedom. Also, the example set by the administration encouraged anti-black activities among certain classes of whites. A mob in Cincinnati burned a black section of the city, and in Chicago packinghouse workers voted to boycott employers who hired blacks.

This was not the whole story, of course. Lincoln's policy was dictated by pragmatic considerations, which Douglass understood although he criticized them. Lincoln, in order to win the war, felt he could not alienate the pro-slave sentiment of the Border States nor the anti-black sentiments of many Northerners. By the same token neither could he alienate the abolition wing of the Republicans, growing in strength and led by such redoubtable fighters as Benjamin Wade and Joshua Giddings of Ohio, Thaddeus Stevens of Pennsylvania, and Charles Sumner of Massachusetts— to say nothing of obstreperous Kansans who freed slaves, enrolled them in the army, and ignored repeated directives from Washington to cease and desist.

Nor could Lincoln disregard the arguments advanced by black and white abolitionists alike. So long as slavery was undisturbed, they said, so long would the Confederacy remain strong, secure in the labor of black millions which freed whites for military service. So long as the administration avowed only a limited political aim in the war, just so long would it lack the positive support of liberal sentiment abroad—a crucial consideration in view of the Confederacy's drive for foreign recognition and possible intervention. So long as blacks were denied a part in the war, so long would the Union lack the strength and morale to cope with Confederate armies.

Thus, there were divided counsels in Congress, in the military and in the administration, and as the Union suffered successive military setbacks the influence of those who advocated more aggressive war measures mounted. Since the administration had no unified policy toward blacks, except insisting upon the President's prerogative in keeping Emancipation in his own hands, cabinet members, military commanders and a Congress dissatisfied with Lincoln's policy so modified it that the role of blacks in the war had been transformed long before formal Emancipation. And this, we must note, happened without incurring the presidential displeasure which had been visited upon Cameron, Fremont, and Hunter.

Let us trace the major developments in this process. In the summer of 1861 the House of Representatives declared it was no business of Union generals to return fugitive slaves to their masters, and in March, 1862, Congress outlawed the practice. In 1861 Congress ordered the "confiscation" of slaves used in the Confederate army without specifically emancipating them. A year later it voted freedom for the slaves of "rebel owners" and authorized enlistment of black troops in the Union army. In December, 1861, the House refused to reaffirm its resolution that the war was waged only to preserve the Union and pledging protection of slavery where it existed. In the same period Congress ordered compensated Emancipation in the District of Columbia, freed all slaves in the territories without compensation, and approved Lincoln's offer of compensated Emancipation in the Border States—an offer none of the states accepted. In short, Congress was moving toward Emancipation and using the neglected black arm to save the Union.

In the meantime, military commanders and cabinet members were moving in the same direction. In May, 1861, General Butler—the same Butler who promised troops to put down rumored slave insurrections in Maryland—declared slaves escaping to his lines "contraband of war," refused to return them to their masters, and employed them as servants and laborers. Many other generals followed his example. Secretary of the Navy, Gideon Welles, in September, 1861, permitted enlistment of "contrabands" in the navy. A month later, Secretary of War, Simon Cameron, authorized the enrolling of fugitive slaves in South Carolina as soldiers in the Union army—an authority never used by the general involved.

Cameron's successor, the War Democrat Edwin M. Stanton, who forced General Hunter to disband his black regiment, almost simultaneously (August, 1862) gave power to General Rufus Saxton to raise black regiments in South Carolina with "the same pay and rations" as white volunteers. This move reassured blacks who had applauded Hunter's abolition moves while at the same time they were dismayed by his forcible impressment of freedmen into the army. Saxton, using voluntary methods, organized troops who soon distinguished themselves in combat.

Meanwhile, Butler, now operating in Louisiana, accepted into the Union army long established units of free black militia never called into service by the Confederacy. In the process he also enlisted many other blacks, neglecting to inform Washington that his recruiting officers rarely asked whether the volunteers were free or slave. These developments are all the more striking in that Lincoln, in cabinet meetings, made it clear that he was opposed to arming slaves!

If the President did not interfere, it was largely because he too was moving in the same direction. Always sensitive to the pressures of events and opinion, he was impressed by the advice of his ambassadors that some dramatic stroke, such as Emancipation, was essential to head off foreign recognition of the Confederacy. He brooded over the increasing dissatisfaction at home with his conduct of affairs, an outlook he could well understand in view of the failure of his generals in the East to produce significant victories. In these circumstances the arguments of abolitionists took on added weight, and as Lincoln himself put it later, "I felt that we . . . must change our tactics or lose the game." Thus followed (1) the first

American recognition of the independent black republics, Haiti and Liberia, (2) Lincoln's proposal for gradual, compensated Emancipation, and, most significant (3) the preliminary Proclamation of Emancipation in September, 1862. In fact, this last move was more than a change in tactics. It was a revolution in strategy, transforming what had been a war for a limited political objective into a war of liberation, in which the causes of Union and liberty would be indeed, in Daniel Webster's words, "one and inseparable."

It was a policy entailing grave risks, in terms of pro-slave Border State sentiment, of the Northern opinion which wanted no truck with blacks, and of the morale of an army shot through with race prejudice. No less a dignitary than General McClellan, commander of the Army of the Potomac, put the issue bluntly to his commander-in-chief. In July, 1862, when talk of Emancipation was in the air, McClellan told the President that "forcible abolition" should not be contemplated "for a moment," and warned that, "A declaration of racial views, especially upon slavery, will rapidly disintegrate our present armies." Douglass remarked that the general's "ideas of the crisis make him unfit for the place he holds."

Black pleasure with the preliminary proclamation was tempered by fears that political pressures might succeed for its modification or withdrawal before its effective date, January 1, 1863. They, as well as Lincoln, knew that while Northern response was favorable, it fell far short of what had been expected. Their fears were stimulated by the elections in the fall of 1862. Democrats increased their seats in the House from 44 to 75: key states which voted Republican in 1860 went Democratic; New York elected as governor Horatio Seymour, an avowed enemy of Emancipation who counselled against military conquest of the Confederacy. But Lincoln was not dissuaded. "I never in my life," he said in signing the final proclamation, "felt more certain that I was doing right."

While blacks thoroughly approved of Lincoln's final proclamation, they were gravely disturbed by his belief that the two races could not live together peaceably and productively as free people in one country. His solution was voluntary colonization abroad. Lincoln put his case to a black delegation in August, 1862, in a curious way, seeming to blame the blacks for the war. If it were not "for your race among us," he said, "there could not be war, . . . without the institution of slavery, and the colored race as a basis, the war could not have an existence. It is better for us both, therefore, to be separated." Since whites were unwilling "for a free colored people to remain with us," it would be advisable for "intelligent colored men" to set the example by settling elsewhere. Following Lincoln's lead, Congress appropriated $600,000 for voluntary emigration of slaves freed under the Confiscation Act of 1862 and by passage of Emancipation in the District of

Columbia. A bemused Lincoln gave official sanction to schemes of shady white promoters to settle freed blacks in Central America and on a small island off the coast of Haiti. Such promoters hoped to profit from exploitation of both the natural resources of the areas and the labor of the blacks. The Central American attempt came to nothing, but the island project did attract more than 400 emigrants—and nearly a hundred of them died from hunger and disease before Lincoln ordered return of the survivors in February, 1864. Congress thereupon cut off colonization funds.

How did blacks respond? Lincoln might well have argued that his proposals were in the spirit of those suggested by black militants, such as Martin R. Delany and Henry Highland Garnet, who in the 1850s urged black emigration from the United States. Further, early in the war, a considerable number of black leaders, including Garnet, William Wells Brown, and H. Ford Douglass, joined in promoting emigration to Haiti—a project which also proved to be disastrous.

Colonization, whether under black or white sponsorship, found little favor among blacks. Meeting after meeting recalled the contributions of blacks to the American Revolution and to the War of 1812, and insisted that the United States for all its faults was *their* country, and made it plain they had no intention of leaving. Boston blacks resolved, "That if anybody wants us to go, they must compel us." Robert Purvis, the famous black leader of Philadelphia, excoriated Lincoln's position as a product of the "insane and vulgar hate" of whites for blacks. Frederick Douglass thought colonization "an opiate to the troubled conscience of the nation," and recommended, "Instead of sending any of the loyal people out of the country, at this time our nation should hail with joy every loyal man, who has an arm and a heart to fight for the United States."

For blacks, January 1, 1863, was a historic day: "the greatest event of our nation's history, if not the greatest event of the century," as Douglass put it in hailing issuance of the final Emancipation Proclamation. Critics at the time were quick to point out that the proclamation freed no one. Slavery in Union territory was left untouched, and in the Confederacy Jefferson Davis did not make it a habit to enforce Lincoln's decrees. Blacks knew better. The forces of freedom let loose by the proclamation were irreversible; if Jeff Davis did not enforce it, black slaves would. The black grapevine in the South carried the news, minus the fine print. As Union armies neared, slaves streamed off the plantations, clinging to the men in blue despite ill-treatment, hunger, disease, and a death rate so high that

Grant wondered if the race would survive. Mary Chesnut, wife of a Confederate Senator, noted the change in black attitude in the family butler: "I taught him to read as soon as I could read myself . . . but he won't look at me now. He looks over my head, he scents freedom in the air."

"Slavery can be abolished by white men," observed Douglass, but liberty and equality could be won only by blacks themselves. Buoyed up by the Proclamation's sanction for black soldiers—even if only for garrison duty—blacks pressed their campaign for all-out participation in the war, including combat duty. This time there was no hesitation on the part of the administration—and the garrison duty limitation was largely ignored. Within two weeks of the issuance of the Proclamation, Rhode Island was authorized to enlist blacks and shortly thereafter Massachusetts received similar power. Blacks responded so readily that what was to become a historic regiment—the 54th Massachusetts—was soon filled and another, the 55th, was organized.

Acting through the states, however, proved too slow to meet the manpower needs of an army suffering from high casualties, mounting desertions and declining white enlistments. In March, 1863, Adjutant General Lorenzo Thomas was sent to the Mississippi Valley with sweeping powers to raise black troops and provide officers for them. By the end of the year he had organized 20 black regiments; before the war was over he had recruited 76,000 blacks, both through voluntary enlistment and impressment. Officers' commissions went to whites—a practice which offended blacks but also helped to reduce prejudice against blacks in the army. So great were manpower needs, however, and so impressive the black military record, that in February, 1864, the federal draft, which already applied to free blacks, was extended to slaves. Altogether, the army raised nearly 100,000 black troops in the South, while many thousands more were enlisted by Northern state recruiting agents. Such volunteers were charged off against these states' draft quotas, and thus eased pressure on whites. Loyal masters of slaves drafted by the federal government were compensated: $100 if the slave were actually drafted, $300 if he volunteered. In either case, the slave was declared free.

Prejudice in the ranks may have been diminished by Thomas' policy, but it had already shown its strength in Washington, D.C. Stanton's pledge that blacks would receive equal pay and rations with whites was held unlawful. Blacks, regardless of rank, and regardless of their being in combat or other units, were paid seven dollars a month—the pay of an army laborer —compared to a white's pay of eleven dollars. The additional monthly clothing allowance of three dollars, paid to whites in cash, was withheld from blacks. Black volunteers received none of the federal bounties paid to whites. Families of white soldiers were aided by cities and states, but little was done for families of black troopers.

Few blacks could hope to become officers. Although 180,000 blacks were enlisted during the war only about a hundred were commissioned, and most of those were in the Louisiana militia taken into federal service in 1862. General N.P. Banks in 1863 frankly avowed his purpose to get rid of *them*. Lorenzo Thomas, despite his strenuous efforts to raise black troops, expressly prohibited appointment of blacks as officers. Many commanders, persuaded that blacks were not fighters, persisted in using blacks as laborers, although many such blacks had been trained as combat soldiers. Medical care, inadequate for whites, was even worse for blacks, which helps explain their incredible death toll—more than 68,000, about 37 percent of their total number. Perhaps most disheartening, the administration for long took no steps to protect black prisoners from being sold into slavery, nor to take reprisals against the "no quarter" policy of some Confederate commanders toward surrendering black troops.

So, black enthusiasm perceptibly cooled. Even Frederick Douglass lost heart. In August, 1863, he informed his friend, Major George L. Stearns, who headed the recruiting efforts in Massachusetts, that he could no longer serve as a recruiting agent in good conscience because of the government's failure to protect black prisoners from Confederate wrath. Stearns promptly assured him that action was being taken, to which Douglass replied sadly: "The poor colored soldiers have purchased this interference dearly. It really seems that nothing of justice, liberty, or humanity can come to us except through tears and blood."

Tears and blood were indeed the portion of many black soldiers. In July, 1863, the 54th Massachusetts Regiment made its place in history. Without food or rest for two days and nights, it led an assault on Fort Wagner, in Charleston Harbor, fighting its way to the top despite murderous fire, before being forced back. The regiment, made up of slightly more than 600 men, lost more than a third of its members. This instance of black courage was far from unique: it was duplicated at Port Hudson, Louisiana; Milliken's Bend, Louisiana; Nashville, Tennessee; and in Grant's final campaigns in northern Virginia. In one battle there, blacks won 14 of 37 Congressional Medals of Honor awarded for heroism. Even skeptical generals, such as Grant, were persuaded that "Negroes will fight"—and some thought that on occasion blacks showed more courage than whites. Count Regis de Trobriand, a French volunteer who eventually became a major-general, reported that during the bloody Battle of the Crater in Virginia in July, 1864, demoralized white soldiers simply "would not move" against the entrenched enemy. Black troops were ordered in, "advanced resolutely, passed over the passive mass of white troops, not a company of whom followed them, and . . . charged under a deadly fire. . . . They even reached the enemy, . . . But they were not sustained. They were driven back. . . ." [1]

Black pride in the record of black soldiers was mixed with doubt that some of the sacrifices had been necessary. It was believed that some commanders deliberately sacrificed blacks as shock troops in order to protect whites. Confederate reports confirmed this. One Confederate officer reported after an engagement that the Union commander had posted blacks so as to draw the most fire, and after defeat had gathered up the white wounded, leaving the "dead and wounded Negroes uncared for." Nor were blacks reassured by reports that in the Battle of the Crater, defeated white soldiers bayonetted their black comrades so as to curry favor with triumphant Confederates.[2] Ironically, it was in that very battle that Grant ordered blacks withheld from the first assaulting party because of the widespread belief that blacks were being sacrificed in such duty!

No matter how bravely blacks fought, they still fought as victims of discrimination—and as fighting men they were in no mood to accept it. Some deserted in protest. A small unit of South Carolina Volunteers mutinied—for which its sergeant was executed. For 18 months the 54th Massachusetts Regiment refused to accept any pay at all until they were treated as equals. Eventually in 1864 Congress voted equal pay for blacks who had been free when they enlisted—but soldiers who had been slaves had to wait yet another year before their rights were recognized. Also, in 1864 Congress extended to blacks the $100 federal bounty paid to white voluntccrs, and voted pensions to widows and orphans of black veterans. But, as Fred A. Shannon observed, blacks shared in the monetary inducements for enlistment "in far smaller proportion to their total number recruited" than did whites.[3]

In the meantime, the administration took some steps to protect blacks captured by the Confederacy. The ending of the exchange of prisoners early in 1863 resulted in part from Confederate refusal to include black soldiers and their officers. War Department General Order 100 (April 24, 1863) held that slaves enlisted in the United States Army were legally free and therefore not subject to re-enslavement. Retaliation was promised for violation of this "law of nations." Lincoln followed this in July with a

---

[1] Regis de Trobriand, *Four Years with the Army of the Potomac*, trans. George K. Dauchy (Boston: Ticknor and Company, 1889), p. 615. The pioneer black historian of the black soldiers, George W. Williams, was not so harsh in his judgment of the white troops. They were he said, "disorganized and distracted, . . . could neither advance nor retreat." See his *A History of the Negro Troops in the War of the Rebellion* (New York: Negro Universities Press, 1969), pp. 249–50. This is a reprint of a work first published in 1888.

[2] Dudley Taylor Cornish, *The Sable Arm: Negro Troops in the Union Army, 1861–1865* (New York: W. W. Norton & Company, Inc., 1966), p. 276.

[3] Shannon, *Organization . . . of the Union Army* (Cleveland, Ohio: The Arthur H. Clark Company, 1928), II, 161.

proclamation warning that for every Union prisoner murdered by Confederates a rebel prisoner would be executed, and for every black trooper enslaved a Confederate prisoner would be put to hard labor. The Union's firm stance may have deterred some atrocities, but at Fort Pillow, Tennessee, in 1864 surrendering blacks were massacred—and the administration failed to take action. Indeed, Lincoln's proclamation was poorly enforced—except when black soldiers put it into effect, as at Jenkin's Ferry, Arkansas where the 2nd Kansas Colored Regiment wiped out Confederate opposition and took only one prisoner.

But even as the federal government took action to correct obvious injustices there were disturbing signs of white backlash, fed by secret pro-Confederate Copperhead organizations which flourished in some areas, resentment among some labor groups over appearance of blacks in war-time jobs, and opposition to the new federal draft law of March, 1863. In January, 1863, the Democratic-controlled Illinois legislature condemned the Emancipation Proclamation, as did the New Jersey legislature two months later. In March, a white mob in Detroit invaded the black section of that city, shouting that if whites had to fight for Negroes they would kill every black in town. They did kill several—and destroyed so many houses that two hundred black people were left homeless. During July, in New York City, what started out as a protest against the draft turned into an orgy of race hatred. The Colored Orphan Asylum was burned to the ground, and hapless blacks hunted down, beaten, hanged, and burned. Federal troops were necessary to restore order—some of them were detached from Meade's army at Gettysburg, although they were sorely needed to pursue the retreating army of Robert E. Lee.

There were still other sources of black fear during the ensuing election year of 1864. Some white abolitionists assumed that with Emancipation their work was done. They were indifferent; sometimes even hostile, to black demands for the ballot and civil rights. Lincoln's Reconstruction plans as publicly revealed allowed no place for black men, although the President had written privately to the new governor of Louisiana suggesting that the ballot be extended to "the very intelligent" blacks and to black war veterans. The Reconstruction policy of Lincoln's Radical Republican opponents, represented by the Wade-Davis Bill, likewise kept government in the hands of white men only. The proposed 13th Amendment, abolishing slavery, passed the Senate but failed to get the necessary two-thirds vote in the House.

In addition, war weariness was rife in the North, talk of a negotiated peace was in the air, and the belief was spreading that peace with the Union could be obtained if only Lincoln would drop his stand that acceptance of Emancipation by the South was the necessary condition for any peace talks. Democrats appealed to this sentiment with their declaration that the war had proved a failure and called for a negotiated peace to restore the Union—with no mention of Emancipation. Their nominee, General McClellan, certainly was no man to calm black fears.

So strong was the Democrats' appeal that Lincoln himself despaired of his re-election—and this boded ill for black hopes. Frederick Douglass, meeting with Lincoln in August, was distressed to find the President so pessimistic that he "wanted some plan devised by which he could get more of the Slaves within our lines. He thought now was their time—*and that such only of them as succeeded in getting within our lines would be free after the war was over.* . . . The President only has faith in this proclamation of freedom during the war, and . . . believes the operation will cease with the war." [4] Lincoln's mood arose in part because in the face of the resurgent Democrats the Republicans had split. Radicals dissatisfied with Lincoln's cautious policies had entered their own ticket, headed by General John C. Fremont, and prominent among the general's backers were militant blacks, including Douglass. Other blacks rallied to Lincoln. Symbolic of the deep feeling of many was the presentation to the President of a specially bound copy of the Bible by Baltimore blacks. Said their spokesman: "Hereafter when our children shall ask what mean these tokens, they will be told of your worthy deeds, and will rise up and call you blessed."

The gloom was swept away in September. In August, Admiral Farragut took Mobile, thus sealing off one of the few remaining Confederate sources of supply. In September, General W.T. Sherman took Atlanta, the great railroad hub and manufacturing center. Shortly afterwards General Philip Sheridan routed Confederate forces in the Shenandoah Valley, Virginia, stripping Lee's army of its food supply. The war was no longer a failure, and Northern opinion veered sharply. The Fremont ticket faded from the scene, and black as well as white critics of Lincoln, including Douglass, rallied to the President's cause. For blacks the re-election of Lincoln was significant in itself, but also significant was the size of the Unionist victory in the House: sufficient votes were now present to carry the 13th Amendment. The new House never had the opportunity. The same House which rejected it in 1864 passed it January 31, 1865. Before the year was out the 13th Amendment had become part of the Constitution. At long last, slavery in the United States had been officially abolished forever.

Actually, slavery had ceased to be viable in the South even before the war ended. In January, 1864, General Patrick R. Cleburne, speaking on behalf of a group of Confederate officers, urged the arming of slaves, and

---

[4] Philip S. Foner, ed., *The Life and Writings of Frederick Douglass* (New York: International Publishers, 1952), III, 423–24. Italics in original.

if the use of black troops meant the end of slavery, so be it: "As between the loss of independence and the loss of slavery, we assume that every patriot will freely give up the latter." [5] Cleburne was too optimistic. President Davis prohibited discussion of the topic in the army. General Howell Cobb thought the idea ridiculous: "If slaves will make good soldiers our whole theory of slavery is wrong." But repeated Confederate military reverses and a crumbling home front emboldened others to speak out, including General Robert E. Lee, who, in January, 1865, urged employment of black troops "without delay," regardless of "the effects which may be produced upon our social institutions." Two months later Davis signed an act of the Confederate Congress authorizing enlistment of slaves in the army, with Emancipation limited to those freed by their owners and by the states in which they lived. It was too late—Lee's surrender was only a month away.

In the meantime, the Confederate Government, in a desperate and unsuccessful last-minute bid for foreign support, offered to abolish slavery if Britain would grant recognition. In short, just as the North had chosen Emancipation to help save the Union, so the Confederacy decided to sacrifice slavery to preserve its independence. In both cases the destiny of the black was central to the issue of survival—but in neither section were whites prepared to accept the implications of their own decisions.

Emancipation, yes; equality, no. This was a major Northern white attitude confronted by blacks throughout the war. However, the exigencies of the times, abolitionist pressures, massive black protests, and the record of black troops—all combined to bring about some modification of discrimination, at least as far as the federal government was concerned. Thus, in August, 1861, despite the Dred Scott decision (which was still the law of the land), the United States issued a passport to the militant black clergyman, Henry H. Garnet, declaring him to be a citizen. In another repudiation of the Dred Scott decision, the United States Attorney General held in 1862 that all persons born in the United States, regardless of color, were citizens. Three years later John Rock became the first black lawyer admitted to practice before the U.S. Supreme Court. Lincoln himself set a precedent: he was the first president to counsel with black men, including Frederick Douglass, of whose criticism he was well aware. How was Douglass received? "Just as you have seen one gentleman receive another," reported Douglass.

[5] James M. McPherson, *The Negro's Civil War* (New York: Vintage Books, 1965), p. 242.

State action came more slowly, and then only after black organizations exerted such pressure as they could, aided by white allies. Beginnings were made in ending school segregation in the many areas where it existed, although courts continued to uphold the principle. Laws prohibiting blacks from testifying in court against whites were repealed, and so for the first time victims of white thieves, rapists, and swindlers gained formal court protection. In 1865 Illinois finally repealed its notorious "black laws" partly as a result of a massive campaign engineered by blacks outraged by a court decision in 1863 temporarily enslaving free blacks who had violated the laws by entering the state. Indiana soon followed. Discrimination in restaurants, hotels, and theatres continued: even Massachusetts, the pioneer state in school desegregation, did not protect black civil rights until 1865. Street cars, of vital importance to blacks since few of them could afford private carriages, were either barred to them, or when permitted on, blacks were compelled to endure open platforms, regardless of the weather. Despite repeated black protests Washington cars did not permit black riders until just before the end of the war. Philadelphia, another scene of black protests, steadfastly refused to end discrimination until 1867—and then only through state legislation.

Whatever concessions they might make to blacks, Northern whites were adamant in denying them the franchise. Only in New England states, excepting Connecticut, did blacks have free access to the ballot. New York effectively denied the vote to most blacks because of property qualifications, and Ohio achieved the same goal through requirements for a certain amount of white "blood" in black voters. Other Northern states simply denied all blacks the right to vote, and voted down all proposals to end the practice. Blacks persisted in their efforts, however, and in 1865 organized a National Equal Rights League to direct the campaign for the right to vote. Their efforts met with success only with the passage of Reconstruction legislation in 1867, and then blacks got the ballot only in the South. Not until ratification of the 15th Amendment did Northern states reluctantly open the polls to black Americans. In short, Northern whites were willing to accept black blood to help save the Union; they were not prepared to have black minds help govern it.

Thus far we have discussed the Northern black man's war—what of the Southern black? Free blacks, of whom there were about 182,000 in the Confederacy, were as divided in their feelings as those in the North, but as in the North, many rallied to the national cause. In Louisiana they formed volunteer military organizations which became part of the state militia in 1861. In Alabama, the prosperous mixed-descent black community of Mobile volunteered en masse, were turned down by the Confederacy, accepted by the state in 1862, and a year later received into Confederate service. Requests for military service also came from organized groups in Virginia, Tennessee, and Arkansas—requests politely rejected. Offers of free blacks to work on fortifications were speedily accepted. Other free blacks throughout the Confederacy contributed money or goods and subscribed to Confederate war bonds. Significantly, none of the units accepted into military service were ever used in combat. How could one justify slavery if black men were fit to be soldiers?

Why were so many free blacks willing to support a government frankly based on black slavery? In part because some were slaveowners themselves—the prosperous black societies of New Orleans, Mobile, and Charleston were made up of people of mixed descent, linked by blood with leading white families of the region, and sharing their values. Also, many Southern blacks loved their own land and dreaded intrusion by the alien Yankee.

Basically, however, the free black response represented an attempt to identify with the white cause, and so to bring about improved status for themselves and a relaxation of the onerous legal restrictions on such freedom as free blacks enjoyed.

In this hope they were disappointed. Whites welcomed expressions of support from the "better class" but they continued to look with suspicion on the mass of poor free blacks, who were viewed as a source of disaffection among slaves. Thus, the restrictions on free blacks were tightened, rather than relaxed, although doubtless it was the poor rather than the well-to-do who felt their force. Nevertheless the lot of the poor free black did improve. He was exempt from military service and his labor was in demand. Regular employment at wages better than he had ever enjoyed gave him a new feeling of confidence, which whites found "impudent." And, incredible though it may seem, some blacks did see service in the Confederate army. As persons not subject to conscription, free blacks were able to hire out as substitutes for whites unwilling to go. How many went is not known, but Walter L. Fleming, the noted Southern historian, reported that he himself knew of two white men "who hired Negro substitutes . . . and the Negroes having been killed in battle, the whites were forced to go." [6] This practice ended early in 1864 when the Confederacy ordered drafting of free blacks as laborers and teamsters in the army.

Black slaves, of course, had no choice. From early in the war many were impressed into non-combat army service as cooks, teamsters, and laborers—although it should be noted that in battle such "non-combat" blacks were as vulnerable to wounds and death as were armed troops.

[6] Fleming, *Civil War and Reconstruction in Alabama* (New York: Columbia University Press, 1905), p. 206n.

Although masters received the wages of their black draftees, they were not happy with the treatment slaves received: all too often slaves returned sick and weak. Slaves not only toiled in the army; they continued to toil in the fields, producing food and other necessities for the Confederacy, as well as in ordnance factories, salt works, iron foundries, and coal mines. Their labor released thousands of white men for military service. Out of that service grew a self-serving white mythology which eventually found its way into history books: the happy slave tending faithfully to his task, protecting mistress and her children while dear "ol massa" served at the front. Such a picture helped to sustain Southern white morale while it provided potent propaganda for Peace Democrats in the North.

Even while they repeated this tale in endless variations, planters took no chances. "Home guards" were organized to guard against feared black insurrections. Patrol laws were tightened to make sure no blacks were on the roads after dark. Slave codes were reinforced and increased restrictions on free blacks imposed. The Confederate government encouraged planters to "run off" slaves to safe areas when threatened by Union invasion. So intense was the fear of slave rebellion that many blacks suffered dire punishment for supposed plotting, although the evidence is far from clear as to whether the alleged plots were genuine or products of white hysteria. In Alabama in 1861, many slaves were executed for plotting "hellish insurrection." The provost marshal at Natchez, Mississippi, reported in July, 1862, that in the previous year, 40 blacks had been hanged and a like number imprisoned. In Virginia, that same year, 17 blacks, slave and free, were executed for organizing rebellion.

That Confederates had some basis in fact for fear of overt black hostility is clear. Early in 1863 slaves in Lafayette County, Mississippi, drove out the overseers and divided among themselves the property of their masters. In a number of states—Virginia, Alabama, North Carolina, Arkansas, and Florida—slaves escaped into swamps and mountains, formed armed bands, sometimes in collaboration with white Confederate deserters, and lived off the country, depriving loyal Confederate farmers of hogs, cattle, and food. In February, 1864, about 1200 slaves impressed for war work in Mobile, Alabama, fled the city. Many enlisted in the Union army.

The rebellious slaves were a small minority, of course, but their attitude was indicative of the fact that the closed society of slavery had not destroyed black personality. Most blacks stayed on the plantations, cautiously waiting the trend of events, but increasingly showing attitudes which whites found disquieting: "insolent," "uppity," "impudent." Contributing to this new slave response was the breakdown of the cotton economy, which transformed slaves from assets into liabilities. While the price of slaves mounted in terms of depreciating Confederate currency, it declined in constant gold terms. In states such as Mississippi, most dependent on cotton, planters encouraged slaves to sell produce on their own or to hire their own labor. In extreme cases slaves were turned off the plantations to fend for themselves as best they could.

The true sentiment of the "happy" plantation blacks was demonstrated when Union armies neared. By the thousands they streamed to the army camps, and trekked after the troops despite fearful mortality from disease, hunger, and lack of shelter. Lacking any federal program to aid the blacks, private philanthropic and religious organizations tried to fill the gap until Congress finally acted in March, 1865, setting up a Freedmen's Bureau to provide emergency aid for black and white refugees. Some generals made the blacks unwelcome, but others made good use of them. Slaves knew the terrain: every trail, path, stream, and swamp was as familiar to them as they were alien to Yankees. Often ex-slaves had firsthand knowledge of the disposition of Confederate troops in the vicinity. Thus, they provided invaluable military intelligence and furnished yeoman service as scouts and guides for Union patrols. The most eloquent testimony to this black contribution to Union victory came from Confederate General Patrick R. Cleburne in January, 1864, when he argued for enlistment of blacks in the Confederate service: "All along the lines slavery is comparatively valueless to us for labor, but of great and increasing worth to the enemy for information. It is an omnipresent spy system, pointing out our valuable men . . . , revealing our positions, purposes and resources." [7]

If slaves thought freedom meant salvation, in all too many cases they were speedily disillusioned. Since there was no federal policy relating to disposition of blacks in Union occupied areas each commander was on his own, and many followed the example of General N. P. Banks in Louisiana, who leased out former slaves to white, often Yankee, speculators who took over abandoned plantations. In this situation, blacks soon found themselves worse off than under slavery. Their experience was reported by an official of the Western Sanitary Commission: "If they were only paid their little wages as they earn them, so that they could purchase clothing, and were furnished with provisions promised, they could stand it; but to work and get poorly paid, poorly fed, and not doctored when sick, is more than they can endure." Even so, few wanted to return to slavery.

There were Northerners who went South to do well, and there were also Yankees who went to do good—and to the latter blacks responded with warmth and friendship. Freedmen's aid societies, both religious and secular, provided not only the necessities of life but also the luxury of

---

[7] McPherson, *The Negro's Civil War*, p. 242.

education. Most notable was the American Missionary Association, which opened a school in Virginia as early as September, 1861, with a black teacher, Mary Peake. So responsive were blacks to schooling that by 1866 the various societies maintained 760 teachers in the field, and had reached 150,000 pupils (of all ages) at a cost of $3,000,000. In the Sea Islands of South Carolina, young New England idealists and abolitionist but hard-headed businessmen undertook an experiment to prove both that blacks were educable and that free black labor was more productive than slave. The experiment was successful on both counts, and as Willie Lee Rose has pointed out, succeeded in another area not particularly pleasing to some Yankees: blacks eventually sought management of their own affairs, and given the opportunity, did so with marked success.[8] Corroborative evidence came from the colony set up by the Union Army at Davis Bend, Mississippi. There blacks not only managed their own affairs, but also the profitable production and marketing of their crops, despite such problems as poor weather, insect pests, and other natural hazards of farming.

For a variety of reasons the Union Army itself engaged in black education. With the raising of black regiments it was found essential to reduce illiteracy, especially among black non-commissioned officers. "School tents" were set up in black outfits, in which white officers, black chaplains, and other literate blacks introduced soldiers to the rudiments of learning. In Louisiana, General Banks, smarting under criticism of his "legalized slavery," sought to placate critics with a black schooling program which by July, 1865, had 126 schools in operation with 230 teachers and 15,000 pupils, in addition to 5,000 adults who were taught at nights and on Sundays. In Mississippi, Grant's superintendent of freedmen, John Eaton, took over schools run by private societies. Before the war was over there were 30 schools functioning, with 60 teachers and 4400 pupils. The black response to education was enthusiastic. In Mississippi an official involved in the school program reported, "Only an enthusiastic desire for improvement could lead any people to put forth the efforts which the freed people are making to procure instruction." In the South Carolina Sea Islands a skeptical Yankee commented that if whites achieved as much under such difficult circumstances, "they would be regarded as prodigies."

Blacks hungered for learning; they hungered even more for land. Without it, they perceived, they would continue to be subordinate to those who possessed it. Prince Rivers, a black Union Army sergeant who was later active in South Carolina Reconstruction, put the case dramatically: "Every colored man will be a slave, and feel himself a slave, until he can raise his own bale of cotton and put his own mark upon it, and say, 'This

---

[8] Willie Lee Rose, *Rehearsal for Reconstruction* (New York: Vintage Books, 1967), pp. 298, 303, 311, 314–16.

is mine!'." During the war it appeared as if this black hope would be realized. The Second Confiscation Act (1862) authorized seizure of the property of active rebels, and powerful voices were raised, in and out of Congress, urging distribution of seized lands among former slaves. The blacks who toiled so industriously at Davis Bend and in the Sea Islands did so largely because they understood the land would be theirs.

Land was the crux of a meeting in December, 1864, when the victorious General W. T. Sherman and Secretary of War Stanton met in Savannah, Georgia, with black leaders, including former slaves, to discuss the problem of the thousands of blacks following Sherman's troops. The black answer was clear: Put the young men in the army, turn over land to their families, "and we can soon maintain ourselves and have something to spare; . . . We want to be placed on land until we are able to buy it, and make it our own." The result was what James M. McPherson calls "the possibility of a truly revolutionary land reform program." [9] Sherman's Order No. 15 set aside exclusively for blacks hundreds of square miles of coastal lands, ranging from Charleston to Jacksonville. Each freedman's family was allotted 40 acres, with provisionary title until Congress issued final regulations. More than 40,000 families had settled in the area by June, 1865.

Black hopes were buoyed still further in March, 1865 when Congress, in setting up the Freedmen's Bureau, authorized the bureau to set aside confiscated and abandoned lands for use by former slaves and "loyal" white refugees. Each male citizen was to receive 40 acres for three years, during which time occupants "may purchase the land and receive such title thereto as the United States can convey."

The hopeful blacks were bitterly disillusioned. Despite the protests of white abolitionists and black farmers the valuable lands of the Sea Islands were sold at auction by the federal government, most of them going to Yankee speculators. Of nearly 77,000 acres involved, blacks were able to buy fewer than 5,000. The Davis Bend colony lands were restored to their owners by President Andrew Johnson, as were the lands covered by Sherman's Order No. 15. The Freedmen's Bureau provision remained largely a dead letter. Thus, the former slaves, victims of unpaid labor all their lives, were now in freedom turned out to take their chances in a harshly competitive society, without land, without property, often still illiterate.

The war, as Douglass said in a sanguine moment, was a "revolution" for blacks. Slavery was abolished; blacks made citizens, accepted as soldiers,

[9] McPherson, *The Negro's Civil War*, p. 299.

assured formal equality before the law, and former slaves given promise of land. But the revolution was far from complete. At the war's end most Northern and all Southern states denied blacks the right to vote, and black civil rights were still largely unrecognized throughout the nation. Discrimination in jobs and housing was still rampant, and soon after the war the earlier promise of land was repudiated. But most blacks were undismayed. With a new sense of strength and a confidence born of their war experiences both free and freed blacks sought, and partly won, during Reconstruction, realization of freedom with civil and political equality.[10] That this experiment in race relations failed was due less to black faults than to white consensus on an answer to the question posed by the war: what was to be the role of black men in the United States? The white answer was: free, but not equal. To a generation of blacks which had fought and sacrificed for freedom *and* equality that answer was as unacceptable as it is to blacks today.

[10] Robert Cruden, *The Negro in Reconstruction* (Englewood Cliffs, N.J.: Prentice-Hall, Inc., 1969), Chaps. 3, 4, 7.

The Starving People of New Orleans Fed by The United States Military Authorities. *Harper's Weekly.* June 14, 1862.

CHAPTER VI

THE POOR MAN'S WAR

"It having been resolved to enlist with Uncle Sam for the war, this Union stands adjourned until the Union is safe or we are whipped." [1] This resolution of a Philadelphia labor union typified the response of organized labor to the events at Fort Sumter. Entire local unions enlisted en masse; in others so many members joined the army that the organizations were disbanded. Previously, the labor unions, weak though they were, had actively sought to avoid war by endorsing various compromise moves, principally the Crittenden proposals to extend the Missouri Compromise line to the California border, thus protecting slavery south of the line while assuring free territory to the north. Now that war had come, union leaders rallied their men to the larger Union. William H. Sylvis of the iron molders and

[1] Quoted in Philip S. Foner, *History of the Labor Movement in the United States: From Colonial Times to the Founding of the American Federation of Labor* (New York: International Publishers, 1947), p. 308.

Martin Boyle of the coal miners helped organize companies among their men, while others volunteered for active service.

What of the people who remained at home?

Their first problem was elemental: lack of jobs. The loss of more than $200 million owed Northern creditors by Southerners sent shock tremors throughout the entire business community, resulting in a wave of bankruptcies. The ending of both the supply of cheap raw cotton and the huge Southern market dismayed New England, with its heavy dependence on cotton textiles. Further, businessmen were worried on the one hand by the effects of the war on the economy, by uncertainty as to the financial policies of the new administration, and by possible British intervention, while on the other they shared the general optimism that the war would be short. Deciding to take no chances, they retrenched, and retrenchment meant unemployment so widespread as to cause suffering in every Northern city. By June, 1861, Phillips Brooks, later a famous clergyman, noted that in Philadelphia, "People are getting dreadfully poor." His words could have applied equally well to other cities.

By the summer of 1862 the doubts of businessmen were resolved. Administration policies were proving favorable, British intervention was less and less likely, the war was going to last a long time—and there was money in war orders. Now there was expansion, rather than retrenchment, and jobs became so plentiful in munitions factories, woolen mills, packing houses and other war-related industries that employers complained of labor shortages. But now wage earners and people on fixed incomes, such as teachers, office workers and government employees, confronted a new threat: inflation. A wartime scarcity of goods, federal tax levies on each step of the production of goods, an outpouring of paper money ("greenbacks") from Washington, a new protective tariff system which effectively curbed foreign competition, and unhindered profiteering drove up prices farther and faster than wages. A careful, conservative estimate of living costs indicates that between 1860 and 1864, when inflation was at its worst, consumer prices rose 76 percent. In the same period, daily wages rose only 42 percent; fixed incomes, of course, lagged behind even more.[2]

The resultant drop in living standards was mitigated to some degree by overtime work, the contributions of wives and children who went to work to supplement family income, and money sent home by soldiers. Even so, there was hardship. Coffee, sugar, and butter became so expensive that they

[2] Ethel Hoover, "Consumer Price Index, 1850–1880," in *The Economic Impact of the American Civil War*, ed. Ralph Andreano (Cambridge, Mass.: Schenkman Publishing Company, 1967), p. 222; for wage rates, see *Ibid.*, p. 220.

disappeared from the tables of many wage earners. Families economized to such an extent on food, clothing, and shoes that in September, 1864, a New York merchants' journal declared that lack of consumption had caused almost "a stagnation" in the trade of mass consumed staples. That same month a staunch Republican newspaper in industrialized Massachusetts reported "absolute want in many families while thousands of young children who should be at school are shut up at work that they may earn something to eke out the scant supplies at home." [3]

Another element in the economizing of the poor was their preparation for the inevitable return of hard times, when only their savings would guard them against utter destitution. Bank deposits in Eastern cities nearly tripled during the war, reflecting in some degree the multitude of accounts of less than $100. Jay Cooke pitched part of his war bond campaign toward workers, and sold an undetermined amount to machinists, shoemakers, clerks, cigarmakers and others of the working poor.

Most wage earners tried to scrape by as best they could, but a growing minority strove to protect living standards by forming unions, notably among skilled craftsmen and artisans. With some of these another motive was evident: through organization they hoped to stem the growth of mechanization of industry which came about in response to the mounting demands of the war—a growth which menaced not only the wages but also the jobs and social status of men trained in the earlier traditions of craftsmanship. Three national craft unions already existed among printers, iron molders, and machinists and blacksmiths (the last included both occupations). These now added to their own local unions and their veteran members helped other workers organize new local unions where no national union was yet established.

These unions were independent organizations, confined to one craft in one locality or shop. Their growth is indicated by a report in *Fincher's Trades' Review*, the leading labor journal of the day. In December, 1863, there were 79 local unions reported, covering 20 different occupations; a year later, there were 270, embracing 53 occupations. Nearly all excluded black workers. Women workers, often employed in the "needle trades" where wages rarely exceeded $3 a week, formed their own unions not only to improve wages but also to obtain shorter hours: New York newspapers reported that sewing girls in that city made from 17 cents to 24 cents a day for a 12-hour day—and had to supply their own thread!

A major element in the spread of unionism was its success. Often the mere threat of organization was sufficient to bring concessions from employers. Confronted with organization, the employer could hardly afford

---

[3] Springfield *Republican*, Sept. 6, 1864, quoted in James Ford Rhodes, *History of the United States from the Compromise of 1850* (New York: The Macmillan Company, 1904), V, 203.

to shut down his plant when business was booming and labor in short supply. Given the strategic advantage of labor and the widely publicized flaunting of their new found opulence by wartime profiteers, union demands sound modest. Early in 1864 New York longshoremen asked $2.50 for a nine-hour day, and building craftsmen also wanted $2.50 per day—usually for a ten-hour day. Such wage issues were in most cases resolved through bargaining, but increasingly employers balked and strikes were the result: the number of strikes rose from 38 in 1863 to 108 the following year. Strikes called to halt mechanization were rarely successful, in contrast with those arising from wage issues. Indeed, so auspicious were the times and so concerned was labor with probable postwar unemployment, that the unions mounted a campaign for the eight-hour day.

Labor's confidence in its new role was reflected in the growth of trades' assemblies in nearly every major industrial center, including New York, Boston, Pittsburgh, St. Louis, Chicago, and Philadelphia. Such assemblies provided mutual aid for local unions, but in addition they sponsored free libraries and reading rooms and cooperative stores to secure savings for union members. Some, as in Chicago and Boston, published newspapers of their own, usually as a result of printers' strikes. Such papers were generally ephemeral, but the *Boston Daily Evening Voice* spoke for New England labor for three years and the Chicago *Workingman's Advocate* represented western views for thirteen. The latter was edited by Andrew C. Cameron, one of the few leaders who openly advocated admission of black workers into unions.

But local unions and assemblies were vulnerable. During wartime labor scarcity they could make gains, inadequate though these might be in view of uncontrolled inflation—but how could these be maintained after the war, when the labor market would be swamped with returning soldiers, and unemployment rising from the end of war orders? Given the Northern railroad network, how could local unions in Philadelphia strike effectively when strikebreakers could be hired from as far away as Detroit or Chicago? Without national unions, how could labor influence policy in Washington or halt the rising tide of anti-union legislation in the states? Such considerations led to the formation of 13 national unions during the war years, including such diverse occupations as locomotive engineers, cigarmakers, coal miners, carpenters, and tailors.

During the war, then, organized labor developed a new national consciousness, as contrasted with the localism of previous union movements— and so great was the momentum that many new national unions continued to emerge in the postwar years. Further, unionism had sunk its roots so deeply into such basic industries as railroading, coal mining, iron and steel, and construction that while employer hostility and economic collapse (as in the 70s) might weaken organization, they could not destroy it. Conscious of their strength, union men displayed a new sense of confidence—a "feeling of manly independence," in the words of William H. Sylvis, the militant leader of the iron molders.

To employers, this was anathema. Long accustomed to dealing with labor as they saw fit, employers viewed the union movement as a threat to business and to the rights of property. Like Southern slaveowners, Northern employers viewed their workers as contented men corrupted by outside agitators, "uneasy spirits, pregnant with the leaven of discontent, and whose words, constantly dropping, are full of the seeds of trouble," according to the Employers General Association of Michigan in 1864. Unless agitation was curbed, said the association, "it must result in widespread beggary . . . suffering, bread riots, pillage, and taxation." [4]

To forestall such grievous consequences some employers refused to deal with unions at all, and when strikes resulted, they recruited strikebreakers from among blacks, recent immigrants, and women. Others used prison labor, available through the standard practice of renting out prisoners to private contractors at rates ranging from 30 cents a day in New Jersey to $1.16 in Massachusetts. In nearly all such cases the unions lost. Even among employers who dealt with unions there were many who refused to recognize them as the legitimate representatives of the workers. But employers soon found, as had labor, that individual efforts were inadequate to promote their interests, and they too organized, into craft, local and state associations, such as the Michigan organization already mentioned.

Through such bodies employers hoped to frustrate the unions' playing off one employer against another and to prevent individual employers from making arrangements with unions which would give them competitive advantage. Such bodies also helped enforce the "yellow dog" contracts, designed to keep active union men out of shops and factories by requiring workers to pledge that they were not and would not become union members. The associations also promoted the effectiveness of employers' blacklists of union activists. Such devices, however, were not sufficient to stop the burgeoning union movement in a time of labor scarcity, and so the associations turned to the state legislatures for aid. Proposals to penalize those responsible for strike activities failed in New York and Massachusetts, thanks to intense union opposition, but they were approved in Pennsylvania, Illinois, and Minnesota.

Other evidence of employer influence on government was apparent.

[4] Quoted in John B. Andrews, "Nationalisation (1860–1877)," in *History of Labour in the United States*, John R. Commons *et al.* (New York: The Macmillan Company, 1918), II, 27.

Active recruitment of black troops in the South was partially due to suggestions of New England businessmen that such a policy would relieve a labor shortage in their area resulting from too many workers being taken into the army. Also on pleas of labor shortages Congress passed a contract labor law in 1864 designed to enlarge the number of immigrants and an American Emigrant Company was speedily organized to take advantage of it. Offices were set up abroad to hire prospective workers, and others were established at home to attract employers, who paid a fee to the company for each worker delivered. The employer, however, had a built-in advantage: the law provided that he could charge off against the wages of the immigrant all costs of bringing him over, for a period of up to one year. This provided the employer with an incentive to pay as little as possible and authority to use the immigrant as he pleased—and often that proved to be as a strikebreaker. Although relatively few immigrants came as a result of the law, union men naturally looked upon it as a means to undermine wage standards and destroy the unions.

They resented even more the formidable alliance between employers and army commanders which developed in 1864. When munitions workers at a plant near West Point, N.Y., went on strike to raise wages to $1.50 a day troops were moved in, martial law declared, four of the leaders arrested and held without trial for seven weeks before they were released. Meanwhile, the strike collapsed. In New York City longshoremen on strike were replaced by soldiers for the loading of government vessels. Locomotive engineers, who had succeeded in halting operations of the Reading Railroad, were compelled to return to work when the army took over the line. A miners' strike in Pennsylvania also failed after military intervention.

In the West, some commanders went even further. General William Rosecrans, ruler of Missouri under martial law, not only broke strikes in St. Louis but also prohibited all organization of labor: "No association or combination shall be formed or continued, . . . having for its object to prescribe to the [business] proprietors . . . whom they shall employ, or how they shall conduct the operation thereof." [5] Another provision called for blacklisting of union activists. When some were arrested, unions were forbidden to demonstrate in protest. In Louisville, Kentucky, General Stephen Burbridge issued a similar order.

Despite such developments, union leaders did not waver in their support of the war or the Lincoln Administration. They were aware that the President had intervened in a strike in the navy yards on behalf of the workers, and that early in 1864 he had ordered General Rosecrans to withdraw soldiers from printing plants in St. Louis where they had replaced

[5] Leon Whipple, *The Story of Civil Liberty in the United States* (New York: Vanguard Press—American Civil Liberties Union, 1927), pp. 167–68.

strikers. Some visited the White House and returned with glowing accounts of the president's friendliness to labor. Nevertheless, the increasing use of troops against strikers put them in a quandary. On the one hand they could not ignore developments so destructive to the union cause. On the other, they had no desire to embarrass the administration nor to encourage the Copperhead peace propaganda making headway among some workers, exemplified in a resolution adopted by the Chicago Trades' Assembly calling for an end to a war in which workers' interests were sacrificed and their only role was to "bear its burdens and shed their blood in the ranks."

The response of the leaders was to denounce military intervention in purely civilian disputes, attributing it to "upstarts" who abused their authority. The remedy, they said, was to carry labor's grievances to the White House: on the basis of the record, if Lincoln knew of abuses, he would correct them. In the meantime, unions must not allow such occurrences, dangerous though they were, to diminish labor's support of the war. Many unions adopted resolutions similar to that of the 1864 convention of the Machinists and Blacksmiths: "Our rights and interests as workingmen, . . . and our duty to our country . . . require that we should use every means in our power to aid our government" in putting down "this most wicked and unnatural rebellion."

Such sentiments were not universally shared by workers—certainly not by men who worked at poorly paid, hazardous, and uncertain jobs, such as longshoremen and coal miners, men whose every effort to improve their lot was ruthlessly suppressed. Since many of them were Irish, there was an added depth to their feeling, for the Irish were victims of discrimination and segregation, looked down upon by a native public which regarded them as fit for its dirty and dangerous work but not acceptable in decent society. In short, they were the "niggers" of Northern society. But poor as the Irish were, there were people even poorer and even more victimized—black people—and when employers used blacks to break strikes of longshoremen the cup of Irish bitterness was filled to overflowing. American society was not only willing to let blacks take the jobs of white men—through police protection it encouraged them to do so. Nor were Democratic editors and politicians lacking to inflame white workers further with the prediction that Emancipation would aid the hated employers even more by opening up the North to a flood of cheap black labor which would drive white men out of jobs.

The manifold grievances of the Irish found expression in opposition to the draft, as did the grievances of many other poor men who were not Irish. To them it was an embodiment of class privilege, excusing the wealthy from military service if they paid a commutation fee of $300 each time they were called or cancelled the obligation once and for all by hiring substitutes, who received fees which went as high as $1500. (Those who could afford it, thought it a bargain. They furnished 118,000 substitutes and paid for 86,000 commutations.) Poor men who could never afford such fees saw themselves trapped into fighting a war for the sake of black men who would take white men's jobs when it was over, while white employers stayed safely at home. Their ire was not lessened when draft boards overlooked eligible native-born men and called up disproportionate numbers of Irish, German, and other foreign-born men.

The most sensational explosion of feeling occurred in New York City in July, 1863, just after the battle of Gettysburg. The city had long been a source of disaffection, nurtured by Tammany Hall, some newspapers, and merchants still grieving over the loss of their Southern connections. These helped set the stage, as did longshore employers who a month before had broken a longshoremen's strike by bringing in black replacements under police protection. Feeling was still running high when published draft calls showed that the poor and foreign-born were preferred to preserve the Union. Led by enraged longshoremen, mobs sacked draft offices, burned the Colored Orphans' Asylum, plundered homes of the wealthy, and murdered such blacks as they could lay their hands on. The police proved unable to deal with the three-day violence. It was quelled only when confrontations of mobs with troops dispatched from Gettysburg resulted in great loss of life. Lesser riots ensued in Boston, Newark, and elsewhere.

The riots were dramatic, sending waves of apprehension throughout the North, but perhaps more significant was the prolonged resistance to the draft itself. Potential draftees were not required to register, as they are now. The job of locating them was in the hands of enrolling officers, who went literally from house to house to get the necessary information. It proved to be an almost insuperable task in urban slums and mining towns: wives, mothers, children, and the men themselves proved adept in furnishing false or misleading information. The enrolling officers then resorted to payroll lists of employers, confirming the poor in the belief that government and employers were leagued against them. Feeling rose to such a pitch that in some cases the officers were beaten or killed, while more frequently the officers' business places were sabotaged or burned. Many resigned rather than take the risks involved.

Of course, in one way or another the government obtained draft lists— but when it tried to draft men it encountered evasion or outright resistance. More than 160,000 drafted men slipped away before induction, bound for Canada, the Far West, and the South. Resistance flared up in many areas, most notably in the coal regions of Pennsylvania, Indiana, and Illinois, long characterized by violent class war. On the one side were the operators, many of them small, engaged in a ruthless competitive struggle in a chaotic industry; and in Pennsylvania, they confronted the superior power of railroad companies which owned coal mines and did not hesitate to use that power to crush small scale competitors. On the other side were the miners, living in isolated mining towns, bound together by ties of family, nationality, and religion. They struggled not only to raise wages but also to correct such conditions as unsafe mines, company housing, and company stores which exacted high rents and high prices. Such gains as the miners made were won only after violent outbreaks. During the war concessions on wages were far from catching up with rising prices.

In this atmosphere of mutual hostility came the draft, and miners were quick to see in it a measure to destroy their unions, a suspicion little allayed when company officials were often chosen to enforce the law. And indeed, operators did look upon it as a means of reasserting their control. In calling for federal troops to put down opposition in Pennsylvania, coal operators said such a move would correct the "state of lawlessness . . . which has made the name of miner a terror to all law-abiding citizens." In their turn, miners organized into armed bands, their ranks strengthened by returned war veterans. These bands provided havens for Union deserters and successfully disrupted draft operations. Only when overwhelmed by superior military force were they suppressed. A somewhat similar resistance took place in the marble quarry regions of Vermont.

At the time it was the fashion to blame the outbreaks on the Irish, who were believed to be by nature turbulent, lawless, and violent; or upon the pro-Confederate underground organizations which actively promoted draft resistance. Few pointed out that the miners challenged the government not from disloyalty but out of desperation—desperation because there seemed to be no other way of registering their protest against a system which ignored basic human needs. Without real grievances to feed on, the subversive propaganda of the Knights of the Golden Circle and similar organizations would have had little influence. In the successful labor unions, Irish workers proved as loyal and responsible as others. Further, let us note that bitter class conflict persisted in the coal fields well into the present century, regardless of whether the miners were Irish, Polish, Hungarian, Italian or native-born American.

The basic problem of the Southern poor, like that of their Yankee counterparts, was inflation. But if inflation brought hardship to Northerners, it proved disastrous to the poor in the South. Reluctant to impose the heavy taxation needed to finance the war, the Confederate government relied largely on paper money. Together with an increased issue of private bank notes, this resulted in a stock of money by January, 1864, 1100 percent greater than in January, 1861, according to a careful analysis made by Eugene Lerner. Professor Lerner also notes that the situation was made even worse by the rapid circulation of currency within the Confederacy and by a decline in the output of goods and services.[6] The government tried to halt the inflationary spiral in February, 1864, but it did so in such a way as to penalize the poor. Holders of currency in excess of $100 were required to turn it in in exchange for its equivalent in interest-bearing bonds. The poor, who possessed few $100 bills, had to turn in such bills as they had at the rate of three old dollars for two of the new. In short, one-third of their cash was in effect confiscated. To be sure, the measure slowed inflation for a time, and thus benefitted the poor to some degree, but soon the upward spiral of prices resumed.

The result was that by the end of the war the cost of living in the Confederacy had gone up 30 times, while money wages increased only 10 times. In short, real wages—the amount of goods and services which can be purchased in money wages—fell two-thirds below the prewar level, according to Lerner's calculations.[7] As in the North, the fall in living standards was modified by overtime earnings and by wives and children going to work in offices, mills, and factories. In the South, moreover, some workers got part of their wages in kind—in cloth or flour, for example—which helped stretch their money wages. The Tredegar Iron Works in Richmond, which possessed its own mines and packing houses, sold food and fuel to its employees at prices below the going market rate. Other workers supplemented their wages by working plots of land for food. As against this, workers found it increasingly difficult to use their money, for as the war went on merchants were more and more reluctant to accept Confederate currency. Those who did marked up their prices accordingly.

As inflation mounted, so did destitution. By December, 1862, the governor of Mississippi found that high prices were "putting the means of living beyond the reach of many of our poor citizens." Half the population of New Orleans, it was reported, were hungry. John B. Jones, the "rebel war clerk" in Richmond, whose diary has become famous, noted in January, 1863, . . . "none but the opulent . . . can obtain a sufficiency of food and raiment." [8] Most eloquent were the letters flowing from the countryside to soldiers at the front, telling of want at home. One such tells its own tale:

[6] Eugene M. Lerner, "Money, Prices and Wages in the Confederacy, 1861–1865," in *The Economic Impact of the American Civil War*, ed. Ralph Andreano, pp. 31–32.
[7] In Andreano, *Economic Impact of the American Civil War*, p. 45.
[8] John B. Jones, *A Rebel War Clerk's Diary*, ed. Earl Schenck Miers (New York: Sagamore Press, Inc., Publishers, 1958), p. 152. Jones, a noted author and editor in pre-war days, returned South from New Jersey as war broke out. Almost immediately he was appointed chief clerk in the Confederate War Department and served in that capacity until the end of the war. His diary was first published in 1866, the year he died.

"Last night, I was aroused by little Eddie's crying. I called and said, 'What is the matter, Eddie?' and he said, 'O mamma! I am so hungry.' And Lucy, Edward, your darling Lucy; she never complains, but she is growing thinner and thinner every day. And before God, Edward, unless you come home, we must die." [9]

Of course, steps were taken to alleviate distress. Private charities doled out meagre supplies of food, with special attention to families of soldiers. Some cities temporarily provided meat and bread for their hungry at "fair" prices. States and the Confederate government experimented unsuccessfully with price controls, while joining in the chorus of denunciation of profiteers who, by hoarding available food and clothing for sale on a rising market, proved themselves "even worse than the Yankees."

Such measures dealt with the symptoms, not the causes, of distress, and so provided little relief for the poor, except to provide them with a visible enemy—the profiteer. As conditions became worse unrest mounted, especially in the cities, where people were almost entirely dependent on their wages. Besides, in the cities the poor could daily contrast their wretchedness with the luxurious living of those making money out of the war, could see shops plentifully supplied, not only with food and clothing but also with silks and wines imported through the blockade. The underground rumblings of discontent erupted into action early in 1863—and significantly, in view of the planter tradition of passive white womanhood, the leadership was taken by women.

During March, groups of poor women in Salisbury, North Carolina, Atlanta, Mobile, and other cities raided stores and appropriated food and other supplies. One of the slogans in Mobile was ominous: "Bread or Peace." A few weeks later the Confederate capital was itself rocked by a major riot. Several hundred women, joined later by men, marched into Richmond's business district, sacked stores, and helped themselves to food, shoes, clothing, millinery, and jewelry. The governor threatened to have troops fire on the mob, but a plea by Jefferson Davis persuaded the women to return home—carrying with them the valuables looted from the stores. The temper of the people was such, noted Jones, that if the governor had carried out his threat, "he would have been hung, no doubt." [10] The following day another women's demonstration for bread was broken up by the city guard, and two battalions of Confederate troops were ordered into the city to put down further anticipated demonstrations, while censorship was employed to prevent the news from leaking to the North. Leaders of the women were arrested and jailed. Nevertheless, women in the countryside followed suit—but in a different way. They organized in small, armed bands

[9] Quoted in Ella Lonn, *Desertion During the Civil War* (Gloucester, Mass.: Peter Smith, 1966), p. 13.

[10] Jones, *Rebel War Clerk's Diary*, ed. Earl Schenck Miers, p. 184.

which raided mills and country stores, took flour, corn, cloth, and thread—and disappeared. Authorities attributed the outbreaks, not to hunger, but to undercover Union agents and to foreigners!

Men's responses to the crisis in living standards were more orderly—although that made them no less reprehensible to Confederate authorities. Men usually resorted to strike action to get higher wages, hoping to take advantage of the labor shortage, and building on the experience of the few unions established in the South before the war. Even so, they could make only limited gains, for as the war went on the labor market was flooded with cheap slave labor, skilled and unskilled, rented out by planters who had comparatively little use for slaves so long as cotton production was curtailed. In effect, black slave labor set the limits on wages beyond which free white labor could not go. The Confederate government was there to enforce the limits and since the draft law of 1862, it had little hesitation in sending strikers into the army.

Early in the war, strikes for higher wages were generally successful, as at the great Confederate arsenal, the Tredegar Iron Works, and at shipyards in New Orleans—outcomes which pleased neither employers nor Confederate authorities. When workers struck in 1862, they found both aligned against them. Railroad machinists in Virginia were drafted; lithographers ended up in a military prison; Richmond printers were indicted for conspiracy. Two years later telegraphers in Georgia who went on strike were speedily drafted. Women strikers in a government drug factory were fired and their places taken by strikebreakers. Postal workers who threatened to strike fared a little better: sufficient concessions were made to keep them at work. But by that time the Confederate government had a more potent weapon to keep labor in line: the new draft law of February, 1864, which abolished all exemptions hitherto granted industrial workers and put them under the technical control of the government as effectively as if they were formally in the army.

Neither strikes nor riots brought improvement in the lot of the poor. Indeed, their condition became even worse as Union armies extended their zones of occupation, for people in threatened areas poured their currency into the still safe regions, providing still another stimulus to higher prices at the same time that food and other supplies became scarcer. In February, 1864, Governor Joseph E. Brown of Georgia found that in many parts of his state "the prospects of suffering for bread are alarming," while later the governor of Virginia warned that many citizens were "in danger of absolute starvation." The urban poor were the more embittered because all around them still were the signs of good living among merchants and speculators, who seemed to thrive despite the laws passed to curb them.

Rural poverty can only be described as grim. The draft swept the countryside clean of young able-bodied men, so that the work on family farms was done by old people, children, and women—few of whom could handle the heavy work necessary to produce good crops. Further, as tools and implements wore out they could not be replaced. What food was produced was subject to the 10 percent Confederate tax in kind; and food was also subject to impressment by the Confederate army at prices far below those on the open market. Farms run by women were fair prey for marauding soldiers, Confederate and Union alike. The poor were the more resentful when they discovered that precious food taken from them by impressment officers turned up on the civilian market—another instance of corruption in the army's commissary department which the Confederate Congress had sought to curb in 1863, without much success.

The alienation of the poor was intensified by the draft. The ability of the wealthy to evade military service through the hiring of substitutes was ended late in 1863—but somehow the wealthy found positions in state and Confederate governments in which they were immune to the draft at the very moment conscription authorities were rounding up small farmers and laborers. And, at the time the exemption of industrial workers was abolished, the exemption of planters and overseers was lowered from those having 20 or more slaves to those having as few as 15. It was said the step was necessary to insure white control of blacks on plantations, but poor men looked upon it as another example of class privilege. The War Department clerk, John B. Jones, who was thinking more and more like a poor man because of the stringencies his own family was experiencing, put the poor man's view succinctly in 1864 when he wrote: "the *higher* class is staying home and making money, the *lower* class is thrust into the trenches."

There were no great draft riots as in the North, but resistance was widespread in the areas peopled by the poor—the isolated regions of Florida, Mississippi, Arkansas, and the hill and mountain country of what we now call Appalachia, running from Virginia to Alabama. Many of them had been unenthusiastic about secession in the first place, and they now saw little reason why breadwinners should risk their lives in a planters' war. Conscripts returned home and worked their farms, enjoying the approval of relatives and neighbors who would provide aid, refuge, and protection should officials try to pick them up.

In some places they were so numerous that they organized their own armed bands with their own constitutions—one such band in Florida required members to swear allegiance to the United States! When food and clothing ran short, these guerrillas invaded nearby towns and replenished their supplies or raided farms of loyal Confederates for cattle and provisions. Such men, who were concerned primarily with their own families' welfare, are to be distinguished from other groups of deserters who preyed on the wealthy, not so much for necessities as for money, jewels, and other valuables. The victims, of course, could hardly be expected to note a difference, and their appeals for help resounded throughout the Confederacy. A report from southern Mississippi was typical: unless speedy aid were forthcoming, it said, "every loyal citizen will be driven from [the area]."

In response to the clamor of "loyal citizens" and to the pressing need for military manpower, authorities moved to round up conscripts and deserters. In the guerrilla warfare which resulted, the efforts of the Confederate Conscript Bureau and of state troops met with little success. The homes and business places of enrolling officers were burned, while those who ventured into the countryside were frequently ambushed, beaten, or killed. Naturally, many found it expedient to stay in town and content themselves with paper work. State troops, often made up of boys and old men, were no match for experienced veterans. If a deserter were arrested, he was often freed by mobs, and if any of them were arrested it was almost impossible to obtain convictions. Indeed, so many local officials sympathized with resistance that General John S. Preston, head of the Conscript Bureau charged, with some exaggeration, early in 1864 that "from one end of the Confederacy to the other every constituted authority, every officer, every man, and woman was engaged in opposing the enrolling officer." [11]

The Confederate army then took over. Large expeditions swept through hills, mountains, and swamps, the troops encouraged by promises of furloughs. Conscripts and deserters offered little resistance—in part because some commanders terrorized women and children into urging the men to surrender. In this way, thousands of men were returned to the army—some of them to face death under a new policy of executions to discourage desertion. This did little to improve morale in the army: soldiers still deserted, but now to the Union army. Nor was morale among the civilian poor strengthened. They bitterly resented the taking of their men and the behavior of the troops among them. Even more were they aroused by the terrorism resorted to by some officers when their deserter quarries proved elusive. On grounds that they sheltered fugitives, communities in Florida were burned and their inhabitants confined to a refugee camp—a step which prompted the governor to protest against "warfare upon women and children." In Virginia, homes of "disloyal" families were destroyed and the families themselves deported beyond the Confederate lines.

The actions of the government, together with realization that the war was being lost and a feeling that defeat of the planters would bring a better day for the poor, inspired the organization of secret peace movements such as the Heroes of America, and those included under the umbrella name of the Peace Society. Such organizations were present in the army, as we have noted, but among civilians they were much more widespread. They

---

[11] Walter L. Fleming, *Civil War and Reconstruction in Alabama* (New York: Columbia University Press, 1905), p. 105.

operated in the East from Virginia to Florida and as far west as Arkansas. Some functioned in true underground fashion: members knew each other only by secret signals; they received instructions from men who in turn knew only a few members; and these men were known only to a few trustworthy leaders. In this way, the organizations were relatively immune to penetration by informers; numerous arrests were made, but the societies were rarely crushed.

Peace movements, of course, were not confined to the poor. More "respectable" people in the South were also urging peace, hoping to avert disaster by obtaining a negotiated peace. The societies of farmers and mechanics, however, sought immediate peace on the basis of the need for restoration of the Union, including Emancipation. Considering themselves loyal Union men, they worked to disrupt the Confederate war effort, encouraging and protecting deserters, capitalizing on the grievances of the poor, supplying intelligence to the enemy, and using politics to promote their main objectives. In the last, the sheer numbers of the poor counted. In Alabama in 1863, the peace movements, with the support of deserters and paroled soldiers, helped elect some of their candidates to the state legislature and the Confederate Congress. A year later in North Carolina they provided such strong support to William W. Holden, a member of the Heroes of America, that only a desperate effort by Governor Vance kept Holden out of the governor's chair.

The Confederate government sought to suppress the societies by the use of informers; by requiring all travellers to carry passports and assigning a small army of military police to enforce the requirement; and by suspending temporarily for a third time, the writ of habeas corpus, thus permitting the arrest of suspected persons and confinement of them without trial. In asking for the suspension Davis noted that the country was menaced by "secret leagues and associations," the members of which remained at large because judges paid "too strict regard to the technicalities of the law." Such efforts proved futile. Disillusionment with the planter government, resentment at its impositions, and a feeling that all the sacrifices of the poor had been in vain—such sentiments ran too deep for even an efficient government to handle, and as we have seen, the Confederate government was far from efficient. It is noteworthy that when poorer whites gained political power under Congressional Reconstruction, they were far more hostile in their treatment of the planters than either Yankees or blacks. They were determined that never again would planters be in a position to oppress the poor; they failed to see that in the South as in the North a new order of oppression was in the making.

Plunger

Plunger and Cap

Outside of Shell before filling or covering

Section of Shell

Shell and Solid Shot

Section of Projectile, showing insertion of Lead.

Filling & Finishing Projectiles

The Union Shell

Pouring in the Lead

Shells and Their Manufacture.
Harper's Weekly. November 30, 1861.

CHAPTER VII

THE BUSINESSMAN'S WAR

"War must have money as well as men, and the former the rich have to furnish; and if they do this, it is but fair that they should be allowed to furnish . . . also the men to do their fighting. Besides, there must be some rule that would exempt the men that carry on the business of the country." [1] This postwar rationale for the hiring of substitutes to do the fighting for the wealthy also emphasizes the businessman's attitudes toward the war: he had more important things to do than carry a gun. Thus, of the young men who were to become the titans of nineteenth-century business— John D. Rockefeller, Andrew Carnegie, Philip D. Armour, J. P. Morgan, and others—none saw military service. Generally, the business community otherwise supported the war, contributing generously to the funds of the United States Sanitary Commission, to the relief of soldiers' families, and even, in the case of Cornelius Vanderbilt, to giving a ship to the Navy.

There were some, however, whose enthusiasm was noticeably restrained. Cyrus and William McCormick, the reaper magnates of Chicago, native Virginians, objected to the "coercion" of the South and worked for a negotiated peace. Erastus Corning, President of the New York Central Railroad, cooperated with the obstructionist policy of New York Governor

[1] Quoted in Shannon, *Organization . . . of the Union Army*, II, 23.

Horatio Seymour. In Ohio, Daniel Rhodes, coal merchant and railroad promoter, and father of the future historian, James Ford Rhodes, backed for
governor the exiled Copperhead, Clement L. Vallandigham.

Initially, as we have seen, the war was anything but a boon to business. The wiping out of Southern debts brought disaster to many merchants, as did the collapse of scores of western banks whose reserves were
based on Southern state securities. The uncertainties of business were reflected in sharp drops in activity. Production of pig iron slumped from
920,000 tons in 1860 to 732,000 tons in 1861; coal output also fell off,
though not to the same degree. Railroad building declined precipitously:
1500 miles of new track were laid in 1860; only 720 in 1861. Cotton textile
production dropped steadily during the war; in 1860 it consumed 845,000
bales; in 1864, only 220,000.

But the basis for rapid expansion was already there. As W. W. Rostow
has pointed out, the Northern economy by 1860 had reached its "take off"
point—it possessed all the potential for an ever-mounting per capita output
of goods and services.[2] Two basic obstacles had hindered full exploitation
of the potential: domination of the national government by Southern interests generally unfriendly to Northern industry, and lack of adequate
capital. The war overcame both. The exodus of Southerners from Washington left Republicans in control, and once it became certain that the war
would be prolonged, the federal government pumped into the economy
$3.2 billion in paper promises to pay (bonds and greenbacks) which fur-
nished ground for still further expansion of credit. In addition, Washington sopped up $360 million in new taxes which speedily found their way
into business channels. Out of this horn of plenty poured a flood of war
contracts, amounting eventually to at least a billion dollars. Payments to
soldiers and sailors for wages and bounties totaled even more.

Few businessmen could resist the temptations thus offered. The exigencies of the government were so great and, in the early stages, its procure-
ment methods so slipshod, that it was easy to swindle the government and
ultimately, the troops. As we have seen, soldiers were supplied with uniforms and blankets that came apart in the rain and with shoes that lasted
less than a week. Inferior meat found a ready market, as did obsolete and
useless weapons. Men who did an ostensibly honest business were found
to have given short weight and adulterated their products. Others simply
overcharged. Rifles were produced for $9 each at government arsenals, but
in order to meet its requirements the army also had to purchase similar

    [2] W. W. Rostow, *Stages of Economic Growth* (Cambridge, England: Cambridge
University Press, 1960), p. 95.

guns from private sources at $20 each. Colt revolvers which had sold on the civilian market for $14.50 cost the government $25. The scope of such practices is indicated by the success of a special investigating commission which in 1862 persuaded contractors with claims of $50 million to scale them down by $17 million.

Naturally, many more sought entrance to this commercial heaven than could be accommodated. Thus there emerged a swarm of "influence ped-dlers"—men who, for a fee usually amounting to five percent of a contract's worth, used their connections in government to get clients what they wanted. One notorious case involved an unidentified U.S. Senator who got $10,000 for helping get a businessman a lucrative contract. Those who failed to win favor in government were not ignored, however. Frequently initial contractors had few assets other than their Washington connections. By subletting their contracts to legitimate manufacturers such men made quick profits without putting up a penny of their own money. In that way one gunmaker who was unable to crash the golden gates on his own even-tually landed an order for 200,000 guns—and presumably made his own profit on the deal. Some operating firms enjoying government business simply made a faster buck by turning over all or some of their contracts to unsuccessful competitors—at a price. For instance, in one typical case, a major contractor got an order to deliver beef at 8 cents a pound; the firm then farmed out the work to another company at 6½ cents a pound. This procedure netted the original firm profit of more than $32,000—at govern-ment expense. Corruption was so pervasive that a committee of the House of Representatives spent nearly a year investigating it. As a result of the committee's efforts, and those of Edwin M. Stanton after he became Secretary of War early in 1862, knavery in the business of government was drastically reduced, but it was never entirely eliminated. In the meantime a great many men got rich and sought new ways to add to their wealth.

One such was the illicit trade carried on with the enemy. The need for cotton was so pressing that the Union government in 1862 established a regulated trade in areas occupied by the Union armies, designed to get cotton while keeping war supplies from reaching the Confederates. Army officers were specifically banned from engaging in the trade. But beyond the Union lines were Confederates willing to trade cotton for drugs, guns, ammunition, salt, and other necessities, and back in New England was an insatiable market which by the summer of 1864 was paying $1.90 a pound for cotton which cost less than 30 cents in the South. So sprang up a "bootleg" trade which soon transformed Union-held towns like New Orleans and Memphis into thriving marts through which cotton flowed north and war supplies entered the Confederacy.

The "protection" required to carry on such a great illegal trade was furnished by corrupt army officers and Treasury agents, who not only were paid off by merchants but also engaged in the traffic themselves. Charles A. Dana, special investigator for the War Department, reported with some exaggeration from Memphis early in 1863: "The mania for sudden fortunes made in cotton . . . has to an alarming extent corrupted and demoralized the army. Every colonel, captain or quartermaster is in secret partnership with some operator in cotton; . . . Besides, the resources of the rebels are inordinately increased from this source." Commanders, including Grant and Sherman, called for complete suppression of the trade, but Congress and the administration agreed only on new legislation in 1864 aimed at eliminating both the illegal traffic and corruption in the legal trade.

Another source of easy money was speculation in nearly every essential commodity—wool, wheat, corn, cotton, and oil—as well as in gold and the stock market. There were risks in such enterprise, of course, given a currency which fluctuated widely as the Union's fortunes varied, but there were few in the hoarding of goods subjected to raises in federal taxation, such as cigars, matches, and whiskey. When it became known that Congress would consider such raises, businessmen built up huge inventories of the goods at prevailing prices and sold when prices rose to include the new taxes. Men holding existing stocks thus in effect pocketed the taxes—in whiskey alone, it was said, they netted $100,000,000. It was widely charged at the time that the failure of Congress to impose new taxes on existing stocks was due to corruption.

Investors in more legitimate forms of business also did well. Railroads which had never paid a dividend cleared their debts and went on to pay dividends of 8 percent or more, while firmly established roads such as the Pennsylvania and the Burlington did even better. Stock prices reflected both the profits made and the manipulations of corporation "insiders": Michigan Central stock, worth less than $40 in 1860, cost $150 a share four years later; Reading Railroad stock increased five times in value, while Erie jumped from $17 to $126! The American Express Company, owned by railroads, made so much money that it disbursed not only generous dividends in cash but also in stock. The woolen industry, working night and day to fill war orders, was a bonanza. For the industry as a whole dividends nearly tripled prewar levels, and some individual firms exceeded that gain. One company paid out to stockholders during the war $500,000 more than its entire capital investment of $2,500,000. Even the ailing cotton industry paid off well when it turned to producing finer cloth. Providence, Rhode Island, a center of such activity, reported that cotton profits had never been better. So high were the returns on cotton thread, hitherto monopolized by English firms, that Yankees began their own production.

From this bounty came the conspicuous consumption which so angered the poor and dismayed the more genteel well-to-do. People with more money than they had ever dreamed of sported diamonds and pearls on the street, drove in magnificent carriages behind pedigreed horses, gambled lavishly at the new race tracks built to attract them, patronized luxurious restaurants, and, with an eye to "culture," attended the theater and opera now offered in every large Northern city. Of all this the aging William Cullen Bryant wrote: "Extravagance, luxury, these are the signs of the times; . . . What business have Americans at any time with such vain show, with such useless magnificence? But especially how can they justify it . . . in this time of war?" [3] Men on the make were too busy to heed such questionings, but some shared Bryant's repugnance toward "vain show." The Carnegies, Rockefellers, and Morgans had other uses for their money.

Such young men were appalled at the chaos, waste and inefficiency which they found in business, and they saw in their wealth leverage to bring about a new order of efficiency in which competition would be curtailed, production stabilized, prices controlled, and high returns assured. Thanks in part to their war profits Rockefeller, Carnegie, and Morgan were able to take the first step toward the goals which they attained later in the century. Rockefeller made his initial moves for consolidation in oil refining and by 1870 the first Standard Oil Company was created. Carnegie expanded his iron holdings, partly from the proceeds of successful speculation in oil. Morgan began to eye the possibilities of banking control of industry.

In a sense, they were in harmony with as well as ahead of their times, for the war accelerated the process of concentration in many areas of business. Western Union, gobbling up small lines and taking over competitors, was well on the way to establishing its lucrative telegraph monopoly. Major railroads absorbed lesser roads so they could control trunk line service between urban markets. The railroads serving the anthracite regions of eastern Pennsylvania taught a lesson on how monopoly in one field could be used to extend it in another. Each of the roads operating in the coal fields had exclusive rail rights in its area, and so was able to jack up freight rates 300 percent while rail competition elsewhere was strong enough to hold rates down. But the anthracite roads went further: the higher rates were applied only to shipments from independent operators; coal from the railroads' own mines moved at cost. This gave the railroad mines a decided edge in the flourishing coal market—and they enlarged it by frequently refusing to haul the coal of the independents. In the process many of the smaller operators had little alternative save to sell out to the railroads.

---

[3] E. D. Fite, *Social and Industrial Conditions in the North During the Civil War* (New York: The Macmillan Company, 1910), pp. 273–74.

In manufacturing the process was not so pronounced, but it was noticeable. Shoemaking, a bastion of the independent artisan, was transformed by the war into a stronghold of the factory system, dominated by men who could afford to pay royalties on the McKay sewing machine and provide the steam power to use it most profitably. During the depression in cotton textiles weaker firms closed down. The small manufacturer also found it increasingly difficult to get war orders. Although the army tried to distribute contracts widely it found the problems of dealing with a multitude of suppliers so great that it gradually confined its orders to major producers. Taxation policies also hurt the small businessman. Excise taxes were levied at each stage of manufacture. Thus, a product which went through three firms before completion bore a burden of three taxes, whereas the same product made in one factory was taxed only once. Enjoying this advantage big firms not only outbid small ones for government contracts but also outpriced them in the civilian market. Bankers, of course, took note of this, and thus credit, the life blood of business, was more expensive for small enterprise than for large ones.

To protect themselves, independent producers banded together in price-fixing arrangements. Paper makers nationally, plow makers in Illinois, twine manufacturers in New York, and ice producers in Chicago resorted to such devices, as did local organizations of milk dealers and tavern keepers. On a larger scale, national associations of manufacturers and other businessmen were formed to influence national policy on tariff and taxes as well as to fight labor unions. As E. D. Fite observed, "Combination in every line was the tendency of the hour." [4]

There were, of course, men of wealth who felt it essential to demonstrate concern for the war effort and the larger public good. A. T. Stewart, a New York dry goods merchant who reported an income of more than a million dollars a year and was much criticized for the low wages paid his shop girls, gave $100,000 to the United States Sanitary Commission. This was matched by Cornelius Vanderbilt, also making more than a million dollars a year as a railroad promoter, part of which, said critics, came from dubious contracts with the federal government. Ezra Cornell, a founder of Western Union and its largest stockholder, donated land and an endowment to start the university which bears his name. Matthew Vassar, a prosperous brewer, not only supplied the funds to initiate the first permanent college exclusively for women but also helped to make the idea eminently respectable. Long established schools such as Harvard, Yale, Brown, and Amherst shared in the munificence flowing from war prosperity, as did many hospitals and charitable organizations.

[4] Fite, *Social and Industrial Conditions . . . During the Civil War*, p. 169.

To what extent did all the activity of the war years contribute to long-range economic growth? The answer is a matter of dispute among historians. For long it was held that the war stimulated the growth of large-scale industrialism and so provided the basis for the business expansion which took place later in the century. More recently some students have claimed that the war reduced the rate of economic growth and it has been suggested that the war actually retarded development.[5] Obviously, the diversion of manpower to the army when manpower as such was much more important than it is today served to limit growth, although it was balanced in some degree by enhanced employment of women and children and increased mechanization. And the evidence is clear that some industries suffered. Cotton mills, as we have seen, lacked sufficient raw material. Shoe production actually declined because the market for cheap shoes dropped: Southerners no longer bought them for slaves, and the Northern poor made do with fewer replacements. Railroad construction went down, as did residential building. And, as the war neared its end, canny businessmen postponed investment in plant and equipment, figuring that an end to war inflation would bring lower prices and interest rates.

On the other hand, evidence is equally clear that in some fields the war years witnessed decided increases in output. Coal, a barometer of the times, since it played a fundamental role in the production of iron and of steam, the basic power resource of the day, is an example. Between 1860 and 1865 bituminous (soft) coal output rose 36 percent, while anthracite (hard) increased 10 percent. In 1860 pig iron production was 920,000 tons; in 1864 it reached 1,136,000 tons—an increase of 23 percent—before it fell again in 1865. Despite the low level of railroad building output of rails mounted from 183,000 tons in 1860 to 299,000 tons in 1864. The boom in woolens saw the mills consume 200 million pounds of raw wool a year before the war ended, compared to 85 million pounds in 1860.

Other lines of business shared in the general stimulation. Canning of milk, fruits, and vegetables, an industry just in its infancy, flourished in the nutrients of war orders. The ready-made clothing industry expanded to provide uniforms. Shipbuilders dismayed by the disappearance of the American merchant marine (thanks largely to Confederate depredations which led to the transfer of ships to foreign registry) found ample recompense in Navy orders as well as those of foreign governments seeking the new ironclad warships. Pipe lines were built linking oil fields with railroad connections, and the first oil tankers sailed from Philadelphia.

Other developments were equally significant for the future: A uniform

[5] The basic statement was by Thomas C. Cochran, "Did the Civil War Retard Industrialization?" (1961). It was further developed by Stanley L. Engerman, "The Economic Impact of the Civil War" (1966). Both essays are conveniently included in ed. Andreano, *The Economic Impact of the American Civil War*, pp. 167–79, 198–209.

railroad track gauge was established, preparing the way for coast-to-coast railroad traffic without delays caused by differing widths of track. Iron makers, in order to comply with army requirements, produced iron of better and more uniform quality, and learned how to handle it in large quantities while at the same time machining it to closer tolerances than ever before. Marine engineers produced engines capable of speeds far above those of any ships in existence. At Wyandotte, Michigan, in 1864, experiments in the production of inexpensive steel proved successful, ushering in a new day for American industry.

While businessmen exploited the opportunities offered by the war they also took advantage of the situation to shape national policy to promote both their immediate and long-range interests. Naturally, not all enterprisers saw eye to eye on what those interests were, but the politicians of the Republican Party with whom they collaborated were able to contain and reconcile the divisions. As a result, business obtained legislation which not only shifted the economic burden of the war to wage and salary earners and other consumers but also conditioned the nation's economic development for generations to come.

The tariff is a case in point. As of 1860 Northern business was divided on the issue. The highly efficient cotton textile industry now felt able to compete on foreign markets and was interested in getting cheap Canadian coal to power its mills; coal mine operators wanted foreign coal shut out. Railroad promoters thought inexpensive foreign rails desirable; Pennsylvania iron makers found them most undesirable. The Southern defections from Congress provided the high tariff advocates an opening, and even before the Fort Sumter episode the Republican-dominated Congress had sharply increased import taxes while adding such mass-consumed staples as coffee and tea to the taxable list. In 1862 protectionists resumed their campaign, this time pleading the need for war revenues and for protection of home industries said to be at a disadvantage because of excise taxes recently levied by Congress. Higher tariffs resulted, again and again, until by the end of the war average rates were 47 percent above the prewar scale —and some went as high as 100 percent. Duties on salt were so high as to halt imports—whereupon a leading New York producer doubled its prices!

If the tariff penalized consumers, so also did the government's war finance policy, which, like its other policies, was largely a series of pragmatic responses to problems as they arose. The depression of 1861 resulted in such a withdrawal of gold by depositors that New York banks suspended specie payments in December, and the government immediately followed suit. This left the country with a stock of money inadequate for normal business, far less that of war. Congress then took the unprecedented step of authorizing issue of paper money as legal tender (legally payable for debts) with no backing save the credit of the federal government. Before the war was over $450 million of greenbacks were issued. Their value in terms of gold fluctuated widely, reflecting Union military success or failure —in the summer of 1864 a greenback dollar was worth only 35 cents in gold! Since tariffs had to be paid in gold this resulted in an even sharper price rise of imported goods than tariff schedules indicated—a development pleasing to manufacturers.

Depreciation of greenbacks offered benefits of another kind to investors. Until the summer of 1863 greenbacks were accepted at face value for purchase of United States gold bonds. Thus, when greenbacks were worth 60 cents in gold, an investor could buy a thousand dollar bond for paper money worth only $600 in gold. He would eventually receive in payment $1,000 in gold while in the meantime he received six percent interest in gold. And in 1864 each gold dollar he got in interest brought anywhere from $1.51 to $2.85 in greenbacks!

Greenbacks, however, played a minor role compared to that of borrowing: in 1865 the interest-bearing debt stood at $2.2 billion, compared to a gross debt of nearly $65 million in 1860. Getting the money, however, proved difficult, despite the urgent necessities of the government. Financiers found little attractive in long-term bonds at five or six percent interest when returns were so much higher in the private sector. A bond issue of 1862 sold slowly until depreciation of greenbacks made their conversion into bonds profitable, but even then the purchases were made largely by farmers, workers, soldiers, and shopkeepers reached by Jay Cooke's aggressive sales campaign, which used every gimmick of the day to develop a mass market. Successive issues sold poorly until near the end of the war, when the prospects of victory, doubts about the postwar economy, and an interest rate of 7.3 percent combined to stimulate flow of funds to the Treasury. In the meantime the government paid its bills by borrowing on short-term notes, which the banks used to expand credit, thus contributing to the inflationary spiral.

Eventually, the government sought to spur block buying of bonds by inducing bankers and other businessmen to join a new national banking system. Certainly there was much to appeal to businessmen in any step to bring some order into the existing banking system. Each state chartered its own banks—and some states were liberal indeed in dispensing charters. As a result the banks ranged all the way from Eastern banks which were strongholds of financial power to those which were little more than a temporary cover for swindlers. The result was an unstable system, marked by frequent failures. There was still another aspect which vexed businessmen. Each bank issued its own paper money, and the worth of the money varied from bank to bank, and that problem was compounded by the sheer number of bank notes: it was estimated that in 1862 there were 12,000 different kinds of notes in circulation. Obviously, the development of a national market required a uniform and stable currency together with a dependable banking system. This need was met in legislation passed in 1863 and 1864 establishing a national bank system, but passage seems to have been dictated more by the necessity for bringing funds rapidly into the Treasury than by agreement on the merits of the measures.[6]

In general the legislation provided for the issuing of national bank charters to groups of individuals who deposited at least a third of their capital with the Treasury in the form of U.S. Bonds. They would then receive 90 percent of the bonds' value in the form of national bank notes, which were legal tender. If banks wished to become depositories for government funds (except customs duties) they put up collateral in bonds. The plan thus appealed to the self-interest of businessmen: they got interest on the bonds deposited with the Treasury, they got additional interest on loans made in their own national bank notes (both on the basis of one investment), and they profited still further in lending out government funds deposited with them. To assure stability certain minima of capital were required, stockholders were subject to double liability in case of failure, reserve requirements were established so that banks could meet normal demands upon their funds, and the limit of bank notes was set at $300 million, to be distributed according to the population and banking services of the states. State banks were encouraged to join the national system. If they did not, they were penalized by a two percent tax on their notes.

But while bankers and others might deplore the evils of the existing system, they feared even more those they envisaged in the new. The great Eastern banks, in effect powers unto themslves, and profiting from their role as reserve banks for countless smaller ones, saw little in the inducements of national banking to warrant coming under federal regulation. Indeed, they actively opposed it. Western bankers, thriving on their lavish issues of paper money, wanted no part of a system designed to curtail such issues. Democrats and some Republicans, including such ardent party men as Thaddeus Stevens, viewed the new system as leading to a money monopoly. Thus, by October, 1864, only 508 national banks were organized, and most of these were in the West, where the pressure of farmers and businessmen injured by recent bank failures was effective.

Congress finally resorted to coercion. Early in 1865 it levied a 10 percent tax on state bank notes, which rendered their circulation no longer profitable. By October of that year more than 1500 national banks were in

---

[6] Robert P. Sharkey, *Money, Class and Party* (Baltimore, Md.: The Johns Hopkins Press, 1959), p. 226.

existence. So, the banking legislation had little significance in helping finance the war, but its influence was long lasting: it provided the basic structure of the nation's banking until creation of the Federal Reserve System in 1913.

In addition to the tariff and borrowing, the government also relied increasingly on internal taxation. Less than two million dollars came from this source in 1862, but a year later receipts mounted to $41 million and in 1865 to nearly $211 million. The proportion of government bills paid by taxes rose from six to 16 percent. Practically every manufactured product and every form of professional and business activity was taxed, as were inheritances and incomes. Significantly, excess profits escaped the otherwise almost universal levies. The income and inheritance levies were widely evaded, and otherwise business simply transferred the taxes to the consumer by raising prices to include them—often with a little extra added. And, as has been noted, small manufacturers suffered because the pyramiding of excise taxes put them at a disadvantage with large-scale operations.

The government's new public land policies also proved of benefit to business. Westerners, as we have seen, had long sought a free land policy, and for a generation prior to the war labor spokesmen in the East, such as George Henry Evans, had taken up the cause as a solution to the evils of industrialism. Now Republicans redeemed their campaign pledge of free land by passing the Homestead Act, which granted to a settler 160 acres free (except for a small fee) if he farmed the land for five years. This challenged farmers who possessed the assets and strength to move into the wilderness—but other provisions of the law brought perhaps even more happiness to men who saw profit in the westward march of America. These provided that land claims were transferable, and that settlers could buy land for $1.25 an acre after only six months occupancy. After the law became effective January 1, 1863, speculators moved "settlers" on to the better lands, evaded the law's requirements for improvement of the property, and bought the land after six months. Soon they were offering it to bona fide settlers at a markup of several hundred percent. In the meantime, other speculators took up unsurveyed land and bought it for $1.25 an acre as soon as it was surveyed—all quite legal under the Preemption Act of 1841. Syndicates of Eastern businessmen thus took title to millions of acres of good land before farmers could homestead them. Settlers had to pay speculators' prices or move on.

There was also profit in the federal program of aid to higher education. In 1862 Congress passed the Morrill Act, granting to each loyal state 30,000 acres of public lands for each of its Senators and Representatives, the proceeds to be used to promote agricultural and mechanical education and provide military training for future officers. The law obviously favored the populous Eastern states, but businessmen everywhere took advantage of it. States, eager to get money to pay their war expenses (such as enlistment bounties and aid to soldiers' families), sold their claims, sometimes for as little as 50 cents an acre. In this way Ezra Cornell acquired through the State of New York a half million acres in Kansas, Minnesota, and Wisconsin. No homesteaders shared in this largesse.

This was as nothing compared to grants given transcontinental railroad promoters. With Southerners gone from Washington the advocates of federally subsidized Northern-based routes to the Pacific went unopposed. In July, 1862, Congress chartered the Union Pacific, bestowing on it a right of way 400 feet wide and 10 square miles of land for each mile of road built, plus loans ranging from $16,000 to $48,000 a mile depending on ruggedness of terrain. For security, the government was to have a first mortgage on the road. The government, of course, would also furnish protection against Indian peoples who might not appreciate this invasion of their territories. Immediate cash for the project was to be raised from the sale of 100,000 shares of stock at $100 each. Similar grants and loans were made to the already established Central Pacific, which would build east from San Francisco to meet the Union Pacific pushing west from Omaha, Nebraska. The project not only enjoyed the blessing of the federal government, but also that of many leading businessmen of the day: Leland Stanford, Collis P. Huntington, Charles Crocker, and Mark Hopkins, sponsors of the Central Pacific; Cyrus McCormick in Chicago; A. A. Low, President of the New York Chamber of Commerce, and William E. Dodge, western land speculator and dominant figure in the firm of Phelps, Dodge and Company, which dominated the metals market. Heading the Union Pacific was the reputable Democratic politician, Major General John A. Dix.

Nevertheless, financiers were cautious. They doubted that the road was adequately financed. They wondered how such a road could generate enough traffic to make it profitable, travelling as it did through vast regions inhabited only by Indians. If it should prove a failure, they did not relish private creditors having to wait while government claims got preference. So, while they publicly applauded the venture, they put their money elsewhere. Naturally, the men already involved were unhappy, and communicated their woes to Congressmen, whose sympathies were the more easily aroused because the promoters spent liberally to get more generous terms from the government.

Thus, in July, 1864, a new law was passed: the land grants were doubled; the government security was reduced to second mortgage status; and the stock was increased to a million shares. Money now flowed in, especially when military successes in September augured well both for

Union victory and continued Republican domination in Washington. The lack of capital, however, had had its effect: little actual construction had been completed when the war ended. In the meantime, a small group of Union Pacific insiders had taken over a small Pennsylvania firm, the Credit Mobilier, to which was assigned a basic contract for building the road. The insiders made millions for themselves in the postwar years through inflated construction costs which drained off the assets of the railroad.

Another group of promoters, proposing to build a Northern Pacific Railroad line from Lake Superior to Portland, Oregon, received even more in land grants than did the Union Pacific. They got 20 square miles of land for each mile built in states, 40 square miles in territories. But they lacked something very important that the Union Pacific had: government credit. Without it they could raise little capital, and construction did not begin until 1870, when Jay Cooke undertook its financing.

Businessmen, then, rather than farmers, really profited from the new generous land policies, which were further expanded after the war. Surveying the results, Ray Allen Billington commented, "Probably not more than one acre in every nine went directly to small pioneers, the supposed beneficiaries of the Homestead Act!" [7]

The outcome of the war gave business a new buoyancy and confidence. Great and little fortunes had been amassed, and now sought new conquests, to be managed by the host of army men who had shown managerial skills in service. Wealth awaited shrewd men in bustling cities like Chicago and Pittsburgh, vastly expanded by the war, as well as in the unexploited resources of the South and Far West. Government policy would be favorable, and the public opinion that mattered would be benign, for business now enjoyed both political power and social prestige. The new breed of businessmen that emerged from the speculation and profits and industry of war had complete confidence in itself and in the social system its members represented. They had fed and equipped and armed vast armies, and so made possible the victory that abolished slavery and reunited the nation. To be sure, businessmen had enriched themselves in so doing, but was that too high a price to pay for a nation now free and united? Had not Lincoln himself observed apropos the illicit cotton trade, "And if pecuniary greed can be made to aid us in such effort, let us be thankful that so much good can be got out of pecuniary greed"?

[7] Ray A. Billington, *Westward Expansion* (New York: The Macmillan Company, 2d ed., 1960), p. 703.

The Confederate government, like that of the Union, tried to shift the cost of the war to consumers and to future generations—but much more drastically. Richmond delayed a year after Washington in developing a vigorous tax policy, and its measures were less effective: the Union raised 22 percent of its revenues through tariffs and internal taxes, the Confederacy only 5 percent. Relying on paper money and bonds, the government ran up a debt of more than two billion dollars by the end of the war, most of it in currency. The inflation which resulted was intensified by the tendency of people to spend it quickly before its value further depreciated— by 1865 the Confederate dollar was worth only two cents in gold! Shortage of goods also contributed to the price rise: the increasingly effective Union blockade sharply reduced imports, and the Southern economy itself was able to supply adequately neither the army nor civilians, a weakness which became worse as Union armies reduced sources of supply. In some fields prices were bid up by state and Confederate governments competing in the same markets. Inflation doomed enterprises attuned to a more traditional economy, but it provided a bonanza to men who saw profits in a situation where prices mounted much faster than wages.

No enterprise was more lucrative than that of blockade running—the drama of which has obscured the fact that it became a highly organized business dominated by firms in which English capital was prominent. At first the trade was carried on by small operators, who used existing ships to carry cotton cargoes to various Caribbean ports and to return with supplies thoughtfully provided by Yankee and English merchants. The blockade-runner thus made two profits: one on cotton, for which both Yankees and English were willing to pay well; and the other on imports which fetched high prices. Naturally, this attracted the attention of men able to build new and faster ships, better able to cope with the Union navy. Soon, fleets of new vessels were doing so well that their owners could lose a ship after two trips and still suffer no loss. Actually, many ships did much better: one, which was captured after only eight voyages, netted her owners a 700 percent return on their investment.[8]

So successful was the trade that stock in the companies involved was eagerly bought at fantastic prices: shares in one with a face value of $1,000 sold in 1864 for $30,000 each—and that after the Confederate government had taken steps to compel blockade runners to carry more of the less profitable war supplies. The dividends were equally fabulous, ranging from $800 to $2000 a share; one company even paid part of its dividend in pounds sterling! John Fraser and Company of Charleston, owned by George A. Trenholm, a cotton broker, collaborated with its English sub-

[8] Clement Eaton, *A History of the Southern Confederacy* (New York: The Free Press, 1965), pp. 147–48.

sidiary, Fraser, Trenholm and Company, in a blockade-running enterprise involving nearly 50 ships, which brought the Charleston firm, it was said, profits of $9 million. Ironically, when Trenholm was appointed Secretary of the Confederate Treasury in 1864 one of his duties was to regulate blockade-running!

The need for regulation arose from the obvious fact that the business contributed little to the war effort. The expectation of the Confederate leaders that it would help bring in badly needed supplies proved an illusion. Since there was relatively little profit in such trade, shippers devoted their space largely to high-priced imports—wines and brandies, jewelry, fashionable clothing—for which there was a market among the wealthy. For a time the government made do with a small fleet of its own and with contract shippers, who were willing so long as the freight fees were large enough to compensate for foregoing civilian cargoes. By 1863 such fees had reached a point at which shippers demanded two million dollars for carrying government cargo! In the meantime public clamor had risen against the trade, accentuated by its boldness in advertising luxuries at exorbitant prices while there were shortages of necessities among soldiers and civilians alike. However, little action was taken until February, 1864, when Congress banned imports of luxuries and required ships to devote additional space to war supplies. Trenholm's enforcement of the law brought in more arms and food, but the trade continued to be profitable—and luxuries somehow still found their way to market.

Another lucrative, but less organized, trade was the overland traffic in cotton. Some was carried on by small farmers and planters to get needed food and clothing, but much more was in the hands of merchants operating in Memphis, Mobile, and New Orleans, who traded cotton for precious greenbacks or even more precious gold. Some of the proceeds they hoarded, the rest they invested in supplies likely to bring good prices in the Confederacy: arms, ammunition, quinine, morphine, and salt. Like the Union government, the Confederate government tried to regulate this trade—and on occasion even forbade it—but its efforts were as futile as those of Washington. Alongside of, and under cover of the legal trade, vast illegal operations flourished, with the connivance of corrupt army officers and Treasury agents.

There was also money to be made in building up inventories of necessities—salt, flour, meat, shoes, and cloth, for example—and holding them for sale on a rising market. The traders got their supplies not only from legitimate sources, such as farmers and manufacturers, but also from corrupt quartermasters, who for a price diverted army supplies to the civilian market. The speculators quickly became scapegoats for the ills of Confederate society: they were held responsible for the high cost of living, the increasing misery of the poor, and shortages in the army. Jefferson

David excoriated the "grovelling speculators" who made money "out of the life-blood of our defenders," and editors, preachers and politicians were even more vehement. As we have seen, the Southern poor made traders the special objects of their wrath. To curb the speculators heavy taxes were levied on incomes and profits, but these were evaded, and the speculation went on until the breakdown of the monetary system made it no longer feasible. In the meantime many merchants had accumulated fortunes.

The outcry against the speculators, however, had a psychological value which has been too little studied. It diverted popular attention from the basic causes of inflation—the shortage of goods and the flood of paper money—to a symptom, embodied in a minority against whom popular wrath could be directed while little was done to remedy the source of the people's ills. This was the more easily done because so often the minority was identified as being Jewish. This in turn was a valuable asset to the numerous enemies of Jefferson Davis, who attributed the Confederacy's failures to the sinister influence of Judah Benjamin, the capable and astute —and Jewish— Secretary of War and later Secretary of State. Davis' refusal to part company with Benjamin became a major point of the attacks mounted on the President, especially after Benjamin openly advocated the enlistment of blacks in the Confederate army on the basis of their Emancipation. In short, just as planters blamed slave unrest, not on slavery, but on Yankee abolitionists, so did Confederates deceive themselves that all would be well were it not for speculators, and there would be few of them were it not for Jews.[9]

Opportunities for enrichment in industry were not as great as in the North. The South, which in 1860 accounted for only 8 percent of the value of the nation's manufactured products, had not developed the kind of industrial base essential for rapid expansion. Its great resources of coal and iron had been barely scratched, and its railroad system was patchy and woefully deficient in equipment. Its supply of machines and tools came, not from within, but from the North. Some expansion did take place, often subsidized by state or Confederate governments, resulting in increased output of iron, copper, coal, lead, saltpetre (necessary for the production of gunpowder), and cotton and woolen textiles. Some new works were entirely government enterprises, as in gunpowder, ordnance, and salt. But such expansion was small, and it was more than nullified by military opera-

[9] Expressions of anti-Semitism were not confined to the South. Numerous Union generals blamed Jewish merchants for the illicit cotton trade, and Grant even banned them from his command in the West—an order which was quickly countermanded from Washington. For a brief discussion of the issue see Bruce Catton, *Grant Moves South* (Boston: Little, Brown and Company, 1960), pp. 353–56.

tions and Union occupation, which literally destroyed the assets of many businessmen.

Also, industry was unable to develop such resources as it had because of a chronic shortage of skilled labor. When war came Yankee mechanics went home, and Southern artisans volunteered. Later, capricious administration of conscription put mechanics in the field when the law required they be kept at work. By 1864 the one steam hammer in the Confederacy was idle because no one knew how to operate it! That same year the Chief of Ordnance reported that although the annual capacity of the arsenals under his control was 55,000 rifles and carbines, output was only 20,000—due largely to a shortage of skilled manpower. In similar fashion the departure of Yankee managers and supervisors crippled Southern industry, for training in business was not part of the education of the Southern young. Manufacturers also had a problem which Northerners never did: when machines broke down or wore out, there was no way of replacing them. Some parts and equipment were brought in through the blockade, but the imports fell far short of the need.

Confederate policies also contributed to inhibiting industry. Cotton and woolen mills got blanket draft exemptions for their workers, but in return they had to turn over two-thirds of their output to the government and their profits, for both government and civilian markets, could not exceed 75 percent of the cost of production, a limit later set at 33 1/3 percent. In 1864, as we have seen, all industrial draft exemptions were cancelled, and the manpower control thus given the government was used to control prices still further. In North Carolina, a major cotton textile state, there was no civilian market: the state bought the total output. In other lines as well the Confederate government used its subsidies and its power of conscription to control production and profits. Iron production, for example, was almost entirely preempted by the government until an acute shortage among civilians forced the government to permit producers to sell half their output to the civilian market. Railroads were made subject to seizure if they failed to comply with orders of the Quartermaster General, who was given control over nearly all equipment. Late in the war railroads, as well as other forms of transportation, were put directly under the control of the War Department.

Businessmen bitterly protested the profit limits, of course, as well as the controls which kept them from benefiting as much as they would have liked from the civilian market. But they found ways of getting around the regulations. Manufacturers inflated their costs, and since they kept their own books, both government and civilians had to pay higher prices. Iron producers, as well as others, eventually got more flexible pricing arrangements. Railroads gradually got higher rates on military transport, and compensated for their relatively low level by boosting civilian rates so much that there was a public outcry against them.

But businessmen's difficulties were far from overcome. The Confederate government was slow in paying its bills—a situation which became worse as the war went on. Some bills were never paid! Even more disturbing were the tax laws, which seemed to favor planters at the expense of urban businessmen. Under the law of 1863 planters and farmers had to pay the tax in kind, which took a tenth of their produce, but business had to cope with a multitude of taxes, some of which could be passed on to consumers and some of which could not. The property tax of eight percent and the occupational taxes of varying amounts could be shifted to consumers—but the income tax, which rose as high as 15 percent on incomes of over $10,000 a year could not, nor could the 10 percent tax on profits.

The following year these taxes were renewed, also new levies on profits were added which were subject to an additional 10 percent tax while excess profits were taxed at a rate of 25 percent. To be sure, planters were now taxed for their land and slaves—but at their 1860 value in terms of United States currency while taxes were paid in depreciated Confederate money. Complaints brought about revision later: land and slaves purchased currently were to be taxed according to the price paid. In 1864, also, planters who lost slaves impressed for military labor either through escape or death were compensated through an appropriation of over $3 million. No such consideration was forthcoming for men who lost mills and factories during the war.

The distribution of taxation reflected planter influence at Richmond, but it also represented a response to a public opinion inflamed over high prices. Southern businessmen had never enjoyed the prestige in their section that Yankees accorded their men of business, and now industrialists were lumped together in the public mind with food and clothing hoarders as "extortionists." Editorial writers denounced manufacturers as "odious monopolies grinding the poor," and the clamor against railroad rates was such that a Congressman suggested taxing the roads $10,000 for each worker exempted from the draft. William Gregg, the South Carolina textile magnate, urged his sons to leave a business in which honest men were pilloried as "rogues."

The public had ample ground for its feeling. While prices mounted, so did dividends and stock prices. Gregg's own mills paid huge dividends, and the stock in one in 1863 sold for nearly 10 times its face value. That same year Virginia levied taxes on 120 firms on the basis of net earnings of at least $3 million. A woolen mill in the state in one year paid dividends amounting to more than twice its invested capital while a paper company in two years returned to its stockholders nearly six times its capital! Railroads paid off debts and declared astonishing dividends. But appearances were deceiving—the returns, paid in a rapidly depreciating currency, were also taken out of capital. Funds which should have gone into replacement of rolling stock and machinery—which were not to be had—were distributed to stockholders with a generous hand.

Some of the income accruing from blockade-running, trade with the enemy, speculation, dividends and stock sales was spent in the same kind of conspicuous waste as characterized the North, and brought forth the same kind of criticism of those who flaunted their wealth in the midst of suffering. But a good deal of it was also invested with an eye to the future. Real estate boomed in such urban centers as Richmond, and precious stones were bought as much for their intrinsic worth as for their prestige value. Confederate money was exchanged for gold and United States greenbacks, and these were hoarded. Much Southern wealth found a safe haven in England. Men caught with large holdings in Confederate bonds and money at the end of the war, and businessmen whose plants and equipment had been destroyed, as well as planters and farmers whose lands were in the way of armies, suffered from the war—but there was also no small number of canny Southerners who prospered during—and after—the conflict.

Northern farmers shared with businessmen in the war boom, after the shock of war had caused a drop in prices generally and distress in the Mississippi Valley from loss of the Southern market for hogs and corn. Then came recovery as war demands for food and clothing became urgent and foreign markets suddenly and astronomically expanded. Farmers found themselves in an ideal situation: they could pay off their debts in depreciated currency while markets would take all they could produce at unheard of prices. Farm income rose both in terms of greenbacks and gold to its highest point in the nineteenth century. Between 1860 and 1864, the last full war year, the wholesale farm price index more than doubled, while the general price index rose 82 percent.

Wool growers and wheat farmers did particularly well. The army's demand for wool was insatiable, and despite a tremendous increase in the wool crop, wholesale prices climbed steadily from a low of 82 cents a pound in 1861 to a high of $1.77 in 1864. Wheat farmers owed as much to Britain's food crisis as to the war for their prosperity. Beginning in 1860 that country had some poor crop years, and the deficiency could not be met by its nearby suppliers—France, Germany, and Russia—who were themselves in difficulties. Britain then turned to the United States, where it had bought nearly 4 million bushels in 1860 for a dollar a bushel. As a result of that and European purchases exports in 1861 went up nearly 800 percent at a price of $1.20 a bushel. The outward flow of golden grain continued: 107 million bushels altogether in the years, 1862–1865. In the last year the export price was $1.90 a bushel. The Western farmer saw in this a highly satisfactory reward for hard work; for the government it had other implications. Since the exports were paid for in gold, they eased the financial strain on the Treasury. And Britain's dependence on Northern wheat was not without its effect on Anglo-American relations.

The tremendous increase in output, despite a sharp reduction in farm manpower occasioned by the absence of so many farmers and laborers in the army, was due largely to more widespread use of farm machinery. In 1861 farmers used 125,000 reapers; five years later 375,000 of the machines were in use. Use of other machines showed similar increases. This development, together with the vast new markets, had significant social implications. The decline of subsistence farming was accelerated as farmers found it both necessary and profitable to direct their efforts toward the market. In order to tap that market they had to increase their capital investment in machinery. Men lacking the cash or credit to do so were squeezed out. Farmers in the army who had to depend on their wives and children to carry on during their absence were in sore straits when the war ended. Their farms had run down and often they possessed too little capital to compete with neighbors who had prospered while they were away.

There were few gains for Southern planters and farmers. Cotton production was restricted, and what was produced brought low prices because the blockade restricted the market. It irked planters that money was being made in cotton—by manufacturers who got cheap raw material and sold the product at inflated prices, and by traders who dealt with the enemy or ran it through the blockade. Repeated suggestions that the Confederate government buy the crop to bolster its commercial and diplomatic position were not heeded. When planters turned to food production they benefitted from high prices, but like the yeoman farmers they were not able to exploit the situation to the fullest, especially if they were in areas of ample food supply. Their output was subject to the 10 percent tax in kind, as well as arbitrary impressment by army agents at prices far below the market level. Later, land and property, including slaves, were taxed, and when businessmen complained that the tax law favored the planters the latter retorted that businessmen generally avoided paying their full tax bills while landowners could not so easily conceal their assets—unless they were in remote areas where army and Treasury agents did not enter.

Under such circumstances, slaves became liabilities to many planters.

As we have seen, some turned out their slaves to fend for themselves or encouraged them to grow their own food and market the surplus. Others rented slaves to industry. Still others had to yield to impressment of the blacks into Confederate service. The first weakened the authority of the slaveowners, while the other two resulted in rapid depreciation of the "property"—for all too often such slaves died or returned to their masters in poor condition. But most slaves still toiled on the plantations (until Union troops arrived), barely earning their keep; nevertheless, planters as a whole remained adamant against Emancipation. Proposals for arming and emancipating slaves were blocked until the last weeks of the war—and then Congress voted only enlistment and not unconditional freedom.

Planters and farmers, too, were particularly vulnerable to the vicissitudes of war. The shortage of iron and skilled labor meant that outworn tools, implements, and equipment could neither be repaired nor replaced. Farms near army camps were fair prey for hungry troopers—the Confederate cavalry being especially dreaded because of its notorious depredations. Farms and plantations in the way of contending armies suffered, no matter who won. As Confederate fortunes waned, some commanders adopted a "scorched earth" policy in retreat, cutting wide swaths of destruction so as to deny anything of value to the enemy, while individual soldiers plundered what they could. The Yankees lived off the land when possible, destroyed property deemed of value to the rebels, and looted when it was profitable. As a result, Southern agriculture was slow to recover: in 1870 the value of farms was still 47 percent below the 1860 level.

But not all planters and farmers were impoverished. The Chesnut family, for example, suffered some privations toward the end of the war, but their Mulberry Plantation remained intact, and Mrs. Chesnut noted other planters in South Carolina who had "saved their cotton and their estates, their mills and farming utensils." Such planters, ironically, entertained Jefferson Davis on his abortive flight to Texas.[10] Besides, many areas never felt directly the withering hand of war. When these areas were taken over by Union forces, many planters and farmers took the oath of allegiance and quickly thrived on the sale of cotton and foodstuffs—paid for in greenbacks, too! Louisiana planters, for example, became a major source for cotton shipped out of New Orleans. Obviously, such men were in a favorable position to take advantage of the business opportunities opened up by Reconstruction.

[10] Hudson Strode, *Jefferson Davis: Tragic Hero* (New York: Harcourt Brace Jovanovich, Inc., 1964), pp. 190, 204, 206.

Contrabands Escaping to the United States Bark "Kingfisher," Off the Coast of Florida. *Harper's Weekly. July 12, 1862.*

THE
WAR
THAT
NEVER
ENDED

The war resolved some major issues: slavery was abolished; the dominant role of the federal government in the nation's political structure was firmly established; and the supremacy of business values in nearly all aspects of American life assured. United again, America once more looked outward, pressuring the French to leave Mexico, acquiring Alaska, and seeking a naval base in Santo Domingo. The still outstanding issues with Great Britain were adjusted peacefully under conditions which signified British acceptance of the United States as a major power. One basic issue, given new magnitude by the war, was not resolved: the place of free black people in a society which felt it could now, without apologies for slavery, avow itself as the one truly democratic nation in the world. Blacks were now free. Were they also to be accepted as equals? In short, was white America

191

prepared to meet the moral commitment to equality set forth in the Declaration of Independence.

Given the presence of several million blacks, the issue could not be evaded—but neither was white America willing to meet it. The result, for more than a century, has been a series of adjustments, which took four major forms. First, in the immediate postwar period, blacks were accepted as free, while the problem of equality was left to work itself out gradually in the future. Second, during Reconstruction, came a short-lived national commitment to equality, during which blacks enjoyed a status and dignity unequalled until recent years. Third, a retreat from equality which lasted well into our own century, characterized by the reduction of blacks to second-class citizenship, both in law and in custom. Fourth, within the last generation, a renewed commitment to the national ideal, marked both by significant improvement in black status and by a development of black power and black militancy rarely seen since Reconstruction.

Nevertheless, despite the gains made in recent years, the basic issue remains unresolved. Racial tensions continue high; the National Advisory Commission on Civil Disorders warned in 1968 that unless existing trends were reversed the country was moving "toward two societies, separate and unequal."

Thus the past joins with the present: the unresolved issue of the Civil War casts its shadow a century later. White America's failure to honor its commitment to equality in the past (except during Reconstruction) bequeaths to the present generation of whites the psychic conflict involved in adherence to the nation's principles and the practise of racism. For blacks this has meant a dilemma of their own. For long now they have sought equality—but always with the consciousness that their struggle was circumscribed by the limits set by white society. Struggle as they might, blacks realized bitterly that they were not masters of their own fate. The consequence of past decisions has been an abrasive coexistence of the races, in which the black minority ever feels at a disadvantage.

But if it is true that the past conditions the present, it is equally true that the past does not determine the present. Man makes his own history, each generation shaping the heritage it will pass along to future generations. Who knows, the present generation of young Americans, both white and black, may so contribute as to bring to an end the war that thus far has never ended.

A SELECTIVE BIBLIOGRAPHY

Following is a list of references which should prove of value to readers who wish to pursue further an interest in the Civil War. The emphasis is on recent work, particularly on that related to the problems discussed in this book. Even so, many worthwhile books have been omitted because of space limitations and to their authors, my apologies. However, for the reader who wishes a more extensive bibliography, there is now available a handy, comprehensive source in paperback: David Donald, *The Nation in Crisis, 1861–1877* (New York: Appleton-Century-Crofts, 1969). Now to my own list.

ADAMS, GEORGE W., *Doctors in Blue: The Medical History of the Union Army in the Civil War* (New York, Henry Schuman, 1952). An excellent introduction to an often neglected aspect of the war.

ANDREANO, RALPH, ed., *The Economic Impact of the American Civil War*, 2nd ed. (Cambridge, Mass.: Schenkman Publishing Company, 1967). A valuable collection of essays exploring some of the economic problems arising from the war.

APTHEKER, HERBERT, ed., A *Documentary History of the Negro People in the United States*, Vol. I (New York: The Citadel Press, 1951). Source material for understanding the blacks' role in the events leading to the war.

BERWANGER, EUGENE H., *The Frontier Against Slavery: Western Anti-Negro Prejudice and the Slavery Extension Controversy* (Urbana, Ill.: University of Illinois Press, 1967). A pioneer study of white racism in the Old Northwest and how it shaped public policy.

BRODIE, FAWN M., *Thaddeus Stevens: Scourge of the South* (New York: W. W. Norton & Company, Inc., 1959). An incisive biography of the Radical Republican who has been the victim of a bad press—historically speaking.

BROCK, WILLIAM, R., ed., *The Civil War* (New York: Harper & Row, Publishers, Inc., 1969). A short collection of interpretive essays containing much new material.

CASH, W. J., *The Mind of the South* (New York: Vintage Books, 1960). A reprint of a classic, first published in 1941, by a Southerner on the factors that have gone into producing a distinctive Southern character.

CATTON, BRUCE, A *Stillness at Appomattox* (New York: Pocket Books, Inc., 1958). An engrossing account of the closing campaigns of the war in which military history is portrayed in human terms.

COMMAGER, HENRY S., *The Blue and the Gray: The Story of the Civil War as Told by Participants*. 2 vols. (Indianapolis, Ind.: Bobbs-Merrill & Company, 1950). Valuable source material from officers and enlisted men.

CORNISH, DUDLEY TAYLOR, *The Sable Arm: Negro Troops in the Union Army, 1861–1865* (New York: W. W. Norton & Company, Inc., 1966.) A good basic survey of the problems of black troops and the black soldiers' responses.

COULTER, E. MERTON, *The Confederate States of America, 1861–1865* (Baton Rouge, La.: Louisiana State University Press, 1950). A standard, informative history by a traditionally-minded Southern historian.

CUNNINGHAM, H. H., *Doctors in Gray: The Confederate Medical Service* (Baton Rouge, La.: Louisiana State University Press, 1958). A pioneer account of how the Confederacy cared for its sick and wounded—another long neglected aspect of the war.

DEARING, MARY R., *Veterans in Politics: The Story of the G.A.R.* (Baton Rouge, La.: Louisiana State University Press, 1952). The early chapters disclose how immediate postwar disillusionment of Union veterans led to formation of a powerful lobby, the Grand Army of the Republic.

DONALD, DAVID, *Charles Sumner and the Coming of the Civil War* (New York: Alfred A. Knopf, Inc., 1960). A significant re-appraisal of the Radical Republican Senator who suffered much at the hands of older historians.

DUMOND, DWIGHT L., *Anti-Slavery: the Crusade for Freedom in America* (Ann Arbor, Mich.: University of Michigan Press, 1967). A vigorous reinterpretation of the role of abolitionists.

EATON, CLEMENT, *A History of the Southern Confederacy* (New York: The Free Press, 1954). An excellent summary, by a Southern historian.

———, *The Freedom-of-Thought Struggle in the Old South* (New York: Harper & Row, Publishers, Inc., 1964). Invaluable account of Southern outlooks in the prewar decades.

ELKINS, STANLEY M., *Slavery: A Problem in American Institutional and Intellectual Life* (Chicago: University of Chicago Press, 1959). A basic and highly controversial view of the black experience as shaped by slavery.

FILLER, LOUIS, *The Crusade Against Slavery, 1830–1860* (New York: Harper & Row, Publishers, Inc., 1960). A valuable, comprehensive account of how anti-slavery sentiment spread throughout the East and West.

FITE, EMERSON D., *Social and Industrial Conditions in the North During the Civil War* (New York: The Macmillan Company, 1910). This work remains the standard source for the ground it covers.

FONER, PHILIP S., *The Life and Writings of Frederick Douglass*. 4 vols. (New York: International Publishers, 1950–1955). Indispensable for understanding the changing black responses to problems arising before, during, and after the war.

FREEHLING, WILLIAM W., *Prelude to Civil War: The Nullification Crisis in South Carolina, 1813–1836* (New York: Harper & Row, Publishers, Inc., 1966). A case study demonstrating how the states' rights doctrine was promoted to defend slavery.

GENOVESE, EUGENE D., *The Political Economy of Slavery: Studies in the Economy and Society of the Slave South* (New York: Vintage Books, 1967). A sophisticated, stimulating Marxist study of the prewar South.

JORDAN, WINTHROP D., *White over Black: American Attitudes Toward the Negro, 1550–1812* (Baltimore: Penguin Books, 1969). A basic, indispensable analysis of the origins of white racism.

KRADITOR, AILEEN, *Means and Ends in American Abolitionism: Garrison and His Critics on Strategy and Tactics, 1834–1850* (New York: Pantheon Books, 1969). A revealing examination of the complexities of the abolitionist movement.

LITWACK, LEON F., *North of Slavery: The Negro in the Free States, 1789–1860* (Chicago: University of Chicago Press, 1961). Essential in understanding Northern white reaction to black freedom before the war.

LONN, ELLA, *Desertion During the Civil War* (Gloucester, Mass.: Peter Smith, 1966). A reprint of a valuable source first published in 1928.

MANDEL, BERNARD, *Labor: Free and Slave: Workingmen and the Anti-Slavery Movement in the United States* (New York: Associated Authors, 1955). One of the few significant studies of the role of labor in the war crisis.

McPHERSON, JAMES M., *The Struggle for Liberty: Abolitionists and the Negro in the Civil War and Reconstruction* (Princeton, N.J.: Princeton University Press, 1964). Scholarly study of the relationships between white abolitionists and black people—which were not as clearly defined as one might suppose.

————, *The Negro's Civil War: How American Negroes Felt and Acted During the War for the Union* (New York: Vintage Books, 1965). Black America's varying reactions to the war set forth in highly readable form.

NEVINS, ALLAN, *Ordeal of the Union*. 8 vols. (New York: Charles Scribner's Sons, Inc., 1947–1971). The most comprehensive general treatment of the war and its background.

PRESSLY, THOMAS J., *Americans Interpret Their Civil War* (New York: The Free Press, 1965). A comprehensive view of interpretations of the war to the early 1950s.

QUARLES, BENJAMIN, *Frederick Douglass* (Englewod Cliffs, N.J.: Prentice-Hall, Inc., 1968). A valuable, brief introduction to the viewpoints of the famed black leader.

————, *Black Abolitionists* (New York: Oxford University Press, 1969). A pioneer study of a neglected subject.

RANDALL, JAMES G. and DAVID DONALD, *The Civil War and Reconstruction*, 2d ed. rev. (Boston, Mass.: Raytheon Education Company, 1969). An updated version of the standard one-volume work.

ROSE, WILLIE LEE, *Rehearsal for Reconstruction: The Port Royal Experiment* (New York: Vintage Books, 1967). The fascinating account of how former slaves proved that freedom worked during the war years.

ROZWENC, EDWIN C. ed. *The Causes of the American Civil War* (Boston, Mass.: Raytheon Education Company, 1961). Interpretations offered both by people of the time and by later historians.

SHANNON, FRED A., *The Organization and Administration of the Union Army, 1861–1865*. 2 vols. (Cleveland, Ohio: Arthur Clark Company, 1928). Still the standard work on the subject, containing much more material than the title suggests.

SIDEMAN, BELLE B., and LILLIAN FRIEDMAN, *Europe Looks at the Civil War: An Anthology* (New York: The Orion Press, 1960). An interesting collection of conflicting views on the American war.

SMITH, GEORGE W., and CHARLES JUDAH, eds., *Life in the North During the Civil War: A Source History* (Albuquerque, N. M.: University of New Mexico Press, 1966). Provides many insights into the behavior of Northerners during the war years.

STAMPP, KENNETH M., *The Peculiar Institution: Slavery in the Ante-Bellum South* (New York: Vintage Books, 1956). A vigorous challenge to the stereotype of the contented slave, with significant material on the domestic slave trade.

————, *The Causes of the Civil War*, Rev. ed. (Englewood Cliffs, N. J.: Prentice-Hall, Inc., 1965). A brief, useful, look at how editors, politicians, and others in the prewar period viewed the issues, together with interpretations of various historians.

STRODE, HUDSON, *Jefferson Davis: Tragic Hero* (New York: Harcourt Brace Jovanovich, Inc., 1964). A sympathetic account of Davis' problems as Confederate President.

STUDENSKI, PAUL, and HERMAN E. KROOS, *Financial History of the United States*, 2d ed. (New York: McGraw-Hill Book Company, 1963). The chapters dealing with national economic problems before and during the war provide important background information.

TREFOUSSE, HANS L., *Benjamin Franklin Wade: Radical Republican from Ohio* (New York: Twayne Publishers, 1963). A pioneering reinterpretation of a Radical Republican.

WADE, RICHARD C., *Slavery in the Cities: The South, 1820–1860* (New York: Oxford University Press, 1964). A significant study in the complexities of slavery—and the pressures that were modifying the institution.

WILEY, BELL I., *The Life of Johnny Reb* (Indianapolis, Ind.: Bobbs-Merrill and Company, 1943).

———, *The Life of Billy Yank* (Indianapolis, Ind.: Bobbs-Merrill and Company, 1952). Both works are invaluable sources for the reactions of ordinary soldiers to the problems of war.

WILLIAMS, T. HARRY, *Lincoln and His Generals* (New York: Vintage Books, 1952). A vivid, short account of the problem of developing military leadership in the Union.

INDEX